Theaters of Madness

Insane Asylums and Nineteenth-Century American Culture

BENJAMIN REISS

The University of Chicago Press

CHICAGO AND LONDON

BENJAMIN REISS is associate professor of English at Emory University. He is the author of *The Showman and the Slave: Race, Death, and Memory in Barnum's America* and an editor of *The Cambridge History of the American Novel* (forthcoming).

The University of Chicago Press, Chicago 60637
The University of Chicago Press, Ltd., London
© 2008 by The University of Chicago
All rights reserved. Published 2008
Printed in the United States of America

17 16 15 14 13 12 11 10 09 08   1 2 3 4 5

ISBN-13: 978-0-226-70963-5 (cloth)
ISBN-13: 978-0-226-70964-2 (paper)
ISBN-10: 0-226-70963-9 (cloth)
ISBN-10: 0-226-70964-7 (paper)

Library of Congress Cataloging-in-Publication Data
Reiss, Benjamin.
Theaters of madness : insane asylums and nineteenth-century American culture / Benjamin Reiss.
p. cm.
Includes bibliographical references and index.
ISBN-13: 978-0-226-70963-5 (cloth : alk. paper)
ISBN-10: 0-226-70963-9 (cloth : alk. paper)
ISBN-13: 978-0-226-70964-2 (pbk : alk. paper)
ISBN-10: 0-226-70964-7 (pbk. : alk. paper)
1. Psychiatric hospitals—United States—History—19th century. 2. Psychiatric hospitals—Social aspects—United States—History—19th century. 3. Hospitals in literature—United States—History—19th century. 4. Mentally ill, Writings of the, American—History and criticism. I. Title. [DNLM: 1. Hospitals, Psychiatric—History—United States. 2. Medicine in Literature—United States. 3. Cultural Characteristics—United States. 4. History, 19th Century—United States. 5. Mentally Ill Persons—History—United States.
WM 49 R378t 2008
RC443.R43 2008
362.2'10973—dc22
2007043179

For Jo Ann and David Reiss

Contents

Acknowledgments

MOST OF *Theaters of Madness* was written under strange circumstances. As a faculty member of Tulane University's English department, I left New Orleans with my family in the wee hours of the morning on August 28, 2005, less than thirty-six hours before Hurricane Katrina reached the city. A computer disk in my car's glove compartment held drafted chapters and research notes for unwritten ones; that disk was, for several excruciating weeks, practically the only connection I had to my professional life. But with the extraordinary support of my family, I was able to find a safe haven— both physical (in Boston) and emotional—in which to finish the bulk of the manuscript. The experience was not one I would wish on anyone, but it did give me new reasons to appreciate my wife Devora, our children Isaac and Sophie, my in-laws Risa and Philip Nyman, my sister Sharon Baker, and my own parents, to whom this book is dedicated.

That bittersweet writing year was a hiatus, as it turned out, between my time as a faculty member at Tulane and at Emory University, where I have begun a wonderful new intellectual life. Thanks especially to Michael Elliott and Frances Smith Foster for facilitating that transition. The support of many friends at Tulane and in New Orleans was also sustaining. To Neil Boris, Gaurav Desai, Jim Elliott, Geoff Harpham, T. R. Johnson, Maurya Kilroy, John Lovett, Supriya Nair, Molly Rothenberg, Felipe Smith, Teresa Toulouse, and Molly Travis: thanks for the memories, and for your continued friendship.

My Katrina year miraculously began to fall into place when Mary Crane of Boston College's English department—at that point a complete stranger—arranged an office and a visiting scholar position for me at BC on practically zero notice. Her colleague Carlo Rotella gave me a hearty welcome and what turned out to be excellent publishing advice. I was startled and grateful to find that monthly installments of my Award to Louisiana Artists and Scholars from the Louisiana Board of Regents (granted to me to allow me to finish the manuscript) were uninterrupted by the storm; thanks especially to John Wallin and Carrie Robison of the BOR for their help and reassurances. New and renewed friendships in the Boston area with Carrie Bramen, John Plotz, and John Stauffer helped pull me through the writing process as well as the challenges of life in limbo. Thanks also to Larry Buell for his support, his advice, his deep knowledge of Emerson, and his constructive criticism. Among the other far-flung colleagues who helped me back on my feet—intellectually and otherwise—I extend curtain calls to Rachel Adams, Lenny Cassuto, and Bob Levine.

Much of the research for this book was conducted at the American Antiquarian Society, where I was a National Endowment for the Humanities fellow from 2001 to 2002. I hereby add my thanks to the chorus of awed gratitude offered by early Americanists who have been fortunate enough to work at that magnificent institution. Among the staff members who helped nurture my project, Nancy Burkett, Joanne Chaison, Ellen Dunlop, John Hench, John Keenum, Jim Moran, Caroline Sloat, and Bill Young deserve special mention. I am also grateful for the camaraderie and intellectual community of my fellow fellows, especially Pat Cohen, Jo Radner, and David Silverman. A Larry J. Hackman Fellowship at the New York State Archives provided sustained access to crucial institutional records. Thanks to Jim Folts for help at the archives.

Along the way, I've hit up numerous friends, acquaintances, and strangers for their knowledge, advice, practical help, and criticism. Among them are Holly Allen, Tom Augst, Michael Bosak, Chris Castiglia, Russ Castronovo, Helen Deese, Ellen Dwyer, Maryrose Eannace, Paul Erickson, Robert Gross, Jay Grossman, Rip Lhamon, Bettina Manzo, Michael Newbury, Charles Rosenberg, Mike Sappol, Ike Schambelan, Matt Sharpe, Caleb Smith, Nancy Tomes, Elizabeth Young, Georgina Ziegler, and David Zimmerman. Jessica Mitchell was an outstanding research assistant. Finally, Alice Oldfather and Jeffrey Gordon were—once again—gracious hosts; may there always be research trips to Albany.

Portions of this book appeared in different form in *American Literary History* (chapter one) and *ELH* (chapter three); thanks to the editors of those journals (especially my new colleague Jonathan Goldberg) for their support.

At the University of Chicago Press, Emilie Sandoz and Mary Gehl helped fine-tune the manuscript. And thank heavens for Robert Devens, whose good sense and great good cheer have seen this through. (But a warning to his prospective authors: he will not let you sound like a hectoring robot—not even for one paragraph!)

INTRODUCTION

———— ✳ ————

Sanative Culture

IMMEDIATELY UPON acceding to the presidency after the death of Zachary Taylor in July 1850, Millard Fillmore was thrust into the roiling debate over the extension of slavery to new territories gained in the Mexican War. This debate would result in the Compromise of 1850, a watershed event in the years leading up to the Civil War.[1] In October of the same year, Fillmore wrote a letter to Dorothea Dix, the reformer and tireless advocate of state and federal construction of insane asylums. He expressed his horror at Dix's findings that large numbers of the insane were held in prisons and at the fact that the North contained disproportionately more lunatics than the South; but he professed himself pleased with the new asylum at Trenton, New Jersey, which had "forms more light and airy" than the one in Tennessee. What really fascinated him, though, was a specimen Dix had sent to him of a "lunatic's poetry to Jenny Lind, which," wrote Fillmore, "is a very creditable production. I am not certain but the partition which separates madness from genius is much thinner than most of us suspect."[2]

Why would a president embroiled in the bitterest dispute in the history of the Republic take the time to comment on a lunatic's poem composed for a popular singer? Of all the grounds for comparing New Jersey with Tennessee in 1850, why would Millard Fillmore choose the issue of ventilation and lighting in their insane asylums? From this vignette, Fillmore may come across as out of touch with reality, preoccupied by trifles. But what I hope to convey here is that Fillmore's interest in the poetic efforts of an antebellum "lunatic" is not evidence of an intellectual failing or a sentimental indulgence that distracted him from national affairs. The precise meaning of the poem to Fillmore—why it caused him to reevaluate the line between genius and madness—may be obscure, but the *fact* of its meaning something to him at such a moment is evidence of the importance of debates over the proper treatment of insanity in the national political realm. The year 1850 may have been a critical moment in the discussion of slavery and territorial expansion, but it was no less crucial in the national discussion about mental illness. Dorothea Dix, in fact, was a crucial player in Fillmore's administration; aligning himself with her highly popular mission was a politically shrewd maneuver. Beginning in 1848, Dix had taken her crusade to finance insane asylums national. In that year, she proposed selling off five million acres of federally owned land in order to endow public asylums, which had hitherto depended on funding from state legislatures and the patronage of municipalities. The high point of this effort would come in 1854, when the House and Senate passed a bill based on her proposal. (The bill's supporters, however, were unable to overcome President Franklin Pierce's veto.)[3] Even the detail about airy hospital wards was not an idiosyncratic concern. Such matters as proper heating and ventilation obsessed architects of the new asylums: under the miasmic theory of illness, doctors assumed that noxious human exhalations could spread disease, and so asylum superintendents took great care to ensure proper air flow in their buildings. This concern penetrated the culture so deeply that Herman Melville's Captain Ahab—like the president who reigned as Melville wrote his famous whaling book—thinks of hospital ventilation as he navigates treacherous waters. As he is about to lower his boat for a third and final time to capture the white whale, he pauses for a moment to consider the wind that whips him on toward his goal: "A vile wind that has no doubt blown ere this through prison corridors and cells, and wards of hospitals, and ventilated them, and now comes blowing hither as innocent as fleeces."[4]

I hope to recapture in this book the texture of a time when the treatment of the insane was a central topic in cultural conversations about democracy, freedom, and modernity, rather than what today is a sporadic discussion about insurance parity for mental health, the effectiveness of various "wonder drugs," or the occasional scandal about warehousing indigent patients and those who do not respond to drug therapy. I find in that past something both usable and cautionary. In mid-nineteenth-century America, the condition of the mentally ill seemed to demand—and to a large degree received—national attention and the full creative energy of a group of dedicated reformers. According even to the French historian Robert Castel—a sharp critic of institutional psychiatry—there was something progressive

about the nineteenth-century asylum movement, in that its architects refused to view madness as a "pre-ordained destiny." Instead, because they
believed "that man is the product of his own works, his living environment,
that he may be overwhelmed by his very conquests, broken by the changes
and chances of history," it was also man's duty to repair those minds that
had been broken by the modern world.[5] In pursuit of this goal, they en-
listed almost the full range of cultural resources in rehabilitating the mad.
At that time, insane asylums were surprising centers of cultural activity. The
buildings themselves were magnificent structures with verdant grounds, often featuring working farms and sometimes even zoos, and they attracted
streams of tourists who wanted to satisfy themselves that their state was
providing humane treatment for its most unfortunate citizens. Inside, many
featured debating societies, lecture series, literary journals for patients, daguerreotype workshops, and fairs. Patients were taught in schools, preached
to in chapels, encouraged to participate in dramatic groups, and coached in
the arts of polite conversation. The energy that reformers devoted to restoring the mad to the realm of reason, however, was ultimately channeled in
ways that produced new forms of inequality in the social realm and conflict
in the cultural realm. Asylum superintendents promoted normalization of
one way of life and stigmatized those who stubbornly held to modes of
conduct and expression that were outside of those norms. In this regard,
Castel writes of "the almost inevitable failure of the totalitarian institution,
in so far as the person detained was obliged to break with his culture and
repudiate his group and class affinities, for the sake of a plan for his own regeneration in which he had had no part, because it merely expressed what
his masters had decreed."[6] This regeneration targeted a population well beyond the asylum walls. The asylum movement had designs on breaking not
just what Erving Goffman called the "presenting culture" of lunatics but
on the entire pathological world outside of their orderly domain; asylums
became at once laboratories for purifying the national culture and theaters
where this process could be observed.[7]

Imagined as sources of psychic and cultural renewal, asylums in practice
left a legacy of stigmatization of the insane and deepening cultural fissures
in the national fabric. In this way, their managers were both utopian dream-
ers and forerunners of today's cultural scolds, those authority figures who
tell us what to read, listen to, and watch in order to protect the social order.
As a literary scholar by training, I find the centrality of literary and cultural
activity to the asylum movement's conception of mental health (and the
good life) worth saluting. And yet this is not a work of nostalgia. My study

also points to some of the dangers that emerge when cultural activity is put to such nakedly instrumental uses: when culture is used as a tool to police social norms rather than to push against them, when it becomes a means to standardize human behavior rather than to explore its amazing diversity.

FROM THE EARLY 1830s until just before the Civil War, a great utopian movement to rehabilitate the insane resulted in the construction of dozens of publicly funded asylums, primarily but not exclusively in the Northern states. There, patients were attended to by medical staff who controlled their diet, exercise routines, drug intake, and—not least importantly—cultural pursuits: their habits in literature, worship, handicrafts, and the like. The environmental and cultural emphases were borrowed features of the "moral treatment" movement that had been developed by nonmedical, typically religiously oriented practitioners in eighteenth-century Europe, such as William Tuke, founder of the York Retreat in England, who believed that madness could be tamed in a loving, if firmly disciplined, environment.[8] From the late eighteenth century through the middle of the nineteenth on both sides of the Atlantic, medical practitioners co-opted the rhetoric and many of the practices of such lay healers. Although asylum physicians insisted that insanity was at its roots a disease of the brain that called for medical intervention, they also believed that mental illness often had a psychological or "moral" etiology, and that a carefully controlled environment was as essential to the cure as the administration of medical treatment. One could go mad from a blow to the head, from the inhalation of poisonous vapors, from indigestion, from masturbation, from hereditary predisposition, or from another disease, although asylums' annual reports and other writings of asylum superintendents also include such causes as excessive study, religious enthusiasm, anxieties over work, and even "blowing Fife all night," "reading vile books," and "extatic [sic] admiration of works of art."[9] Accordingly, patients' cultural and social activities were to be nurtured and closely monitored under the ever-watchful eye of the asylum superintendent.[10] The moral treatment movement—transposed into a medical key—gained systematicity in nineteenth-century asylums. Virtually every element of patients' quotidian routines attained therapeutic significance, but such activities as reading, writing, performing plays, worshipping in chapel, and learning useful—even marketable—skills were considered especially significant components of treatment, since they demonstrated the ability of the patients to internalize and reproduce the codes of behavior and thought endorsed by the authorities. Diversion was the key: at a time when the specialization encouraged by a market economy led to what physicians feared was a morbid tendency for the mind to run down one obsessive track, the asylum promoted a healthful range of cultural pursuits, aesthetic vistas, and useful occupations. Under some circumstances, these activities could even reshape the patient's brain and restore health.

To the extent that patients could produce creditable poetry, learn to work efficiently, comport themselves respectably, and advertise that skill in published literary works or stage performances, they justified massive public and private expenditures in this early form of social engineering. Cure rates in the early decades of American institutional psychiatry were routinely listed at upwards of eighty or ninety percent (although these figures were later shown to be faulty[11]); to its advocates, the asylum movement's medical/moral treatment paradigm was a revolutionary program, one that virtually guaranteed a right to mental health for all citizens. And the management of patients' cultural lives—promoting a healthful variety of correct cultural practices and suppressing activities deemed dangerous—was a central tool in maintaining an orderly democracy and producing sociable subjects fit to sustain it.

This logic was accepted, often uncritically, by many of the period's influential thinkers and cultural agents. For instance, although Nathaniel Hawthorne sometimes portrayed asylums as spaces of punishment rather than cure, he casually accepted the asylum movement's central therapeutic premises in his novel *The House of the Seven Gables*. Cloistered in that famous domain, the elderly Hepzibah Pyncheon "had grown to be a kind of lunatic, by imprisoning herself so long in that one place, with no other company than a single series of ideas." Her brother Clifford is even further gone, and is at one point threatened with being sent to a public asylum. But their young cousin Phoebe, whose arrival on the scene eventually sanitizes the house from the apparently contagious threat of insanity, has perfectly internalized the moral treatment regimen.

Unless she had now and then indulged her brisk impulses, and breathed rural air in a suburban walk, or ocean-breezes along the shore—had occasionally obeyed the impulse of nature, in new England girls, by attending a metaphysical or philosophical lecture, or viewing a seven-mile panorama, or listening to a concert—had gone shopping about the city, ransacking entire depots of splendid merchandize, and bringing home a ribbon—had enjoyed, likewise, a little time to read the Bible in her chamber, and had stolen a little more, to think of her mother and her native place—unless for such moral medicines as the above, we should soon have beheld our poor Phoebe grow thin, and put on a bleached, unwholesome aspect, and assume strange, shy ways, prophetic of an old-maidenhood and a cheerless future.[12]

Phoebe's "moral medicine" consists of activities that were sanctioned in almost every asylum: walks in nature, soothing the mind with music and stimulating it with lectures, carefully partaking of the variety of cultural pursuits that nearby cities had to offer, carefully mixing communion with nature and sociability. In a sense, she self-medicates according to the moral treatment plan, inoculating herself so that she will never need to have the program administered to her involuntarily, or slip into a delusional and dysfunctional dotage like her kinfolk.

Ralph Waldo Emerson would seem even less predisposed than Hawthorne to accept the logic of an institution devoted to regularizing and standardizing behavior through cultural programming, but at points in his writing he, too, seems unquestioningly to accept its central premises. Sounding much like Hawthorne's narrator, he wrote in "Experience":

> Health of body consists in circulation, and sanity of mind in variety or facility
> of association. We need change of objects. Dedication to one thought is quickly
> odious. We house with the insane, and must humor them; then conversation
> dies out.[13]

What seems merely a figurative way of speaking (over-specialization is like "hous[ing] with the insane") takes on a more personal and urgent character when we learn that Emerson had two brothers who were committed to McLean Asylum, and that he sometimes wondered whether the family's "constitutional malady" might affect him as well (chapter 4 will explore Emerson's close encounters with madness and institutionalization in detail). In a sense, his career as an essayist—and a generalist—could be read as an attempt to avoid "dedication to one thought," to promote "variety or facility of association" so that he need not "house with the insane." Such comments suggest the precariousness with which Emerson—like so many—guarded his own sanity at a time when the malady of madness was being diagnosed with unprecedented frequency, but they also reflect his sense that the insane could be wrenched out of their condition by training and a change of environment ("we need change of objects"). Phoebe's therapeutic shopping and playgoing are the "diversions" that asylum physicians thought central to jolting the mind from its morbid track; for Emerson, it is a constant mental motion ("we live amid surfaces, and the true art of life is to skate well on them")[14] that keeps him from going under.

Culture in the asylum was part of a systematic attempt to make the skating safe, to turn patients into so many little Phoebes, whether they wanted this or not.[15] Their cultural pursuits, then, carried a tremendous ideological baggage: the weight of an enormous institutional structure bore down on the patients, and the fulcrum bearing this weight was often the pen held in the hand of a maniac. In the case that interested Millard Fillmore, Jenny Lind sang a song; a patient heard it and was moved to write; an asylum physician read the resulting poem, approved of it, and showed it to a well-connected reformer; the reformer sent it to her friend in the Oval Office; the president read it, appreciated it, and wrote to the reformer, suggesting that he would support her endeavors. This poem is just one piece of flotsam in the broad flow of culture that entered into and poured out of these novel institutions in the nineteenth century. Through their barred windows came noises from the outside world: novels, poems, minstrel shows, songs, hymns, fashions, lectures; and back out through the windows, patients and doctors alike sent a stream of commentary on topics ranging from slavery to Shakespeare, from women's rights to temperance. Some of these elements of culture were endorsed by the doctors and served as models of and incentives for correct modes of speech and behavior. Tea parties, choir singing, walks in the countryside, lectures on the possibilities of reforming human character and on the best steps toward maintaining physical and mental health, the formation of debating societies, guided reading of scripture, temperate forms of worship, and elocution lessons — all of these presented a rational, polite, elevating model of culture that came from the top down, uplifting the patients whose minds and behavior had been unstrung by the pressures of life in the nineteenth century.[16]

Patients came from different worlds, sometimes feeling themselves above, but more often below, the doctors. And so, especially in the state-run institutions, there were the patients' guilty pleasures: fast dancing, drink, gambling, cheap novels, minstrel acts, pornography, religious revivals. These activities were all said to produce mental instability, even in some cases to deform the brain. Some were banished outright from the asylums (and sometimes smuggled back in), but others went through a kind of medical alchemy that transformed them into something sanative. Samuel Woodward, the superintendent of the State Lunatic Hospital in Worcester, Massachusetts, wrote that despite the moral hazards associated with dancing in society at large, within his institution it was:

> an exercise of the right kind, and very harmless in a hospital where every movement is in the hands of the officers. . . . There may be some institutions, in the vicinity of large cities, where this amusement might be objectionable, most of the inmates being from a small circle in extent; the intimacies and associations formed at dancing parties might not be desirable abroad. In my

own experience I have not met with any difficulty of this kind and the amusement has been more gratifying to a large class of patients, and more beneficial in its results, than any other mere amusement.[17]

Woodward's comments on dancing were echoed by D.S. Welling, the chaplain at the state asylum in Columbus, Ohio, who placed this vice-turned-virtue in the same category as card playing. Despite the "great evil" arising from these activities' "fascinating influence," their encouragement of "dissipation and frivolity," and even their tendency to induce "mania," such diversions within the asylum could be employed in a way that was "healthy" and even "curative."[18]

> No exercise is more healthful for persons of sedative habits than dancing; yet there are many modes of exercise more proper. I shall not now discuss the morality of the question as an exercise for healthy and sane people, but will say that it is very proper for lunatics in an Asylum to engage in it, and none but lunatics or sick persons should resort to it. Card playing is one of the most beneficial recreations that can be taken in the Asylum. It is an attractive and amusing exercise, and while it most powerfully engages the attention it does not fatigue the mind by study. . . . Some are thus cured, and many others greatly aided in their recovery.[19]

What these two reevaluations of "low" cultural practices reveal is that the asylum was not just a space for restoring the rationality of the insane; it was also an institution devoted to the purification and rationalization of culture. In a more focused and urgent way than their allied institutions of reform—the lyceum, the public school, the temperance society, the penitentiary—insane asylums adopted the role of the prefecture in a sort of neocolonial cultural warfare. Dedicated to upholding order and improving the unruly natives, they fought against a frustrating enemy who now seemed to endorse the mores of the rulers, and now spoke in code, concealing threatening gestures under a veil of incomprehensible cultural forms and gestures.[20] Accordingly, as this book will show, psychiatrists devoted a surprising amount of energy—if not subtlety—to such enterprises as theory of drama and literary criticism, which they saw as establishing the official rules for what Michel Foucault called "public hygiene."[21]

In his important book *The Discovery of the Asylum*, David Rothman analyzed the world of the asylum superintendents (the contemporaneous term for what we today call psychiatrists) as driven less by medical theories and innovations than by a critique of Jacksonian society.[22] Although insanity could result from a staggering variety of somatic and "moral" factors—all of which affected some compartment or "faculty" of the brain in different ways—the superintendents uniformly attributed the rise of insanity to faulty social organization.[23] Their critique of society, Rothman shows, strikes at what we recognize today as central ideals of Jacksonian, and even contemporary, American democracy: social mobility, political participation, and intellectual and religious freedom. These were not bad things in and of themselves, the asylum superintendents believed; rather, these hallmarks of the progress of civilization created conditions that led to mental strain. In the words of physician Edward Jarvis, an influential figure in the defense of asylum values:

> In this country, where no son is necessarily confined to the work or employment of his father . . . many are in a transition state, from the lower and less desirable to the higher and more desirable condition. . . . The mistake, or the ambition, of some, leads them to aim at that which they cannot reach . . . and their mental powers are strained to the utmost tension. Their minds stagger under the disproportionate burden; they are perplexed with the variety of insurmountable obstacles, they are exhausted with the ineffectual labor.[24]

The institutions that Jarvis and others promoted offered a clear hierarchy and sense of order, routine, and discipline to counterbalance the dizzying variety of options and obstacles of modern life. But if modernity and democracy wrought damage to the brains of American citizens, they also provided solutions, in the form of the asylums themselves. According to Amariah Brigham, superintendent of the New York State Lunatic Asylum, "The more there is of liberty . . . more numerous are the chances of mental derangement; though this does not prevent our allowing, that liberty is favorable also to the expansion of human reason."[25]

A significant focus of these reformers' social critiques was on the cultural forms thrown up by modern life. Card playing and dancing were hardly inventions of the nineteenth century; but cheap newspapers and novels, bawdy stage performances, and the rough-and-tumble culture of taverns provided quick fixes and new dangers for an increasingly rootless population unbound by traditions and communities. Physicians' writings give particular attention to reading. According to the influential psychiatrist Isaac Ray:

> The multiplicity of books and of readers, not only evinces a degree of mental activity which, a century ago, would have been regarded as scarcely within the bounds of possibility, but much of the literature of today is of a kind not calculated to promote the mental health. It is more or less directly addressed

to the lower sentiments of our nature, thereby impairing that supremacy of the higher which is indispensable in a healthy, well-ordered mind. . . . He . . . whose reading is calculated only to inflame the imagination with pictures of unhallowed enjoyment, to banish every manly thought and pure emotion, to extend the empire of passion, and induce him to fill his measure of happiness with things that perish in the using, is weakening all the conservative principles of his mind, and facilitating the approach of disease.[26]

Reading the right sort of thing, of course, could be enormously instructive and stabilizing for patients. But according to John Galt—who brought the largely Northern system of medical and moral treatment to his asylum in Virginia—doctors should have a thorough knowledge of the cultural habits of their patients and even develop a "course of reading" for patients who tend to read in a "desultory" manner.[27] Even the Bible, Galt believed, could be dangerous in certain contexts (especially when read by those with religious delusions), and so he urged that access to the Bible be restricted depending on the psychological state of the patient.[28]

This system of cultural—rather than simply social—control was thus an important part of the power dynamic that Rothman and (even more influentially) Michel Foucault analyzed in the history of the asylum. The emergence of institutional psychiatry in postrevolutionary France, wrote Foucault, brought into being a system of "social segregation that would guarantee bourgeois morality a universality of fact and permit it to be imposed as a law upon all forms of insanity."[29] But was this imposition ever really achieved? A sense of the struggle that ensued at every point in the management of the institutions is something that—as numerous critics have pointed out—Foucault's *Madness and Civilization* does not address.[30] Before the 1850s, insane asylums in the United States met with little organized political and intellectual opposition, but the system still faced internal and external resistance. Doctors struggled with the public and legislatures to secure and maintain authority over their institutions; they struggled with attendants to implement their policies; and they struggled with patients to accept their dictates.[31] Meanwhile, patients struggled with their families, their communities, their employers, and—most importantly—themselves to retain a sense of dignity and personal autonomy amidst the overwhelming pressures to abject themselves.

In posthumously published lectures that revisit the terrain of his famous *Madness and Civilization,* Foucault recognized the importance of these struggles, and in a sense recast them as critical to the management of the insane (and—in his characteristically sweeping gestures—the management of the modern self). Power in the asylum was not granted to an individual or a specific group, but rather, was relational; what these nineteenth-century institutions brought into being was the "procedure of continuous control" over bodies and behaviors. This power was no longer a matter of segregation and interdiction, as Foucault had conceived of it in his earlier work; instead, he portrayed the asylum as a "battlefield" in which medical authority was engaged in a more or less constant "scene of confrontation" with patients, the goal of which was "wearing down" the mad and forcing them to accept the dictates of the institution passively, without resistance. This is a crucial point for Foucault, since he argued that the asylum and related institutions brought into being a modern type of control—the "microphysics of power," or a "disciplinary power"—that no longer relies on sovereign authorities who hand down edicts, command allegiance, and levy penalties and punishments. Rather, it is a "capillary" network that opens up perches for constant monitoring and surveillance, a network whose function is to control rather than to punish, one that is intended to run itself rather than operate at the will of a person or particular group. It is a network, Foucault argues, that envelops us in a "tissue of writing" that records our "bodies, behavior, and discourse"—a "pangraphic panopticism" that pervades our sense of who we are.[32] Case notes in a nineteenth-century patient's file are the prototype for all those minute interventions by unseen yet all-seeing authorities who—sometimes subtly and sometimes not—shadow us, monitor us, scribble down facts and figures, and force us to monitor our behavior. Whether she knows it or not, Phoebe's shopping trips are conducted under the watchful eye of the authorities; the eye has simply been internalized.

The Foucault known to readers familiar with *Madness and Civilization* was of a piece with the protest movements of the 1960s and 70s that questioned the legitimacy of institutions (especially state-sponsored ones) that propped up the power of the ruling classes. But the positions Foucault arrived at in these later lectures are more in line with my concerns here: the point is not to blame the architects of the asylum for shutting away the mad but to understand how a story of humanitarian intervention is also a story of domination. And yet there is still in this posthumously published work a tendency to load the dice. The doctors' theories of cure are laid out only in fragments so that we can never hear them apart from Foucault's own practically panoptic perspective—with the result that doctors come across as cogs in a dehumanizing machine rather than as human beings with complicated motivations, talents, and limitations. And the patients, with whom Foucault's sympathies seem to lie, are virtually silent. For all his reportage from the front lines of this foundational battle for the modern soul, Foucault—like Rothman and most of the asylums' historiographers—relies almost exclusively on the word of the authorities, or what James Scott calls the "public transcript" of institutional life.[33] Foucault's focus is always on how bodies are controlled, and for this, one can perhaps content oneself with the perspective of the authorities. But the goals of the asylum movement were larger than controlling bodies: for them the fate of the culture was at stake. And since one of my presuppositions in this book is that culture flows upward from below and can never be thoroughly controlled by those in power, it is imperative to listen closely to those whose cultural expression was placed under maximum pressure.

Looking to the cultural activity of nonelite actors as signs and sites of social struggle has by now become a central, even defining, operation in cultural studies. The idea of culture as a "whole way of conflict," however, undergoes some strange permutations when it is applied to life in the asylum.[34] One ordinarily works in one place and worships, watches a show, writes a poem, or reads a book in another. If the poem or the show offers a sense of resistance to or release from the hierarchies of the workplace, the boss usually does not find this out. But in tightly enclosed spaces such as the asylum—what Erving Goffman called "total institutions"—where patients are under the constant surveillance of the authorities, every act is monitored and folded back into the hierarchical structure of the institution.[35] One would ordinarily imagine, for instance, a card game as a site for nineteenth-century workers to curse the boss or at least suspend the ordinary rules of bourgeois conduct; but for Reverend Welling, it could support the morality of the official asylum regime. This does not mean, however, that the "constant punitive pressure" that Foucault describes ever produced an entirely docile population, one that it succeeded in fully "wearing down." Conflict was meant to be leeched out of asylum culture, for sure, but paradoxically, this only created new conflicts. According to a former patient named William Hotchkiss, "The card-playing produced a decidedly bad effect upon some inmates," who imagined that they were in a gambling house, "and this would set them raving."[36] Whether they were raving because they had relapsed into madness or because they did not want to play by the doctors' rules he did not say.

Being caught up in such a program meant, for many patients, having one's world turned against oneself. Strange new cultural hierarchies could emerge. If card playing was refashioned to uphold the official order, sometimes even singing hymns could be subversive: Hotchkiss tells of another patient, "an elder of the Presbyterian church," who was forbidden to sing hymns in the evening and passed his time doing nothing but playing checkers.[37] Accepting the authorities' cultural proscriptions meant turning the ordinary tools of expressivity, freedom, and autonomy into a jailhouse of words, ideas, and practices. An 1845 article in the *American Journal of Insanity*—the main organ of early psychiatric thought—calls asylum amusements a superior means by which "refractory youths, and wild young men and women, are tamed at the shortest notice."[38] The documentary traces of these amusements record a painful awareness of this function. To write in an asylum journal, perform in a stage play, or worship in chapel was only to redouble the acute self-consciousness of ordinary life in the asylum, where every action was scrutinized like a stage play. "The history of disabled people in the western world," writes Rosemarie Garland Thomson, "is in part the history of being on display, of being visually conspicuous while being politically and socially erased."[39] Psychiatry in the nineteenth century was something of a spectator sport. Promoters and superintendents of asylums encouraged visitors because they wanted to raise funds, gain approval from legislators, allay public suspicion about the institutions, and demonstrate that the harsh treatments of the past had been replaced by humanitarian kindness. And so asylums were popular tourist destinations, where ordinary citizens could bask in the glory of their Republic's benevolent treatment of the most unfortunate. Day-trippers brought picnic lunches to eat on their verdant grounds and stopped in to chat with doctors and patients, and virtually all of the great travel writers of the day—from Charles Dickens to Harriet Martineau—felt that no account could be given of the national character without a stop at a lunatic hospital.[40] In its first decade of existence, the New York State Lunatic Asylum at Utica averaged 2,700 visitors a year, outstripping Mammoth Cave in Kentucky, a leading tourist attraction.[41] (The patients' families, however, were generally not allowed to visit, as the superintendents feared that they would create obstacles to treatment.[42])

Asylum tourism also allowed visitors to indulge in some of the spectatorial pleasures that they might be too ashamed to pursue in public, at the popular freak shows of the day.[43] Doctors and patients alike were aware of the prurient side of these ostensibly humanitarian visits. Pliny Earle, superintendent of the elite Bloomingdale Asylum in New York, asked, "Why should [people] visit asylums for the insane, with no higher purpose than to be amused at the freaks of an idiot or the ravings of a madman—to gratify that idle curiosity, which would be equally well satisfied by the antics of a monkey, or the raging of a famished lion?"[44] Earle did not so much try to combat this curiosity as to elevate it, to turn it into a kind of literary fascination with the wondrous capacities of the minds of the insane, which could be demonstrated through their writings. Earle shows that one patient, however, in his fantastical hallucinations, appeared to turn popular fascination with the insane into an element of his psychological struggle. "An intelligent clerk," this man believed that bumblebees came out of his back and produced changes in the moon, that "Nick Biddle's Bank-books" also came out of his back, as well as "a large collection of bones, nails, screws, buckles, horse-shoes, locks, &c., which he had collected in his rambles, and deposited under his bed. He requested that they might be sent to Peale's Museum, as remarkable curiosities, inasmuch as they all came from various portions of his body."[45]

This patient's desire to donate the fantastical emanations of his body to a museum that straddled the never-quite-separate worlds of nineteenth-century science and popular culture appears to represent his desire to have some say over the uses to which his person was put, in both confinement and display. Perhaps it also points to a desire to escape from the stultifying refinement and imposed civility of his captors for a world of popular culture that represented the freedom to look and be looked at without judgment. But of course the lunatics, like the human wonders of the world of "the freaks" that Earle disparaged, had no such options. The display of freaks, like that of lunatics, involved actors who were usually coerced and who had limited life options aside from displaying their disabilities or deformities to "norms"[46]; the difference was that the performances of freaks generally emphasized their aberrance, whereas the confined lunatics acted out a script in which they were overcoming their deviant tendencies and mental disturbances and returning to a state of civility. At any rate, whether for amusement or edification, all of the public gazing and prying only intensified the normal theatrical state of things in the asylum, where even a meal became a test of one's ability to act appropriately. To be cured was to go through an elaborate stage show, and sanity was revealed as the mastery of artifice. As one lunatic author put it: "It is deemed a matter of consideration whether this noble temple of humanity, should not be converted into a giant theater and that Mr. Macready [the great Shakespearian actor] be invited to superintend over it."[47]

President Fillmore scrutinized the results of one such staged expression and found it passable. Clearly, writing one successful poem would not be enough to win a release from the asylum, but mastering expression of a rational sequence of thought in a decorous and formal manner was a significant therapeutic achievement in the behaviorist program of the moral treatment. The patient who wrote to Jenny Lind (and, unintentionally, to the president) may well have found the poem an agent of effecting or demonstrating a cure and therefore an avenue of release from the asylum. The artificial, heavily scrutinized, character-effacing cultural pursuits of the asylum could in this way be experienced as highly liberating. The asylum poet was a caged bird, but how many anonymous, nonprofessional poets, after all, could boast of having their offerings read and commented upon by the president of the United States? The poem's strange circulation route might make rough sense at a time when technological advances and the development of micro-markets for literature led to a democratization of print culture; all sorts of people were reading works by strangers who were nonprofessional writers.[48] And yet this writer's work received notice, not in spite of his or her subordinate position, but because of it. To be part of a national problem was to make one suddenly visible, to produce a public voice where one had none before.

This tension of an asylum culture that was at once liberating and enslaving can further explain the significance of Fillmore's response to the lunatic's poem in its historical context. While Congress—and the nation—found themselves dragged toward open violence by the pull of one spectacularly controversial carceral institution, the asylum appeared (at least through the early 1850s) as a happy twin of slavery. Indeed, insanity and the asylums that housed the afflicted were always shadowed by the national debates over slavery and abolition. The insane asylum constituted a site no less crucial—and in some ways more complex—for the discussion of individual liberties and their limitations than did the slave system. Both institutions revoked the civil liberties of a confined population in the name of public order and the creation of an efficient labor force, and both housed a purportedly subrational population that was deemed incapable of handling the complexities of life in a modern democracy. Lunatics, like slaves, were deprived of the right to vote, to sign contracts, to make wills, and to hold property. Both blacks and the insane were viewed as children, with the asylum's triumph over madness paralleling the white race's subduing of the black.[49] The difference, however, was that the lunatic, with proper care, might attain adulthood, whereas the black was stuck in a more or less permanent primitive or childlike state.[50] As George Fitzhugh, a preeminent apologist for slavery, put it: "If it be right and incumbent to subject children to the authority of parents and guardians, and idiots and lunatics to committees, would it not be equally right and incumbent to give the free negroes masters, until at least they arrive at years of discretion, which very few ever did or will attain?"[51] The implication, of course, was that in contrast to "free negroes," lunatics would "arrive at years of discretion" if properly cared for, and so the parallels between the systems of slavery and asylum care were jammed even as they were created. Unlike slaves, the insane had their rights and freedoms revoked in the name of restoring them to citizenship.

Especially when the reported cure rates were so high, the asylum could be viewed as a benevolent institution that uplifted the downtrodden and restored them to a place of dignity in American society. Even the preeminent black abolitionist Frederick Douglass seemed to accept this logic. In an 1852 article in *Frederick Douglass' Paper*, readers were told of "an insane colored woman, wife of a respectable colored man" who was sent to the Lunatic Asylum of Indianapolis, only to be "refused admission by the Superintendent, who thought the law did not authorize him to bestow the benefits of the Asylum on a colored person."[52] Rather than drawing a parallel between the incarceration of lunatics and the situation of slaves, Douglass presented this story as an instance of racial prejudice, one in which a black man was denied "the right of all persons having a legal settlement in the State," namely the right to commit his wife to an institution. That he did not protest the right of the woman to choose whether or not to go may be attributable not only to his acceptance of the institution's legitimacy but to his conception of freedom as a masculine prerogative: he seems to be accepting what Elaine Showalter has called the asylum's "domestication of insanity," in which the patriarchal institution was "ruled by the father, and subject to his values and his law."[53] (In Douglass's defense, however, the piece ends on an ironic note that makes his position more difficult to pin down: the woman, he writes, should be admitted because "a colored insane person can disturb a whole neighborhood just as well as if he or she were white.")

Douglass's apparent endorsement of a right *to* psychiatric treatment rather than a protection *from* involuntary incarceration points to the widespread legitimacy of the asylum in the mid-nineteenth century. Only in the following decades, as the moral treatment paradigm collapsed under the weight of its inflated claims, challenges from competing paradigms (most notably the new science of neurology), and the complaints of former patients who exposed the underside of the psychiatric utopia would asylum care in a progressive Northern institution come to seem to many observers like white slavery. (Mental patients in Illinois, one protestor wrote in 1867, were "debased like the negro."[54]) And so, in 1850, the president's enchantment with a lunatic's verse represented a shift in his attention from a paternalistic institution that was tearing the nation apart to one that was almost universally hailed as restoring its psychic well-being.

WHAT FOLLOWS in this book is a series of snapshots of cultural life in the nineteenth-century asylum and asylum life in nineteenth-century culture. Throughout, I am interested in recording the dialectical tension between the institutional processing of culture and the cultural processing of the institution. By the former, I mean the aggressive reshaping of patients' cultural lives that secured the authority of those in power; by the latter, I mean both the patients' recourse to cultural knowledge as a way to navigate their perilous institutional existence, and the representations of the asylum regime by outsiders who were poised to make a difference in the public's perception of institutional psychiatry. The book's chapters fall roughly in two groups: the first three explore the cultural activity of inmates and doctors under the moral treatment regime; the last three reverse the gaze to show what these institutions with new powers to rescind individual liberties in the name of mental health looked like to critical observers from the outside. I do not pretend in either section to achieve thoroughness or even representativeness. Some of the cases I study are transparently exceptional, strange, or offbeat. One reason for this is that as a writer I follow my own nose to places that interest me; another is that I want to resist treating the lives of those on the margins of society as part of a deeper aggregate, an impulse that was behind segregating the insane from the sane in the first place. The subjects of the following chapters are, I hope, treated as individuals caught up in a system that would erase their particularity in order to return them—paradoxically—to a society that valued individual liberties above all. Some of the "mad" poets and other asylum figures assembled here wrote and performed and talked with great skill and insight; this skill was sometimes deployed in disastrously self-defeating ways, and occasionally in ways that secured their release from the asylum. Nonetheless, I make no claims for the artistic greatness of any of my central asylum figures. (The possible exception is the poet Jones Very, a primary subject of chapter 4; but my sense of his literary accomplishment is hardly an original one.) Instead, I have looked for moments of high cultural intensity, where something in a poem or a performance or a social interchange vibrates with violent force against its ideological and institutional contexts. The asylum as a site of cultural exchange can illuminate not just individual texts and institutions but, I think, the whole shape of mid-nineteenth-century culture. The obsession with insanity—diagnosing it, segregating it, reforming it—was not just a question of tidying up the margins; it was a central story that the culture told itself about itself.[55]

The first three chapters of *Theaters of Madness* view nineteenth-century cultural life through the barred windows of the asylum. Chapter 1 focuses on the *Opal*, a journal of patients' creative writing published at the New York State Lunatic Asylum. In this chapter, I reconstruct the psychiatric theory and practice behind the journal's production and examine the ways in which patients used the space provided them to make sense of their social situation and their afflictions. My central claim is that patients responded to the enforced anonymity and "civil death" of asylum life by mimicking an elite, literary anonymity practiced by genteel writers of the period. Rather than using the journal to voice coded protests against authority, many of the authors cast their confinement as a retreat from the overwhelming forces of nineteenth-century modernity with which they had been unable to cope on the outside; and they cast their authorship in a mode that similarly retreated from market forces that their doctors claimed had poisoned the culture.

The second chapter explores the life of a curious blackface minstrel troupe composed of patients at the New York State Lunatic Asylum. Performing several times a year for patients, doctors, and visitors, they turned a famously carnivalesque popular form into a therapeutic diversion for other patients in a display meant to convince the outside world—and perhaps themselves—that they, unlike the black characters they mocked, were capable of rationally managing their affairs in the modern world. The chapter also examines patients' writings about these performances, in which they reflect on how the social categories of blackness and mental alienation resemble one another. This discussion encompasses an examination of the interplay between strategies of confinement and uplift common to plantation slavery, the colonial enterprise, and institutional psychiatry. I use the episode to argue that the "civilizing process," which proved such a potent argument behind Euro-American colonization and enslavement of blacks, also structured the relations between doctors and patients.

Moving from the cultural lives of patients to those of the doctors, chapter 3 resurrects a substantial body of Shakespeare criticism in the first-ever psychiatric journal, the *American Journal of Insanity*. In this work, the physicians cite the Bard as a precursor to themselves, modern mental health specialists, on the basis of his theories and even practices of mental science, and they appropriate his legacy in an attempt to legitimate their new profession. For the early psychiatrists, Shakespeare's medical infallibility both mirrored and masked their own fiercely guarded institutional authority. In their role as critics of modernity who nonetheless were at the vanguard of progress, they appealed to him as a premodern visionary who intuited the modern world but was uncorrupted by it. The chapter concludes with an account of patients reading Shakespeare and responding—sometimes strenuously—to what they perceived as their doctors' misreadings; they used the almost scriptural authority of the Bard to contest the regime of their doctors in much the way that slaves used the bible against the masters who gave it to them.

The final chapters of the book examine renderings of asylum life and the nascent psychiatric profession in literature and popular culture. I am interested throughout in the ways that institutionalization figured both as the fulfillment of a democratic ideal of universal mental health and as the underside of that ideal, characterized by irrationality, physical constraint, and abuse of power.

Chapter 4 poses the question of what the transcendentalist movement would look like if we placed McLean Asylum as the central institution against which the group defined its relation to New England culture. The key figures in the story are Ralph Waldo Emerson and his acolyte Jones Very, the self-proclaimed Second Coming of Christ and writer of visionary poetry, who was confined in McLean Asylum shortly after hearing Emerson's infamous "Divinity School Address" in 1838. Through the writings on Very by Emerson, Elizabeth Palmer Peabody, and others in this philosophical-literary movement, I examine the transcendentalists' guarded accommodation to early psychiatry—a profession that would seem to cut against the core of their anti-institutional thinking, their emphasis on nonconformism, and their radical individualism, but that intersected with the movement in surprisingly frequent and intimate ways. What emerges is a glimpse of the uneasily shared ground of American literary romanticism and psychiatry, both of which movements saw themselves as fortifying the individual against the threats of modernization and social atomization. The chapter concludes with a reading of Emerson's famous essay "Self-Reliance," in light of Emerson's uneasy experience with institutions that housed those unable to manage their independence. Finally, a coda examines Very's poetry from the period during his incarceration and immediately after his release, in which he interprets his travails and his abandonment by the transcendentalists through the filter of his messianic vision, which appeared to survive his ordeal.

Building on a close reading of Edgar Allan Poe's short story "The System of Doctor Tarr and Professor Fether" (a strangely similar story to Peter Weiss's famous 1964 play *Marat/Sade*), I explore in chapter 5 some of the inner contradictions in the ideology of the asylum that Emerson could never quite acknowledge. In particular, the reading opens out to interrogate the place of the asylum in a postrevolutionary, democratic society. In this ominous story, Poe links the emergence of the moral treatment to the outbreak of revolutionary terror in France, and—through terrifying racial imagery at the end—to the uprising of slaves against their Southern masters. Whereas chapter 2 shows how what Sander Gilman has called "the nexus of blackness and madness"[56] could create an opportunity to ponder the possibilities of uplifting downtrodden populations, Poe's story crawls along the psychological underside of that nexus, hinting at the rage of those exploited and confined the name of rationality and order. It is not only the slave system that creates this disorder; liberal democracy is as much to blame. Guided by a Burkean fear of (and a Sadean fascination with) the breakdown of authority, Poe sees the asylum as an instance of the worst kind of bourgeois humanitarian illusion: that civility can put up a good fight against unreason without descending into the abyss of madness.

The final chapter explores some of the cultural forces and gendered dynamics that contributed to the downfall of the moral treatment movement. Much of the focus is on the successful reform efforts of Elizabeth Parsons Ware Packard, a former patient whose exposés of her treatment called attention to the plight of women who were wrongfully incarcerated at the will of their husbands. Packard's twin political goals were to overturn marriage laws that made women defenseless against unscrupulous husbands and to weaken the authority of (male) asylum superintendents to admit patients against their will. The chapter asks why these two movements became linked, and why—in the following century's feminist historiography—psychiatry came so often to be viewed as a tool of patriarchy to silence nonconforming women. The question is more acute when we consider that male patients in some sense had more to lose than did women in becoming mental patients (the rights to vote, to hold property, and so on), and that in some ways men were more stigmatized by early psychiatric views of sexuality than were women. To answer these riddles, I set Packard's text against a background of male- and female-authored asylum memoirs, popular fiction detailing the figure of the woman captive to psychiatry, and doctors' writings on the dangers of male sexuality. I end with a reading of Melville's story, "Bartleby the Scrivener," which can be taken as a commentary on the voicelessness of pathologized males in a period when feminism found an early voice in the cries of female former patients.

Finally, the epilogue seeks traces of the moral treatment in the contemporary scene in psychiatry, literature, and popular culture. While our society remains fascinated by the specter of madness—as manifested in popular memoirs and Hollywood films—we have lost the sense of its broad social implications. And though a chastened, perhaps matured version of the moral treatment's faith in the efficacy of culture in the treatment of mental illness lives on, it does so almost exclusively in elite, private psychiatric hospitals. The widely reported collapse of the state systems follows from this privatization of hope. Perhaps the deepest casualty, however, is the sense that our collective response to our most vulnerable citizens is a measure by which our whole society may be judged.

———— ✳ ————

CHAPTER ONE

Brothers and Sisters of Asylumia

Literary Life in the New York State Lunatic Asylum

Naked, we needed protection, and the hospital protected us. Of course, the hospital had stripped us naked in the first place—but that just underscored its obligation to shelter us.

Susanna Kaysen, *Girl, Interrupted* (1993)

ON OCTOBER 24, 1843, A.S.M., a 38-year-old doctor from Columbia County, New York, was brought by his brother to the New York State Lunatic Asylum at Utica.[1] According to his case file, he was a voracious reader who had been deranged intermittently for about 15 years, with recent bouts of sleeplessness, confusion, loquaciousness, and "irregular habits of dress." In his first year at Utica, he seemed "happy and contented." His new home was, in some ways, a good fit for A.S.M. Founded only ten months earlier under the leadership of the charismatic superintendent Amariah Brigham, the Utica asylum quickly became the nerve center of the newly emerging psychiatric profession (known then by a variety of monikers, perhaps most commonly "asylum medicine") and one of the most innovative centers of moral and medical treatment. The institutional home of the *American Journal of Insanity*—the official organ of the young psychiatric profession—the Utica asylum played a crucial role in formalizing and disseminating key aspects of this mode of treatment. And with its grand, pillared facade, verdant grounds designed by the famous landscape architect Andrew Jackson Downing, a working farm, an annual fair, theatrical productions, and occupational workshops, it was also a tourist attraction for those who wanted to see how this utopian experiment brought light to benighted minds[2]

FIGURE 1. New York State Lunatic Asylum. (Collection of New York State Archives)

(fig. 1). A.S.M. took full advantage of the cultural program at Utica: he joined the patients' debating society; he spent long hours in the library; he composed speeches at asylum anniversaries; and he even found himself formally addressing Millard Fillmore on the president's visit to the asylum in 1851.

In that same year, A.S.M. became the editor of the patients' new literary journal, the *Opal,* and he would become perhaps its most frequent contributor throughout its decade-long run. The journal contained a mixture of fiction, poetry, religious writings, dramatic sketches, occasional pieces, literary exercises, political commentary, patient memoirs, open letters, "healing" narratives, and cultural critique. It is, however, at best an elliptical record of the lives, thoughts, and experiences of the authors. If one wants a straight picture of asylum life drawn from the inside, the *Opal* is bound to disappoint. Accounts of the daily lives of patients are so cheery and sugarcoated as to be beyond credibility. Asylum life is most often pictured as a series of games, theatrical amusements, ceremonies, book-reading parties, learned conversations, and, occasionally, dramatic cures of insanity. The physicians are kindly father figures with nothing but humanitarian impulses; the attendants are professional and respectful; and the patients are intelligent, refined, and creative—if given to bouts of despondency. There is very little writing about madness itself—except for a few articles written from the safe perspective of former patients or convalescents, who narrate their triumphs over illness—and few of the wild flights of imaginative fancy or "the poetry of insanity" that the belle-lettristic superintendent of another institution, Pliny Earle, was beginning to take seriously in the writings of the insane.[3] One could easily forget on reading the *Opal* that the asylum was an institution with unprecedented powers to rescind the liberties of the socially deviant or psychologically aberrant; that the patients were subject to the physicians' haphazard experimentation with serious drugs like opium and to their "cures" for problematic behavior that included cauterizing the genitals of masturbators; that attendants occasionally beat patients who challenged their authority; and that many of the patients themselves were violent, tore their clothing to shreds, smeared their faces with excrement, committed suicide, or sang out their hallucinations into the night.[4]

How, then, do we read the *Opal* if not as a realistic portrayal of asylum life or as an authentic voice of the mad? In a small pool of critical writing on literature produced within asylums, most commentators have agreed that such literary production should be read in terms of its relation to the totalizing power of the institutional authorities. They disagree, however, on whether such writing can ever meaningfully resist institutional surveillance, or whether its sponsorship by the authorities always undermines its subversive potential. In the same year that Foucault published *Madness and Civilization* (1961), Erving Goffman wrote that "house organs"—newsletters written by patients—are little more than vehicles for patients to voice "the institutional line" on issues affecting their lives.[5] Jann Matlock, writing about a nineteenth-century woman's surreptitious asylum journal, arrives at an equally sweeping but precisely opposite conclusion: "Writing in the asylum is always [a] transgression. It is always an attempt to get beyond the asylum, to make sense out of being locked up, to reclaim an identity other than the one conferred by the system, to procure an inviolable space."[6] Maryrose Eannace, the only critic to examine the *Opal* in depth, sees the journal as a "miscellany" that does not speak "in one voice"; ultimately, however, she focuses on the journal's "political" writings, which she sees as "writing to power"—challenging the doctors' definitions of insanity as well as popular images of the insane.[7]

Despite their disagreements, these critics all read patients' writings as responding to a field of power that is already thoroughly established by the doctors, rather than one that is actively created and contested in the scene of writing. I believe it is more productive to read the journal as what James Scott calls a "public transcript" of official asylum ideology, in which patients are made to legitimize the ideology behind their treatment; and yet it also gives us a glimmer of a "hidden transcript," that is, a "critique of power spoken behind the back of the dominant," but disguised by carefully maintained "innocuous understandings of their conduct." The "hidden transcript," writes Scott "is a strange kind of ideological debate about justice and dignity in which one party has a severe speech impediment induced by power relations."[8] Neither the monochromatic voice of the "institutional line" nor a consistently subversive vehicle for "writing to power," the journal was a space in which authority and its subjects spoke to each other and to the outside world on heavily unequal terms: the former in confident, ringing tones; the latter often through linguistic masking, anonymity, and double talk.

The goal of this double talk, however, was not generally to protest the conditions of asylum life or to win one's release. Open protest against the asylum authorities would hardly be sanctioned in Utica's house organ; and winning one's release, after all, would be accomplished more easily by mouthing the institutional line than by subverting it. More often, paradoxically, the jagged or off-key pieces published in the journal represented a resistance that was more perverse and unsettling than direct critique, because it could not quite be pinned down. The journal, for certain writers (especially A.S.M., to whom I will return at the end of this chapter), offered a way to reclaim the meanings of life in the asylum in terms other than those prescribed by the authorities. Claiming their institutionalized lives *as* their identity, these writers apparently embraced the asylum's self-image as a respite from a dangerous world—but they embraced it so tightly that their writings often called into question the central function of the asylum, which was to return them as "normal" citizens to the world from which they were sheltered.

The tacit fiction governing the journal—the "speech impediment" imposed upon patients—turned their removal from the democratic currents of the nineteenth century into an exalted literary opportunity. Having lost their civic identities and the rights of self-possession, enfranchisement, and social—even physical—mobility, the patients were asked to glorify their loss of freedom as an act of humanitarianism, to view their incarceration as the gateway to freedom. The hinge for this process was the writers' anonymity, which had a range of meanings in nineteenth-century literary culture. Anonymity could be the sign of a genteel refusal to play the game of literary commercialism—a sign that one's writing was not motivated by a desire for acclaim and the money that might go with it.[9] Additionally, it could function as a mask used by writers from disenfranchised groups, who often wrote from a position of danger and wanted to protect themselves from some of the consequences of affixing their name to writings that might be scrutinized by those in power (freed blacks in the North, for instance, often wrote anonymously when they published their work).[10]

In reality, the *Opal* writers' anonymity came from yet a third motive: to print their names would risk stigmatizing them and their families. Most of those who wrote for the journal came from bourgeois or even upper-class backgrounds, and their consignment to the asylum marked a loss of social standing as severe as could be imagined in a culture that prized, above all, upward mobility. Accordingly, in crafting their literary personae within the journal's pages, they seemed most often to adopt the first type of anonymity: that of the gentlemen and ladies of standing who actively refused the sordid world of literary ambition and striving. And yet they knew that their stay in the asylum was a function of their inability to maintain the class standing from which they had been alienated. In the journal, they could maintain the fiction of their elevated status, even as they hinted at their anger at the world that had cast them aside. And so their anonymity became something like the veil adopted by the underclass: a mask that could occasionally be lifted to reveal—through wry portraiture and fleeting gestures of pain—the fictionality of the world they portrayed and the cruelty of the one they had left behind.

THE OPAL had at least three forerunners: the *Retreat Gazette,* a newsletter published by patients at the Hartford Retreat for the Insane in 1837; the *Asylum Journal,* put out at the Brattleboro Retreat in Vermont beginning in 1842, and the *Morning-Side Mirror,* published by patients at the Royal Edinburgh Lunatic Asylum in 1845. All were relatively short-lived, and judging from surviving issues and descriptions, none had quite the ambitions or range of the *Opal.*[11] The *Opal* itself originated in the male and female schools that Brigham established for patients whose brains he felt would not be overtaxed by close application to study. In classes of twenty patients that met for two hours a day, the schools gave instruction in hymn singing, arithmetic, spelling, geography, and other conventional subjects; at the end of the month, the scholars met in a chapel to undergo a general examination and read aloud from their compositions. Some of these were distributed within the asylum in a pen-printed journal.[12] By 1850—a year after Brigham died and was replaced by Nathan Benedict—the female patient-scholars had produced a formal collection of their compositions, which they sold at the asylum's annual fair. Several male patients contributed to the first volume, and by the second year a male editor (A.S.M.) had the reins of the journal.

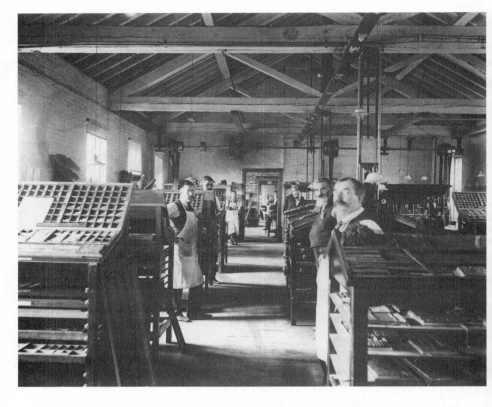

FIGURE 2. Print shop at the New York State Lunatic Asylum. (Collection of New York State Archives)

It was printed on the asylum's printing press, which had been acquired primarily to publish annual reports and the *American Journal of Insanity* [13] (fig. 2). By now the *Opal* was such a success that it was established as a regular quarterly modeled after popular periodicals, such as *Graham's*, *Godey's Ladies Book*, and especially the *Knickerbocker*, the leading literary journal of New York's elite.[14]

The ostensible function of the *Opal* was to furnish the means for the acquisition of a patient library, and in this it was quite successful. Building on the subscription list of the *American Journal of Insanity*, the journal had by the end of its first year 900 subscribers and an exchange list of 330 periodicals, numbers that continued to grow through the mid-1850s. The exchange list provided a wide variety of reading material for the asylum's library, and sales of the journal furnished an elegant collection of "standard works of literature"—650 volumes in the first year alone.[15] Beyond this narrow function, the journal also served to showcase the effects of the medical and moral treatment of patients. This advertising often took the form of paeans to kind physicians, favorable descriptions of daily life in the asylum, and hagiographies of Brigham or Philippe Pinel (the acknowledged founder of the moral treatment movement), whose portrait graced the standard cover of the journal (fig. 3). Some articles portrayed the asylum as one of the crowning achievements of American democracy. In a time of scattered but mounting charges that asylums were contemporary "bastilles" headed by tyrannical superintendents who compelled the inmates to work for nothing and subjected them to severe punishments for the slightest acts of disobedience, the *Opal* presented the superintendents in the image of the founding fathers, guaranteeing a self-evident right of mental health to temporarily damaged citizens.[16] Accounts of Fourth of July celebrations in the asylum always recorded that toasts to George Washington and the Revolutionary heroes were followed by "volunteer" toasts made by patients to the physicians. One ode written for the festivities in 1854 made the equation particularly clear:

> God of our destiny,
> Whose grace doth make us free,
> Teach us the right to see,
>   And seeing—to embrace—
> Oh! Give us self control,
> Let virtue be our goal,
> Pursued with heart and soul—
>   When we shall win the race.[17]

The "freedom" secured by the institution was "the right to see" and to maintain "self control." Orated by a patient whose fundamental liberties and rights—property rights, the right to vote, the right to physical mobility—were taken away by the asylum, this poem performs a reversal with a high ideological charge. It is insanity that takes away those rights, and (if one makes the easy substitution of *superintendent* for *God*) the asylum that—by confining the patient—will restore them.

The meaning of the journal, however, was not simply a matter of what its articles were *about*: the patients' writing was cast as an effect, rather than simply a description, of the moral treatment at Utica. The title (the *Opal*) refers to the precious stone's "singular power of preventing sickness and sorrow," and the journal's purpose was described as "to indicate some phases of the mind, from the State's Retreat for Sorrow, at Utica" and "to exhibit . . .

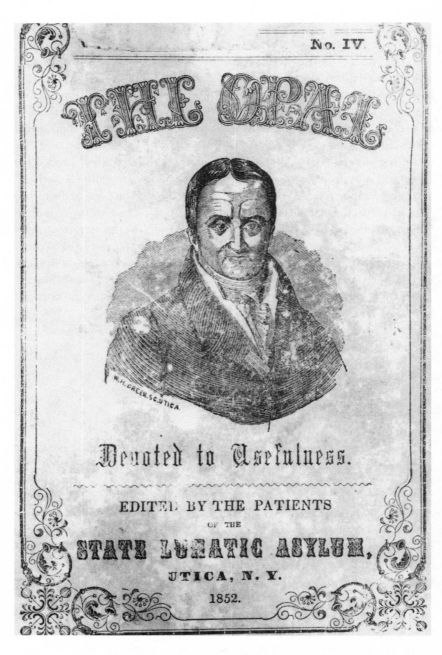

No. IV.

THE OPAL

Devoted to Usefulness.

EDITED BY THE PATIENTS

OF THE

STATE LUNATIC ASYLUM,

UTICA, N. Y.

1852.

FIGURE 3. Cover of the *Opal*, a journal of creative offerings written and edited by patients. (Courtesy of American Antiquarian Society)

the effect of the discipline of this cherished institution in promoting the objects of intellectual benefit."[18] The *Opal* was thus billed as both an advertisement of asylum medicine and a therapeutic tool: it was meant to act on patients' minds by helping them to compose their thoughts in a rational manner and to provide models of healthy cultural activity. Over and against what the doctors perceived as a diseased literary culture, featuring cheap "yellow-covered" novels that kindled "strange emotions" and threatened to "loosen the hold of the mind on eternal principles and allow it to wander on its dim and perilous way" toward "unhealthy" sensations, the *Opal* was a sanitized instrument, a bulwark against a flood of destabilizing cultural trash.[19]

The psychiatric critique of the literary landscape was part of a wider pathologization of American social mobility and the cultural forms that grew out of it. In particular, according to Isaac Ray, market capitalism created a literature of "supply and demand" rather than of timeless verities, and the emergence of commercially driven literature created "a degree of nervous irritability that may easily be converted into overt disease."[20] Readers of popular literature, asylum superintendents pointed out, had minds that were already at maximum tension, given the social uncertainties of life in antebellum America. The unprecedented freedoms that Americans enjoyed in the spheres of politics, labor, and religion threatened their fragile self-control, and they found themselves pushed over the edge by reading novels and newspapers that were not anchored in traditional values.

Overexposure to the dangerous new elements of the antebellum literary scene may have been blamed for many asylum cases,[21] but the *Opal* appealed to a more polite form of literary communication. The journal mimicked the tone of magazines catering to the elite classes, but its function resembled such literary avenues for character formation as lyceums, literary societies, and common schools, which used literature to help temper emotions, focus attention, and enhance religious meditation—often for members of non-elite classes.[22] Cultural reformation, asylum superintendents believed, was an important component in the civilizing function of the asylum, which would turn unruly subjects into citizens fit for democracy and bourgeois family life—it would help bring the victims of a capitalistic, individualistic social order back to civil life. The history of the *Opal* (and related journals at other institutions) makes clear that the asylum authorities had an essentially literary model in mind when they imagined outcomes for their patients. To acquire the polite arts and to learn eloquence, disciplined reading, and correct composition were essential, not only for developing literary sensibility, but also for healthy character formation.

The *Opal*'s restorative work was produced through the labor involved in shepherding patients' writings into print, as well as through cultural reprogramming. The *Opal* was part of what we would today call recreational therapy, but in some ways it constituted a sort of inmate labor and vocational training as well. Some state-funded asylums made labor compulsory for all but the "furiously mad," and although the New York State Lunatic Asylum—among others—prided itself upon the voluntary nature of patient labor there, work was always a key component of the moral treatment movement in asylum medicine.[23] And clearly, the nonfurious were pressured to work. Farming, groundskeeping, and working in small artisanal workshops (including shoemaking, plumbing, and tailoring) were some of the chief occupations of the men; needlework, cooking, and cleaning were preferred for women.[24] "Printing" was also considered suitable labor, and the journal was produced by patient typesetters and printers, with the exception of one paid local man who supervised the printers.[25] Asylum superintendents did not want their institutions to be considered glorified workhouses, and so they made special accommodations to attract a clientele from the elite classes, who were allowed to pay for better accommodations than nonpaying patients and generally were placed in the types of work situations to which their class status had accustomed them.[26] Most of the patients at Utica had limited education and came from laboring and farming backgrounds, but patient case notes suggest that the majority who wrote for the *Opal* paid privately for their care and were well educated. They usually occupied the best wards of the asylum and were often given positions on the *Opal* in part because their physicians recognized that they were unaccustomed to manual labor. Writing for and editing the journal were two of the only kinds of employment in the asylum that did not involve manual labor; in fact, they were not listed in the asylum's annual reports as labor at all.[27]

Some of the writing clearly came out of classroom exercises constructed to divert patients' minds from their delusions or obsessions and refocus them on formal intellectual or creative tasks. As Brigham put it, the underlying principle of moral treatment was "withdrawing patients from accustomed trains of thought, and awakening new ideas. . . . Hence the utility of amusements, music, schools, exhibitions, religious worship, books, newspapers, mechanical pursuits and other kinds of labor."[28] The frequency of acrostic poetry (often on asylum themes) betrays a pedagogical and therapeutic origin. Other writings, while not so formulaic as acrostics, also contain a note of willed mental and behavioral challenge. In an open letter to her parents, a female patient wrote: "I write now for the sole purpose of seeing if I can indite an epistle that will be called by you unexceptionable. . . . This is not a bad school to learn to correct that unruly member the tongue." [29] This "sole purpose" of the letter was probably an urgent one for her, as she appears to have been admitted to the asylum in part because of her propensity for abusive language.

Even when this rhetorical self-consciousness is not so visible in the articles of *Opal* writers, the improvability of patients' minds was a running theme. "In the application of public principles to private life," wrote one patient, clearly struggling to shape his wayward thoughts into an acceptable form, "the danger is that the imagination will lead astray into the mazes of Insanity. . . . Resemblances correspond, and if Editors perceive reason in the *Opal*'s contributors, it surely is entitled to some consideration, and indeed is like a diamond found amid rubbish, shining more brightly in contrast with the surrounding continuities." [30] Outside editors did sometimes perceive something like this. One self-styled "radical reformer" from Alabama, who was agitating for the construction of a new asylum in his state, ran regular excerpts from the *Opal* in his paper to give evidence that afflicted minds could be healed. [31] Occasionally, however, the journal was seen to fail the test of rationality. Some editors delighted in reprinting the more disordered pieces; one made sniping jokes about a rival by comparing his "deranged judgment, deficient information, and vague nomenclature" to "the *Opal*, which is published . . . in the lunatic asylum." [32] However, these jibes only reinforced the idea that the *Opal* served as a barometer of the asylum's success in reforming its inmates.

The Utica physicians left no published records of their editorial policies in managing the journal, but the Brattleboro superintendent wrote that patient contributors to the *Asylum Journal* (the *Opal*'s forerunner) were "allowed to write on all subjects, except those of their hallucinations." Such writing, he felt, would detract from the power of composition to "divert their attention from their delusions, and [present] new objects of thought for their contemplation." [33] His comments may well serve as a template for the *Opal*'s policy. Whether it was the decision of the doctors or the patient-editors, the restriction on "mad writing" was not lost on at least one critic of the journal, who wrote that "the lunatics of the Utica Asylum know too much to put their madness in print." [34] The *Opal* itself frequently proclaimed complete editorial freedom: "Its articles are all written by patients, and under no 'supervision' or restraint [other] than their own *genii*." But there was a catch: "The beloved and honored Superintendent," one editorial announced, "nor either of his estimable Assistants . . . do not advise or supervise in the matter, farther than to express their decisions that such and such individuals, thus desiring—and many are *here,* somehow seized with *author-mania,* who before never thought of the thing, may be furnished with writing material and opportunities to 'improve their gift.' " [35] Editorial freedom was always tempered by contributors' knowledge that writing was a privilege that could be taken away. And there is some evidence of more direct interference. After Dorothea Dix made a visit to the asylum in 1857, the *Opal* printed a cheeky conversation between two female patients. When told that Dix is a philanthropist, one woman asks the meaning of the term, and the other replies that it means "a lover of men," to which the first replies, "Well, then, are we ladies not all philanthropists?" [36] A subsequent letter from Superintendent Benedict to Dix indicates that she was not amused: "I regret that you have been annoyed by our 'Opal'—you shall not appear in it again." [37]

One curious fact about the *Opal* is that its articles received relatively little attention in the writings of the medical authorities who sponsored it. Perhaps this is because the journal's standing as a reflection of its authors' successful internalization of appropriate modes of conduct and rhetoric made such medical commentary redundant. In contrast, some other patient writings were held up by physicians as evidence or even symptoms of their insanity. Brigham, for instance, published in the *American Journal of Insanity* several extracts from (apparently unsent) patient letters home to illustrate how patients can "talk or write themselves into an ungovernable fury." [38] And Maine Insane Asylum superintendent Isaac Ray responded to a former patient's criticisms of his institution by interpreting the author's writing as evidence of a relapse.[39] However, the more common psychiatric stance toward the discourse of the mad was, as historian of science Roy Porter writes, "deafness . . . [e]ven the advocates of 'moral' therapy were not interested in listening to what the mad had to say for themselves, or in direct, person-to-person verbal communication. They were preoccupied instead with what might be called 'behaviourist' techniques of rendering their speech proper." [40] The *Opal* might be read as such a behaviorist project, but the apparent infrequency of direct medical meddling in its editorial affairs suggests that like many other antebellum reformers, the asylum superintendents saw their work as most effective when it appeared to be done by the objects of reform themselves. It was meant to embody, in print form, an outcome of what Richard Brodhead has termed "disciplinary intimacy," a style of reform and pedagogy that worked through "internal colonization, not outward coercion." [41]

This "disciplinary intimacy" worked on patients' sense of themselves as proper citizens—most clearly subjecting deviations from religious, gendered, and class-based norms of propriety to correction. The asylum's setting in Utica is fitting, because Utica was the heart of New York's "burned-over district" of religious revivals, and it was also the center of gravity for antebellum "moral reform," which focused on shoring up traditional family structures during a time of social and economic upheaval. Paul Johnson has interpreted the religious revival movements in the burned-over district as an attempt by the ruling class of proto-industrialists to discipline potentially unruly workers through the use of a religion that stressed internal discipline.[42] However, revivals were often viewed as a mental-health threat necessitating medical reform of character; they constituted an eruption of disorder from below rather than an imposition of control from above, as in Johnson's account.[43]

In the wake of the Second Great Awakening, with old doctrines crumbling, new sects emerging, and revival meetings in even established churches stirring up deep emotional anxieties about salvation and damnation, it is not surprising that "religious anxiety" was listed as a leading cause of insanity in asylum reports during the middle of the century.[44] Brigham wrote a tract about the mental-health threat posed by religious activity in 1835, and though—under severe public criticism—he eventually moved away from its apparent anti-religious message, he continued to monitor patients' religious worship closely.[45] Religion could not be entirely abandoned within the asylum, for few families would send their afflicted kin to a godless sanctuary. Accordingly, a chaplain was hired for weekly services; some patients were given leave to visit area churches; and patients even formed a choir to perform religious music on Sundays and at official asylum events. In-house chapel services, however, stressed public order and discipline rather than the inward transformations and ecstatic revelations that were encouraged in many revivals. Only well-behaved patients were allowed to attend services, and Brigham wrote in the 1844 annual report that "not unfrequently [sic] strangers have been present, and they will bear testimony to the good order and attention of the congregation."[46] Clearly, as the writer of the Fourth of July ode above made clear, it was a god of "self control" rather than the revivalist god to whom the patients were allowed to pray.

Also subject to normalizing reform within the asylum were the gender roles associated with middle-class family life.[47] Some feminist scholars, particularly in the 1960s and 70s, took for granted that women were special victims of these intensely patriarchal institutions; but in fact, asylums included male and female patients in roughly equal numbers.[48] Indeed the asylums were patriarchally organized, with patients' prescribed roles generally mirroring the "separate spheres" that men and women were supposed to inhabit on the outside, but men as well as women were pathologized when they stepped outside of these roles.[49] Perhaps a more productive way of looking at the work of gender in these asylums, then, is to ask what they did to women *and* men on the inside, and to examine patients' writings as signs of patients' strained attempts to fit those roles.

Entries on patient improvement in the case books commonly include comments that patients are acting more "gentlemanly" or "lady-like"—one patient, for instance, is judged to be near a cure when he "holds head up like a man."[50] Case notes are never detailed enough to indicate whether patients' writing was judged in this way, but evidence from the *Opal* does suggest that the voice of sanity and bourgeois propriety to which the patients aspired was a gendered one, with different literary norms associated with each sex. In particular, female writers and editors of the *Opal* tended to stress themes of piety, fashion, and "domestic" scenes within the asylum. Short stories by women usually repeated the conventional sentimental formula of an unusual woman passing through many tribulations (including, sometimes, institutionalization) and then being rescued by love.[51] Rarely do self-identified women writers broach national politics directly—only once is the topic of women's rights mentioned by a female author, who sidesteps taking a position by concluding that in discussions in the female wards "ably are the arguments *pro* and *con* canvassed."[52]

In general, male writers (and especially editors) found for themselves a political and thematic ground far wider than their female counterparts ever occupied. They comment freely on governmental elections, on the activities of abolitionists, and on the political postures of other newspapers and magazines. There is no paper party line, although a composite position includes skepticism of the manipulations of mass politics, sympathy to abolitionism and the colonization of free blacks (a project sometimes compared to the institutionalization of the insane, as chapter 2 will discuss), pro-temperance views, hostility to women's rights, advocacy of strong systems of social deference, and a generally Whiggish orientation. This befits the social standing of most male contributors, whose writings constitute an attempt—often strained—at projecting an image of cultivated masculinity: wearing one's learning lightly, holding one's own in the public sphere and in the marketplace of ideas. However, the "separate spheres" of men's and women's writings in the *Opal* were not as rigidly policed as was life in the asylum's wards, where men and women congregated only rarely, and then in chapel and on special festive days. And characteristically, the strict segregation of the sexes is given jocular treatment in an article by a male patient called "Life at Asylumia," in which the asylum is compared to a fashionable resort hotel, run "upon the Shaker principles." The strain of this arrangement does pierce through the happy facade of the article, however: "At chapel," he writes, "and occasionally upon other occasions, we get a sight of the ladies. God bless them! Which affords us a kind of melancholy pleasure, as it reminds many of us of those from whom we are separated, and of the many happy hours spent in their society; and it also seems rather too much like placing a dainty morsel with sight of a hungry man, without his being able to reach it."[53] For a moment, the site of religious instruction is the scene of a terrible breakdown of the asylum's social order, but the patient-author works cleverly to erase this possibility even as he records it. The sexual frustration of life in the asylum is, of course, quickly transformed into a "melancholy pleasure" of Asylumia—just enough sexual stimulation is permitted to allow a detached, thoughtful, even pleasurable meditation on why one is not permitted to gratify one's sexual hunger.

State-run asylums have often been viewed as tools for the bourgeoisie to control the lower orders and create a more efficient workforce;[54] but the existence of class distinctions within the patient population must complicate this claim. The prominence of well-educated, non–working class patients among the *Opal*'s contributors speaks to the asylum's (and the journal's) additional function as a self-regulating mechanism of the ruling class. Whether the result of editorial policy or simply a loosely agreed upon patient style, patients were generally more comfortable presenting themselves as elite reformers than as wayward souls in need of reform. The trope of "Asylumia," a mythical land peopled by a genteel, sorrowful race who can spread wisdom and light among the benighted and who need in turn only the sympathy and loving kindness of the outside world is the central conceit of this mode of self-representation. An anonymous article apostrophizing Pinel concludes by asking:

BROTHERS AND SISTERS OF ASYLUMIA: What think you of Pinel? Does not gratitude inspire your hearts? That you are enjoying the delightful privileges of Asylumia's resources—that you can interchange the kind salutations of friendship and love—discourse sweet music—range over hill and dale, and like the boy pursuing the butterfly, chase only the brilliants of life or domesticated, weave your beautiful emblems of taste and genius . . . that societies and books, and healthful play—and rides and pretty views, and fruits and flowers, and birds of song and cheerful eyes portentive of gay thoughts are ever cherished in Asylumia's halls. . . . The sons of Asylumia become the emissaries of her vital hope, and bear the balm of cultivated, refined humanity to the most retired arenas of life.[55]

In this picture, enforced removal from the world of material cares and competition has transported patients not to a carceral institution but to a gay resort for the pursuit of elevated thought and feeling. They are being trained not so much to become reformed citizens but enlightened moral reformers, spreading the superintendents' vision of "domesticated" and "refined" harmony throughout the world.

The implied social elevation of the writers is mirrored in the very format of the journal. "The Editor's Table," which spoke as the official voice of the journal, was also a well-known feature of the genteel *Knickerbocker*, and the *Opal*'s version often mimicked the famous "outside" journal's urbane, witty style. Both columns passed lofty and stinging judgment on what they perceived as lesser lights in the publishing field (of one recent book, the *Opal*'s editor writes, "Macauley says of some book that it is as bad as the mutton—badly conceived badly written and badly printed. But he never saw such a book as this"[56]), and both cast their lightly worn learning over any number of topical issues. The contents of both journals, too, were almost entirely anonymous or pseudonymous. The problems of attribution, however, have different but curiously parallel social meanings for each. Literary activity, in the *Knickerbocker*'s worldview, is something carried out by the socially respectable; signing one's real name to a piece indicates only that one desires to make a name or achieve social standing through writing. In this genteel model, authorship is detached from and elevated over the commercial world of hack journalism or popular novels; anonymity (or pseudonymity) is the mark of freedom from worldly concern.[57] The *Knickerbocker* spoke in the voice of a vanishing age of print culture—a "republic of letters" guided by elite white men during the Enlightenment, before the advent of print capitalism and the phenomenon of literary celebrity that it inaugurated. To speak to public questions, one must adopt a public, rather than private voice: this fulfilled the republican ideal of disinterested civic engagement. In this older model, to use Michael Warner's elegant phrase, "what you say will carry force not because of who you are but despite who you are."[58]

The social distinction implied by literary anonymity in an age of literary celebrity is a dynamic satirized by Herman Melville—himself an aggressively mercenary writer in his early career—in his 1852 novel *Pierre*. The young protagonist, an aspiring author of genteel birth, shudders at a literary world that not only requires authors to have their names made public, but often demands that they put their portraits on the title page: "When every body has his portrait published, true distinction lies in not having yours published at all. For if you are published along with Tom, Dick, and Harry, and wear a coat of their cut, how then are you distinct from Tom, Dick, and Harry?"[59] For the authors of the *Opal*, of course, anonymity emanated not from elite class affiliation or republican ideology but from a unique kind of social degradation: any author who hoped to return to the outside world would not want to broadcast his or her associations with the asylum. But the civil death of institutionalization is turned into a kind of rhetorical privilege through the mimicking of the elite literary anonymity anatomized in *Pierre* and defended by the editors of the *Knickerbocker*—a realm in which "cultivated, refined humanity" pursues truth and beauty from a position floating above the strivers—the Toms, Dicks, and Harrys—of the nineteenth-century marketplace.

The anonymity of the journal's authors, however, was a precarious position to assume in the antebellum literary world, for it added to uncertainty about the authenticity of the journal. Another of Melville's novels, *The Confidence-Man* (1856), skewers an era in which the specter of fraud hung over all grand charitable schemes, including the support of the disabled, who sometimes feigned their disabilities to garner sympathy and trust. In the novel's opening pages, a parade of apparent cripples, deaf-mutes, and others claiming pity clamor for the attention—and alms—of the "normal" passengers aboard the steamship *Fidèle*.[60] As asylums and other institutional responses to disability, poverty, and deviance proliferated, the cultural air in nineteenth-century America was thick with overinflated claims, scams, and confidence games; in this atmosphere writers of the *Opal* could not simply assume that their project would be supported on trust alone. Readers of the *Opal*, unlike passengers aboard the *Fidèle*, were not openly being solicited for money. But to the extent that the journal advertised a publicly funded institution, garnering faith in both the *Opal* and the asylum was essentially a fundraising mission. If the journal was seen to be *too* rational and smooth, it might arouse suspicions that it was not produced by the inmates—or at least the really crazy ones—at all.

The writers' anxiety about simultaneously demonstrating the authenticity of their authorship and of their handicap was a situation similar to that faced by black writers, from Phillis Wheatley to Frederick Douglass, who had to combat perceptions that their eloquence must have been ventriloquized by whites. One strategy of these writers was to attach to their publications extratextual supplements from white authorities attesting to the genuineness of their authorship; and in the case of Wheatley, she even underwent an examination by "the most respectable Characters in Boston" to authenticate her work.[61] But these strategies were unavailable to the *Opal* writers, who wrote in deliberate anonymity. Instead, to combat readers' suspicions the patients sometimes used the psychiatric concept of "partial insanity" to explain that the lunatic can appear completely disordered in one realm and completely rational in others; or they argued that doctors (the most likely fabricators) would hardly have the time to contribute articles for the journal.[62] A more subtle strategy was to set rambling and disordered pieces alongside the more conventionally presentable ones. This, of course, risked adding to the public perception that asylum inmates were incapable of producing rational thought, but it did lend credence to the editors' claims that nothing was fabricated.[63]

The problems of authentication and uncertain social identity troubled the authors' self-image of cultivation and perhaps led them to redouble their efforts to project it. This implied social elevation extended from social and political to aesthetic concerns in the journal's pages. In "Poetry and Poets," Etta Floyd (a pseudonymous frequent contributor to the journal) argued that true poetry "refines and elevates the mind"—a notion shared both by the *Knickerbocker* and by asylum medicine. "A person can not be taught to poetize, and for any to attempt poetry-writing because it is, as they hear, the fashion of the day, or to make an effort to versify for the purpose of obtaining a support by the publication of their effusions is an idle and useless affair." A wistful air of melancholy, she believes, a remembrance of better days from a position of lonely isolation, provides the perfect tone for the poet. To pursue the lonely task of poetry requires that one forego the expectation of "the plaudits of all." [64] The enforced solitude and anonymity of her authorial position thus enable a kind of refinement; and she can publish with no regard for the market forces that impel so much poetry writing. Of course, what she does not mention is that her writing participates in a different kind of institutional economy: it may not be supported by the kind of direct exchange so disdained by well-born authors like Melville's Pierre Glendenning, but it depends on a much wider circuit of legislative appropriations and the public support that underlies them.

Consistent with this fantasy of dwelling in an extra-economic literary empyrean realm, much of the journal's writing conveys detachment, airiness, an almost disembodied portrayal of life and writing. Despite the centrality of the patients' social situation to the meaning of the journal, the scene of writing and printing is almost never pictured in *Opal* articles. One never hears, for instance, that a certain piece was composed in a classroom, that an author was living in a particular ward, or that the author had to behave well to be granted writing privileges. In one sense, this is the result of the therapeutic function of the journal, which is to divert and elevate the mind beyond its present course, a course that for many patients must have run incessantly along the walls of their asylum. It is as if the *Opal*'s writers are trying to wrench themselves out of their material conditions and enter a plane of abstraction. This is especially apparent if one compares the journal's hazy picturing of asylum life with the portraits common in exposés written and published by former patients. In these, the drama of the patient's liberation from the asylum is essentially the drama of the texts' coming into existence. Authorities stressed the need to practice surveillance over patients' writing, and so these fugitive texts tended to dramatize their own material existence and create a documentary record that would not be, as Brigham and others insisted, "in the care of the supervisor." [65] Unsanctioned asylum writing is produced on rags, underwear, or the margins of newspaper; it is concealed behind mirror plates, in band boxes and secret pockets. When such texts reach the public—the best-known being Elizabeth Packard's famous exposés of her confinement at a state hospital in Illinois—part of their subversive effect is that they call attention to their own material existence, contrasting their free circulation and expression with the subterfuge that incarcerated writers had to practice. [66]

The abstraction of the *Opal* pieces, then, may be read as a negative sign of the confinement of the authors, insofar as a frank description of that confinement is available only to those on the outside. In one of the few pieces that does attend to the journal's material circumstances, a "contributor" writes a letter to the editor in which she explains that out of curiosity to see how the *Opal* is made she has visited the printing office. One wants to know under what circumstances she and other patients were allowed to enter—especially, given the strict sex segregation within the asylum, whether the office was ever a space in which the sexes could mingle. She gives a cheery account of all that she has learned about printing, but about the social dynamics of her visit we are left without illumination—other than the faintly ominous comment that "the pleasure of this stroll was greatly augmented by the company of our long-tried and worthy friend, the Supervisor of the 1st department, Ladies' Wing, whose smiling phiz [face] added much to the enchantment of the hour." [67]

But while the *Opal*'s abstracted representation of asylum life has much to do with the specific constraints placed on the journal's writers—in which asylum writing, like all asylum life, must be idealized—it also points to a unique set of material advantages granted to *Opal* writers. When a former patient wanted to publish, she had to expend significant resources of social (and often financial) capital. Who would publish, distribute, and read the works of a former patient? A cloud of popular suspicion enveloped these works, a suspicion fed by asylum superintendents' arguments that such exposés were evidence of lingering pathology.[68] Fear of stigmatization might also lead to self-censoring. As the publisher of one asylum exposé wrote, "Few of those discharged cured are willing to recapitulate the circumstances of their own condition, or of their surroundings, while *behind the bars*." [69] And one former patient who wrote a memoir critical of her stay at Utica succeeded only in exposing herself to ridicule for publishing (at her own expense) her view that the walls of the asylum were plastered with human feces and references to one of her doctors as "Bub." [70] A later exposé writer from Utica would refer to her book as creating a public expectation that his own narrative would be simply "a freak of my own insanity." [71] The drama of an exposé's coming into being, then, was not just brought about by evading the asylum's censors but by overcoming the stigmatization of insanity created outside of the asylum.

The staff of the *Opal*, writing anonymously, did not need to worry as much about their writing adding to their social stigmatization. Nor, unlike the exposé writers, did they need to concern themselves with the market pressures of the literary business. The asylum was a state-funded entity with a relatively stable budget. Doctors were drawn to work there in part because of its economic stability during a time when most physicians had to scramble to establish their own practices.[72] The forces of market capitalism, they argued in many writings, were highly pathogenic in that they produced a social instability that encouraged individuals to "aim at that which they cannot reach" and thereby "strain . . . their mental powers . . . to the utmost tension." [73] Former patients who were only "partially restored," superintendents argued, were particularly susceptible to this strain, which might lead them to expose their former institutions in a pathological attempt to attain popular notice and success in the literary marketplace.[74] *Opal* writers, on the other hand, were released from this competitive dynamic. In an era in which the average book publisher stayed in business for slightly more than a year, the *Opal* put out four issues a year for over a decade.[75] The journal was distributed largely through a system of direct exchange rather than sales, and it had practically no advertising, depending as it did on the asylum's state subsidy. Outside of the asylum, one had to sell one's writing in the marketplace of ideas, which could lead unbalanced minds to "aim at that which they cannot reach." The writers of the *Opal*, on the other hand, were given a sophisticated apparatus to publish and distribute their work, virtually freeing them from the mental strain of unrealizable literary ambition.

Despite the image of the asylum as privilege or refuge, it was impossible to read the journal and not know that the writers were on the "other side"—that they were objects, rather than agents, of charity and cultural reform. As a public test of rationality and the possibility of uplifting degraded subjects, the *Opal* bears considerable resemblance to other periodical writings by objects of reform. These include the *Cherokee Phoenix,* a bilingual journal produced by mission-trained Cherokee Indians hoping both to preserve some degree of cultural autonomy and to convince whites that they were good, "civilized" Christian neighbors; the *American Annals of the Deaf and Dumb,* published by the American Asylum for the Deaf and Dumb, and serving both as an instrument of spiritual and cultural uplift for the inmates; the *Freedman's Journal,* a miscellany published by Northern free blacks who wished to demonstrate their literary refinement in order to show their capacity to participate in the public sphere; and the *Lowell Offering,* a journal produced by female factory workers at the paternalistic Lowell Mills, which stressed that institution's efficacy in promoting intellectual advancement, even mental hygiene, among its nonelite population.[76] Comparisons between the *Opal* and the *Offering* are perhaps most apt here. In both cases, the writers of the journals were cultural mediators, packaging and advertising the worldview of the elites for an as-yet-unreformed population; both journals also strenuously avoided mentioning the grueling details of life that might mar the picture of their idyllic and culturally elevating institutions.[77] But in several important respects, the literary work of the "lunatics" differed from that of the "mill girls." Despite limited opportunities, many of the *Offering*'s writers were drawn to the Mills out of a desire for economic independence or distance from family, whereas asylum authors had mostly been committed by family members, against their own will.[78] The mill workers accordingly retained a fundamental freedom of contract that asylum inmates never had; this meant that the *Offering* adopted a strong propagandistic line, which was carefully policed by the editors. As Michael Newbury puts it, the *Offering* functioned as a "recruiting tool" both for new workers and for the retention of current ones, a function totally unnecessary for the captive writers of the *Opal.*[79]

Although it was common knowledge that the patients at Utica were often brought in and held against their will, their lack of social options

allowed on occasion for a more dangerous, even perverse, play of ideas in the *Opal* than the writers of the *Offering* ever had. For example, an article called "A Crazy Man's Common Sense" urged readers outside of the asylum to discount the "crazy" speech of religious fanatics and political radicals: "The crazy have no right of public freedom in speech, and the sane ought not to listen and much less in the least be actuated by the harangues of insanity." [80] This self-canceling advice — coming from a confessed "crazy" person—widens out into an examination of the relation between censorship and incarceration. "Alienation of the natural right of public speech is the just and salutary sequence of mental alienation," he continues. If social deviants are not placed in the asylum, where their incendiary speech will be sealed off from the public, then it is "only outsiders that we blame, not our wandering brother." But in referring to the radical as "our brother," the author suggests an identification with the very speech that he says should not be sanctioned. Suddenly, the asylum becomes not a jail but a fortress, a "castle of defence [*sic*] from an inappreciative world." [81] The piece moves, then, from an initial rejection of deviant political and religious discourse to a vision of the patient community as a band of radicals unappreciated by the sane world. This clearly was not an invitation to radical thinkers to come join the asylum community; but neither was it an acceptance of institutional logic. It seems, instead, a bitter kind of defense against having one's ideas pathologized. That the writer had been "alienat[ed]" from his own "natural right of public speech" and yet managed to test the limits of censorship in print testifies to the strange rhetorical opening provided by a journal produced in an institutional setting that denied civil liberties in order to restore them.

Opal writers, then, were in some senses rhetorically liberated by their own civil death. Their publication within a "house organ" allowed them to develop relatively stable literary personae that were free from the pressures of the literary marketplace; their anonymity and social exclusion removed some of the personal consequences of literary transgression; the physical force behind their confinement removed some of the pressures on overt ideological accommodation; and even their acknowledged insanity sometimes obviated the need to demonstrate their rationality in print. It remains only to be seen how one *Opal* writer—A.S.M.—negotiated his tenuous identity and the literary possibility it generated.

BECAUSE HE never signed his name to his writings, it is not always possible to identify the pieces that were authored by A.S.M.. However, his case notes mention that he is "the editor" of the *Opal* in 1851, the year of the first volume. For most of 1852, the "Editor's Table" columns continue in a similar voice and sometimes make reference to earlier editorial decisions, and the casebooks have him contributing to the journal through at least 1857. Thematic, stylistic, and autobiographical cues make it possible, at least provisionally, to attribute authorship of about a third of the "Editor's Table" columns and of many other pieces to A.S.M. through the ten-year run of the journal.

A.S.M.'s literary urges, however, were not entirely satisfied by writing for the *Opal* and for official asylum proceedings, for he also wrote on the walls. Six years into his stay at Utica, he was removed from the pleasant First Hall, where the more manageable and presentable patients—among them, most of the *Opal*'s contributors—resided. "Removed to [2H]," says the casebook, "for marking with pencil upon the doors & casings & tearing up newspapers &c." He was soon back at the editor's table, conducting himself "with more propriety," but his self-possession—and his stewardship of the journal—were interrupted by bouts of violence, ranting, liquor smuggling, throwing his clothes out the window, eating his own feces, and, one presumes, more scribbling. His astonishing editorial career, then, took shape within an arc of personal havoc, confinement, and a two-decades'-long struggle to express himself within the bounds of his physicians' rules, rather than to lash out in a self-defeating fury.

What is most striking about A.S.M.'s literary persona is its range. He is sometimes topical, referring to popular singers, asylum entertainments, and controversial subjects of the day; but he is also autobiographical, writing reminiscences of his earlier stay in the Bloomingdale Lunatic Asylum, his travels around the country, and his desire for a wife. He constructs and cheerfully engages in battles with other newspaper editors (most of whom seem not to notice); he writes literary criticism; and he pokes fun at asylum visitors who reveal their ignorance of the workings of his institution. In his portrayal of life at the asylum, he often seems contented, sometimes a bit wistful; at other times he hints at thoughts of rebellion, even revolution. He portrays himself as a slave, as an enlightened philanthropist, and as a victim of depression; and he makes startling inversions and connections: blackface minstrels become the most effective philanthropists, slaves educate their masters, Tom Thumb presides over the Independence Day celebrations, and a disapproving "outside" editor is mentally ill and suicide the best cure. His voice is sometimes rambling, but it is always crafty, elliptical, probing, and frequently disarmingly funny. And for all his range,

FIGURE 4. an illustration from the *Opal* 2, no. 2 (February 1852), 50. (Courtesy of American Antiquarian Society)

he clearly meant to develop a consistent persona. Despite the fact that he never signed his name, A.S.M. commissioned an asylum artist to make a woodcut of him to stand at the head of the "Editor's Table" (fig. 4). In this picture he sits at a table with his head in his hands, staring wild-eyed into the distance with a pile of books strewn about him. Books are also stacked against a wall behind him, which appears to have prison bars—or perhaps bookshelves—fastened to it. At first A.S.M. claimed that it was a "faithful and striking" illustration, if somewhat less handsome than he would have liked.[82] But when a local newspaper began mocking the portrait, he wrote that it was "*positively* not" his portrait and that a ham or an oyster would have done in its place, which would especially please his robust rival.[83] This mixture of disguise, self-revelation, self-deprecation, and combativeness is entirely typical.

Unlike A.S.M., many of the *Opal*'s writers, in their obsequiousness and adherence to convention, typify what Goffman has called public "conversion" to an asylum's code of conduct. In this common response to strictures of life in a total institution, the patient takes up the institution's vision of him or herself with apparent enthusiasm, posing as the "perfect inmate" by lavishly praising the authorities.[84] A number of *Opal* articles that recount patients' progress and the efficacy of their medical and moral regimens reflect this strategy. One essay, called "Insanity—Its Causes and Cure," narrates the progress of a patient's own delusions and the means by which his doctors cure him. He concludes that "at present all that can be done for the comfort and restoration of the lunatic, with the means allowed, seems to have already been accomplished in our own noble institution."[85] Not surprisingly, this patient was released shortly after composing the essay, and his doctors reprinted it in the *American Journal of Insanity*.

A.S.M. consistently rejects the position of the convert; his literary offerings almost systematically frustrate—while never openly challenging—the logic of the moral treatment cure. All of his praise for the asylum evinces not so much a desire to become cured but a desire to stay, and thus to resist the designs of his doctors. As such, his writings might be read as an example of what Goffman called "colonization"—an attempt by patients to build up a "stable, relatively contented existence" inside the institution and apparently to dismiss the desirability of life in the outside world. Such patients might occasionally act or speak out against the institutional authorities, but they strategically "mess up" only enough to ensure that they will have "an apparently involuntary basis for continued incarceration."[86]

Goffman's claim that all pathological behavior by patients is a response to their treatment by authorities is too sweeping to be warranted; such extreme behavior as A.S.M.'s eating of his own feces, for instance, was unlikely to have had a simple cause. But even if he was not intentionally acting out, this man's literary career at the *Opal* indicated his strong desire to stay put. His writings often suggest that "normal" life is irrational, frightening, and oppressive, while the predictability and order of life in the asylum made it a safe haven. In a striking piece called "A Dialogue Between Two Southern Gentlemen and a Slave," a slave owner who has made a visit to Northern philanthropic institutions explains to his clever slave Bob that "an Asylum is a retreat from the world's cares, a refuge from sorrows." There follows a wide-ranging conversation between the slave owner, his friend, and Bob about politics, philosophy, insanity, and the running of plantations, in which Bob always proves the most learned of the group, often baffling his interlocutors with his erudition. In such a scenario (as in abolitionist tracts) we might expect Bob to argue for his own freedom, but instead he simply offers the hope that "a Pinel" or "a Brigham" might "alleviate woe" for blacks as they have for the insane. When his master leaves to travel, Bob does not try to escape, but contents himself with perusing the great house's grand library and entering into imaginary conversations with philosophers.[87]

The parallels to A.S.M.'s own situation are clear, although his point is ambiguous. He seems to see himself in terms of the colonizer: he takes subtle jabs at his doctors (they are foolish owners) but endorses the philanthropy of their mission; he is given opportunities to leave but would rather stay in his comfortable surroundings with the fine library and opportunities for self-improvement. Just as the slave delights in outwitting and perplexing his powerful overseers but does not use his intellect to argue his way out of bondage, so A.S.M. delights in a kind of doubletalk that gets him nowhere other than exactly where he is. While I do not claim a high literary value for A.S.M.'s writings (they do not abstract well from their original context), such writings as "A Dialogue" do have a distinctly literary feel. In their clever frustration of meaning, they reach for what Shoshana Felman has called "the literary thing": that is, the dramatization of "a dynamically renewed, revitalized relation between sense and nonsense, between reason and unreason, between the readable and the unreadable." This quality, she writes, is "what makes texts literary, what turns them into events, what constitutes their literary life, their continued emotional and rhetorical vitality."[88] Perhaps what made A.S.M. a lifer in the asylum was precisely his literariness: his refusal to accept final meanings, to make himself fully readable, to package his treatment in the terms of the convert.

At one point, Bob the slave refers to Phillis Wheatley as "the pride of our race" and then undergoes a Wheatley-like examination by his master's friend, who does not believe a slave to be capable of learning and eloquence. Similarly, A.S.M. knew that his writings would not be read with the usual interest given to journals and newspapers. In an 1855 column, he complained that readers "either look upon the OPAL as a literary curiosity, an experiment or a humbug, instead of bowing it a graceful welcome to the circles of Magazine, or even Newspaper fraternization."[89] And yet his literary performance is clearly enabled by this status as a curiosity. Notices about the *Opal* almost never consider the content of its writings, but—as with the famous examination of Wheatley — they look to the form of expression as an indication of the rationality of the authors. Thus, A.S.M. cannot get his ideas to be taken seriously, even exactly listened to — but it is this which, in a sense, liberates him as a writer. A man without a social identity, A.S.M. is writing without the usual incentives and dangers of public speech. He cannot profit from his literary success, but neither can he be stigmatized by failure; his ideas can hardly be taken seriously, nor can they be shot down; he is free to let his mind roam in a way that few editors of commercial papers would have license to do, and yet he is not free to address the basic facts of his situation as a writer. He is writing within unusually severe constraints, but at the same time he is writing almost without concern for consequences.

No other periodical of the day would grant an editor so much space for such cryptic and sometimes even menacing self-indulgences (as when A.S.M. hints in one column that patients might "take a fancy to have a revolution here"[90]). This is because the *Opal* functioned not as a magazine but as a "magazine," a what-if experiment in which patients were allowed to address the outside world *as if* their voices mattered. The fact of their exclusion from civic life (they could not vote, sign contracts, or make wills) constituted the very grounds on which they addressed their public, and so the contents of their writings were always, strangely, bracketed before they were even circulated. What would it mean, the *Opal* implicitly asked its readers, if those you have deemed voiceless actually had a voice? As A.S.M. was acutely aware, this dynamic did not give the writers a voice but a simulacrum of a voice. They were objects, rather than agents, of their own discourse; they were constructed by what they wrote, rather than the other way around.

To have a voice, however — to speak within a real social network — was in A.S.M.'s mind more frightening than to speak within the abstracted realm of the *Opal*. As opposed to the protections offered by the gentle realm of Asylumia, he viewed society outside the walls (or the pages) as tyrannical, deadening. "We are all seeking after society," he wrote, and — echoing Ishmael's question in *Moby-Dick*, "Who ain't a slave?" — responded with a question: "And what is society but a restraint — oftentimes alas! most dreadfully despotic? Yet how cheerfully are these restraints submitted to. Take the case of love, or jealousy, tight boots, or corsets. Is not the thought even, to say nothing of the experience, of them sufficient to still this clamorous cant about liberty?"[91] People seek liberty, and find there the most frightening of restraints. Better are the known restraints of the institution, which liberate the mind. For to write without constraint, he knew, was to scribble furiously on the walls.

A.S.M.'s is a portrait of the anonymity of nonpersonhood; he conveys in print the perverse pleasures of practically abstracting himself out of existence, of entering a literary realm of the undead. But writing in the *Opal* must have occasionally compounded the pain of his situation—as editor he seeks to express, rationally, the logic of the institution that has denied him his freedom because he is subrational. This quality is especially pronounced when read against his shadow career of scribbling, clothes rending, and self-mutilation, in which he appears to be materializing the torment of his condition at moments when he cannot abstract himself into the *Opal*'s pure ether. For him, Asylumia is at once a utopian space in which all the trials of social belonging are left behind and, in its self-conscious fictionality, a reverse image of the confined space he actually inhabits. For A.S.M. and his fellow writers, the *Opal* was both an escape and a reminder that no real escape was possible.[92]

—— ✳ ——

CHAPTER TWO

Saneface Minstrelsy

Blacking Up in the Asylum

BLACKFACE MINSTRELSY has taken many twists and turns through the course of American culture. Originating as a series of song and dance routines traded by black and white workers along the piers and canals of New York in the early 1830s, it quickly developed into a kind of cross-racial musical street theater of the urban proletariat. Characterized by dancing that was alternately fast and grotesque, coarse and, at times, satirical lyrics that were pointed at the moralizers of the upper class and the bourgeoisie, and musical structures that sounded to outsiders like "noise," minstrelsy was the first explosive, propulsive popular form of youth-oriented American performance. By the 1840s, however, numerous performers had managed to cash in on the phenomenon, bringing minstrel routines to stages across the country—particularly in the Northeast—and even across the Atlantic.[1] During this period of commercial takeoff, minstrelsy increasingly fell under the control of cultural entrepreneurs, who successfully broadened its appeal beyond the original audience of rambunctious, sometimes rebellious young men. Professional troupes began to form, and theater managers advertised evenings of "Chaste, Pleasing and Elegant" entertainment safe for a middle-class clientele.[2] The form at this point hardened into a standardized set of routines and playlets with room for improvisation built in, a structure that let customers know what they could expect while also offering the promise of novelty. Increasingly, as it became commercialized, routinized, and stripped of some of its oppositional social content, the minstrel routine also emphasized racist caricature that masked the cross-racial, class-based alliance that had given birth to the form.[3] With a few notable exceptions, the performers at this point were all white men in burnt cork and grease, and the halls in which they performed admitted no black people as spectators. The spectacle that they presented was one of black antics, aversion to work, and unintentional double entendres, which served both as mockery of the unsophisticated or pretentious black characters and as subtle upward jabs at the social elite they presumed to mimic. With an afterlife that stretched from vaudeville stages and early cinema to rock 'n' roll and hip hop, minstrelsy has remained a potent—and generally noxious—vehicle of racial trespass and a seemingly inexhaustible resource for commercial culture.[4]

But of all minstrelsy's many gyrations—more even than those of the perpetually jumping Jim Crow—perhaps none is more surprising than the formation of a troupe of blackface performers among the patients in the New York State Lunatic Asylum in the 1840s and 1850s. Upon contemplating this scene, one is immediately confronted with a set of ironies. In masking themselves, the outcast actors imitated figures who were equally outcast—the slaves and urban Northern blacks who were tarred by blackness much as the actors themselves were stigmatized by the label of insanity. They enacted scenarios of slave life for the ultimate captive audience; and under the watchful eye of the asylum authorities, they turned a famously unruly form into a spectacle of their own capacity for self-control. From behind blackface masks, they spoke to each other, to their doctors (who doubled as their captors), to the curious townsfolk and even politicians who were occasionally given admittance, and to themselves—all in different codes, some still faintly decipherable, others no doubt lost somewhere in the transmission from performer to observer to print record to twenty-first century historian. What actually happened on stage is almost irrecoverable, but most of what remains of these performances is an extraordinary archive of written responses by fellow patients published in the *Opal*. In dozens of articles, poems, dramatic sketches, and strange hybrid pieces, these writers left behind a collective record of excitement, guilty pleasure, disgust, perplexity, fantasy, possibly hallucination, self-reflection, and—most poignantly—cross-racial identification in the face of the minstrel shows.

Reconstructing the strange career of blackface minstrelsy in the lunatic asylum presents an unusual opportunity to watch what happens when an official culture collides with an explosive popular form. First, there is the push-and-pull generated by the authorities' attempts to regulate the patients' behavior through carefully controlled cultural activities and the patients' powerful urges, sometimes unconscious, to express their own alienated feelings. Erving Goffman describes the "disculturation" or "untraining" of subordinates that is invariably a goal of the managers of total institutions: a systematic attempt to dispossess inmates of the culture of their "home world." [5] But while the Utica minstrel shows certainly speak to this process, they also bring into view some of the repressed cultural currents that the asylum regime could not ultimately sanitize. Patient writings often construe a taste for minstrelsy as a cultural relapse into the kind of unruly, nonproductive behaviors that their doctors and attendants tried to stamp out; but their comments on the shows are also a demonstration of their progress in the "civilizing process" that supposedly structured the relations between whites and blacks, as well as between doctors and patients.

The story thus presents us with an unusual encounter—mostly imaginary, but with powerful real-world consequences for the actors—between two marginal groups that were often understood, and misunderstood, in relation to each other. Blackness and madness were two social categories that justified both the social marginalization and custodial care of supposedly subrational populations. Blacks and the insane were denied property rights because they lacked the capacity to manage that most important of all properties: themselves.[6] Surprisingly, however, this linkage sometimes worked to join blacks and the insane not just in a mutually reinforcing cycle of marginalization but also in a discourse of uplift and regeneration. Both groups were the objects of schemes of moral improvement that stretched from locales as far apart as the asylum at Utica to the plantations of the South and on to the former American colony in Liberia. In donning the mask of blackness and the veil of anonymity in the *Opal*, patients traced these routes in a fantastical twinning of self and other, noise and refinement, rationality and madness.

The asylum's stage was the scene of a complex set of desires, imperatives, fears, rewards, and identifications. On the doctors' side, it encompassed the desire for control of the patients' cultural lives, a bone thrown to restive inmates, an opportunity for surveillance and discipline, a therapeutic tool, a chance to display their humanitarian management. On the patients', it was a reward for good behavior, a diversion from boredom, a taste of forbidden pleasures, and an opportunity to advertise one's self-management; but it was also a humiliating reminder of their similarity to the downtrodden figures they portrayed on stage. There are perhaps two main strands here: discipline and race. The goal of the shows was to promote order by carefully managing scenes of disorder. In the fictional world of the show, the disorder that was portrayed on stage was imputed to the blacks who were represented. Their supposed nonproductivity, lack of decorum, and inadequate control of bodily functions (including sexual ones) were the negative example against which the patients were supposed to measure themselves. The discipline surrounding the spectacle was in studied contrast to the antics on stage.

THE SHOWS BEGAN on November 30, 1847, when a group of patients at Utica put on a "great bill" of theatrical fare before their doctors, attendants, and fellow patients. Included were an original play in three acts, a number of songs and recitations, dances, and, to conclude, a sketch titled "ETHIO-PEAN SAYINGS AND DOINGS."[7] The event proved so popular that similar productions were carried off annually, and then as frequently as quarterly, through the 1850s. And almost always, they concluded with "ETHIOPIAN EXTRAVAGANZAS," in which patients delineated the ways of "Sambo, Ned, Jim, Gumbo, Cato, Bones, and Quambo." Not only male patients, but "our fair Southrons"—women who lived in the asylum's South Wing—performed in blackface, a rather rare occurrence in minstrel productions of the time.[8] On at least one occasion, a professional blackface troupe from New York visited the asylum to perform before the patients. The patients were so excited by this that they formed their own troupe, called the Blackbird Minstrels, which gave full-length performances on three consecutive nights in January 1856, with music provided by the patients' own "darkie band."[9] The outside community was sometimes allowed admittance, and even the governor of New York—probably the Whig John Young—attended one performance.[10] A few issues of the *Opal* contain almost nothing but a running commentary on minstrelsy. And all this received the blessings of Amariah Brigham and his successors, Nathan Benedict and John P. Gray.

How did this come to pass? The simple answer is that stage shows were part of the normal routine of asylum diversions, which occupied an important part of the moral treatment program at Utica and other centers of the moral treatment movement. Especially in the winter, when carriage rides, farm work, and other outdoor activities were impracticable, keeping the patients busy was a crucial aspect of managing the asylum.[11] But "diversion" meant more to the physicians than one might consider—it was in fact a central term in their lexicon of treatment. By "withdrawing patients from accustomed trains of thought, and awakening new ideas,"[12] diversions could stimulate "social feelings" among the patients; they promoted exercise and discipline; and they were educative or refining, all of which contributed to mental health.[13]

The historian Michael Katz has written of the "assault on popular culture" waged in the name of an "'orderly, predictable, and regular' routine in early mental hospitals" that was "part of the therapy.'"[14] Clearly, however, some aspects of popular culture—sanitized to meet asylum specifications—were not assaulted outright but were put in the service of therapeutic routines. D. Tilden Brown—Brigham's assistant at Utica and the man responsible for managing "amusements" there—offered something like an industrialist's justification for the apparent frivolity that reigned in the asylum's stage productions. While in general "employment in industrial pursuits, as a moral agent in the treatment of [mental alienation], proves far more efficacious, and in general, more alleviating to the patient than mere recreation," steady and productive industrial employment was not always possible in the asylum, especially in the winter months. And even when such labor was possible, he wrote, some of the patients are so maddened that they "pertinaciously object to all other employment" aside from producing theatrical events. For these, such endeavors provide valuable lessons in "combining present gratification and prospective benefit," or what Max Weber would describe almost sixty years later as the Protestant work ethic. Finally, Brown believed that the hope of participating in the performances provided an incentive for good behavior, and that the spectacle itself was a perfect opportunity for the authorities to practice "that restraining surveillance which [the patients'] conditions require."[15] In short, such activities, far from being frivolous, were instrumental in the disciplining, cultural reprogramming, and management of patients.

And yet there is still something incongruous about a popular form known for catering to the boisterous sensibilities of the working class receiving sanction—even encouragement—in the bastion of genteel reform. Business groups decried "the baneful habit of late hours at night and neglect of business in the morning [that] is the Inevitable Result" of such shows.[16] And early psychiatrists warned frequently of the dire mental health consequences of nineteenth-century commercial culture—popular novels and commercial newspapers were kept out of asylum libraries because they were "a prolific source of cerebral disorder"; and asylum managers were enjoined to refrain from exposing patients to entertainments that stimulated "the lower sentiments or propensities."[17] Indeed, early blackface acts staged all that drove the reformers themselves crazy: a heightened and grotesque sexuality, a release from the confining rhythms of industrial discipline, a general breakdown of social order, even an incipient critique of social authority.

In suggesting that even the supposedly "genteel" later minstrel productions promoted disorder, Eric Lott described "the air of a collective masturbation fantasy" that pervaded the shows, which were sometimes advertised with black figures strumming on fantastically phallic banjos[18] (fig. 5).

THE COAL BLACK ROSE

Philadelphia Published by G.E.Blake No:13 south Fifth street.

FIGURE 5. Minstrel songsheet, 1827

Insane asylums were citadels of the anti-masturbation movement; superintendents wrote volumes on the solitary vice as both a cause and effect
of insanity, and they devised novel ways of stamping it out—from drugs
to beds with straps to "blistering" the genitals of offenders.[19] In the peak
years of the minstrel show at Utica, superintendent Nathan Benedict reported the existence of "one hundred and seven masturbators out of eight
hundred and sixteen cases." The majority of offenders were male patients;
these he treated with a combination of "aphrodisiacs," blisters, and cold
baths, while he experimented with "cauterizing the urethra of females."
When these treatments were not effective, offending patients sometimes
took matters into their own hands (for the second time, as it were): "One
patient in his zeal to conquer this habit subjected himself to severe torture.
Another performed upon himself a painful surgical operation."[20] Although
patients were careful not to let their associations of minstrelsy with sexual

excitement show, one did write in the *Opal* that the craze for popular music, especially minstrel songs, represented a "music mania" that was sweeping through society, affecting even "our own Asylumian abode."[21] What this mania led to she did not suggest.

Still, the superintendents appeared to view the minstrel shows as an effective tool in maintaining order in the asylum, a sort of safety-valve for patients' pent-up frustrations. By far the largest number of patients came from farming or laboring families, for many of whom minstrelsy still must have had a long, class-based appeal. If the upper classes had their libraries, lecture series, and debating societies, then what would motivate the working classes to stay in line? Brown, the assistant physician at Utica, hinted at this when he wrote that it was crucial that amusements cater to "the social position and former occupation of [the asylum's] inmates"[22]; a superintendent at another asylum mentioned that creating a "better supply of cheap and innocent amusements" was an imperative for those concerned with the national state of mental health. This was particularly important for laborers, for whom "amusements constitute almost the only practicable means for repairing the constant waste of nervous energy."[23]

But how could one keep the lower classes in line—and even elevate their condition—with a form of amusement that appealed to the "lower sentiments"? As in the comments of D. S. Welling and Samuel Woodward about the transformations of card playing and dancing from dangerous practices in the outside world into therapeutic exercises within the walls of the asylum (discussed in the introduction), minstrelsy seems to have gone through a similar transformation as it entered respectable realms and eventually passed through the asylum's walls. Even before the asylum's Blackbird Minstrels took the stage, minstrelsy had become an object of reform: its routines were regularized, its songs and dances made less sexually suggestive (at least in their packaging), its protest against the upper classes redirected downward at blacks. In making the minstrel shows "Chaste, Pleasing and Elegant," safe for middle-class audiences, theater managers were doing to popular culture what the asylum directors were doing to their patients.[24] The asylum authorities only extended this process of cultural purification. On the one hand sanitizing popular culture, and on the other creating actors and spectators disciplined enough to enjoy it in rational and orderly terms, the asylum directors were attempting to reorder the whole of social relations as expressed in the stage show.

The few published comments that Superintendent Brigham and his successors made on the productions suggest that they were hardly the raucous affairs that had marked the early days of American blackface minstrelsy, or even the relatively controlled mayhem of the commercial extravaganzas that followed. Instead, the shows were presented in an atmosphere that mimicked the neoclassical trappings of more "respectable" theater (fig. 6). At the first performance, Brigham noted that "a handsome drop curtain has been painted by a patient, representing a view of the Coliseum at Rome, with gladiators in front, and in contrast a view of our Asylum with ladies dancing and promenading near it."[25] Only patients from the first and second wards—the sections of the asylum containing the least unruly patients—were allowed to attend;[26] they were carefully watched by "the resident officers, attendants and assistants . . . and occasionally the managers of the Asylum with their families and a few ladies and gentlemen from Utica."[27] Given such tight surveillance, it is unsurprising that "no evils whatsoever" resulted from the performance. Presumably this meant

FIGURE 6. Amusement hall at the New York State Lunatic Asylum, ca. 1888

no fistfights, riots, thrown vegetables, or other rowdy audience reactions that were hallmarks of early blackface performance; it probably also meant limited audience participation, improvisational openness, or double entendres that still marked the later commercial versions. Patients themselves were aware of the difference between minstrelsy on the outside and the asylum's version. "Pious people say 'they are wicked songs, not fit to be sung,'" wrote one patient about minstrel tunes in the *Opal*; but here in the asylum they perform wonders in casting off despair: "When struggling in 'the Slough of Despond,' the magic numbers of 'The other side of Jordan,' well executed upon a banjo, with a pair of protruding lips caroling the refrain, that 'Jordan am a hard road to travel,' has caused the pilgrim to shake off his burden and go his way rejoicing." [28]

The reformation of popular culture—or the disculturation of patients— can go a long way toward explaining how the blackface shows were made acceptable, even useful, to authorities, but not what they were supposed to *do* for the patients. In an atmosphere where every aspect of the environment—down to the construction of heating vents and the positioning of drapes—was said to influence mental functioning (and even brain structure), how would blackface act upon the brain?[29] One possible answer comes in the writings of John Galt, superintendent of a state asylum in Virginia, and a leading architect of the moral treatment in the United States. Galt believed that amusements should be employed as a "revulsive" technique—that is, as psychological interventions that would make patients recoil from their own delusions. Especially important in this regard was the deployment of "hilarity," which would help "supplant the place of delusive ideas and feeling" by exposing them as laughably incorrect. [30] Evidence that Galt's notion was in currency at Utica comes from a disgruntled former patient, who nonetheless echoes this likely rationale for over-the-top amusements: "If you can get [the insane] to laugh natural, it is quite apt to explode the whole affair; and they will yield their indigo feelings because the ridiculous impression is the strongest." [31]

Galt seems to have been influenced by the thinking of the German psychiatrist Johann Christian Reil, whose theories of dramatic therapy were debated in the *American Journal of Insanity*. Reil devised bizarre theatrical representations of madness with which to confront delusional patients. These, he argued, were an important part of the moral treatment, since theater was a place where "the fixed ideas of madness are confronted." [32] Additionally, such techniques can be traced back even further, to the origins of the moral treatment in postrevolutionary France. Philippe Pinel, for instance, used theatrically staged events to startle or jolt patients into discrediting delusive ideas—for instance, staging a mock trial of a tailor who was convinced that the Jacobins were trying to kill him because he disagreed with their punishment of Louis XVI.[33] It was under this therapeutic rubric of theater that the Marquis de Sade was allowed to develop his stage plays at the Charenton asylum.[34]

Michel Foucault found such acts of "theatrical representation" central to psychiatric practice of the late eighteenth century (or, the "classical age"), in which the medical authority created a scenic version of delusion, carried it through to its logical conclusion, and thereby led the patient to "a state of paroxysm and crisis in which, without any addition of a foreign element, it is confronted by itself and forced to argue against the demands of its own truth."[35] According to Foucault, this "comic purification" of madness through theatrical means was jettisoned in the nineteenth century, which he characterized as ushering in a "return to the immediate" and a "suppression of theater." Medical authorities, he argued, turned to "nature" (and their mastery of it) to do the curing and rejected the earlier age's structured conversations of madness with itself.[36] Brown's and Galt's program in dramatic therapy might seem to refute this sweeping characterization, or at least to represent residual holdovers from the earlier "classical age" and its theatrical tricks. But there is a division in their writing between "comic purification" and something akin to a management technique—a rift, in other words, between theater as therapeutic and theater as opportunity for disciplinary spectacle. Both Galt and Brown agreed that comedy was preferable to tragedy for insane actors, but for different reasons. For Galt, a revulsive "hilarity" produced an opportunity for patients to "supplant the place of delusive ideas and feeling." In contrast to "farce and comedy," performances of tragedy by insane actors or for insane audiences were dangerous because they tended to over-stimulate the emotions. Brown seemed to echo this in writing that "mirth and recreation, no longer frivolous or puerile, become dignified as instruments of cure" when cultivated within the moral treatment regime. But "humorous" dramatic presentations did not, in his view, confront ideas of madness head on—they simply helped to control the patients. The minstrel shows were not direct representations of the patients' delusions, as they had been for Pinel and Reil—they were simply stylized models of incorrect behavior. And their staging would "impel the patient to the exercise of self-control, both by suggesting that propriety of behaviour which will secure participation in such privileges, and by engaging the attention to the exclusion of irrational thoughts."[37] Madness no longer confronts itself on stage.

In the stage shows at Utica, madness was to be tamed, managed, repressed; the mad were treated as objects of rather than agents in their own cure.

Utica's theatrical management of insanity appeared to work, according to Brown. Of the seventeen patients involved in putting on the first performance at Utica, many "have since recovered and left the institution. Others are convalescing. . . . Among these were individuals who believed, or had recently believed themselves to be the especial ministers of divine will; exalted personages, Roman Pontiffs or Secretaries of State; that by a wave of their hand they could control the movements of railroad trains, and vessels on the high seas; who had, previous to admission, been confined in chains, as dangerous, from their homicidal propensities; who insisted on their own idiocy and 'inability to think' even while engrossed in the study of their parts; or whose ordinary conversation denied all attempts to trace coherence or point." None of the asylum physicians left an explicit statement of how such cures happened, exactly, but most probably would have agreed with Brown's conclusion that "undoubted benefits have accrued from the intellectual application, mental discipline, exercise of memory, and self-control of the performers, and from the diffusion of good humor and hilarity among the observers." [38]

Over the following decade, the Utica asylum's programs followed Galt's and Brown's prescriptions for therapeutic (and disciplinary) "hilarity" closely. Stage plays usually involved dialogues of ever-heightening absurdity, such as the patient-authored sketch about the formation of a philanthropic society devoted to prying into the affairs of one's neighbor. [39] And the minstrel shows themselves highlighted the ludicrous: a "Burlesque, a la Jullien," which was a deliberately bad satire of a conductor well-known for his thrilling style, consisting of "a commingling of sounds unharmonious and concord discordant" and long-winded lectures that ended with a temperance plea accompanied by the downing of a glass of liquor. [40] In these familiar minstrel gambits, actors used the mask of cork and grease to systematically invert the principles of "correct" bourgeois behavior and to make detection of that inversion laughably easy—much easier, apparently, than the insane found it to be in their ordinary lives.

WE HAVE NOW the official accounts of how the minstrel shows functioned, or, at least, were meant to function. But what of the patients? How did they respond to the carefully controlled disorder on stage? It is particularly disappointing to find that none of the tiny minority of black patients recorded their impressions in the *Opal* or elsewhere. [41] (Frederick Douglass's newspaper *North Star*, however, reported cryptically in 1851 that "the Nightengale [*sic*] Minstrels . . . recently entertained the inmates of the Utica Insane Asylum with one of their concerts." [42]) Nonetheless, it is not difficult to imagine the humiliation of black spectators (if they were in attendance), who had clung to a tenuous and marginal freedom in the North, only to find themselves labeled inadequate to the task of self-management. Many white former patients referred to the asylum in their memoirs as a kind of slavery, where labor was compulsory and uncompensated, and where patients were subjected to the whims of capricious attendants, with no recourse for complaint.[43] To black patients, slavery must have seemed an ever-present frame of reference; watching fellow patients hoot over the antics of plantation "darkies" could only have compounded the pain of the experience.

Nor do the surviving representations of the asylum minstrel shows give clear voice to the responses of the lower-class white population, who — as shown in the previous chapter — did not generally publish in the *Opal*. But again, one can imagine a particularly poignant sense of alienation among these patients. In contrast to the studied refinement and inoffensiveness of the asylum spectacles, which one patient described as a "kind, polite, and accomplished performance," minstrelsy had emerged as a boisterous and vital set of interactions between the black and white workers along New York's system of canals. Trading dance steps and songs after work and during breaks, these workers at the very bottom of the social order fashioned a form of joyous, riotous noise and motion that served both as emotional release and, just as importantly, social critique of those above them. This "mudsill mutuality," as W. T. Lhamon, Jr., calls it, extended to the subculture of what the reformers called New York's "dangerous classes." [44] A fascinating study by Dale Cockrell shows the prominence of minstrel slang and dance steps in at least one mixed-race gambling hall that was raided by police in 1839.[45] Among the Utica asylum's hundreds of patients classified as laborers, it is safe to assume that least some had worked in the 1820s and 1830s along the canals, one of the fastest-growing industries of the period, just as minstrelsy was taking off; many others knew well the urban terrain of the "dangerous classes." And so what working-class white patients saw on the asylum's stage could only have added to their sense of self-dispossession. Cast against their will into an insane asylum, they were subjected to a performance that appropriated their own form of popular protest against authority, a performance that was deployed in an effort to make them conform, to exercise self-control, and to learn punctuality, discipline, and correct behavior.

What we are left with are the writings of the relatively privileged and well-educated staffers of the *Opal*. As always, their writing is hard to read as directly self-expressive, as the writers seem intensely aware that their offerings will be scrutinized by doctors. Especially in these instances, writing anonymously about masked performances in a scenario in which popular enthusiasm was both elicited and pathologized made the prose all the more guarded and self-conscious—unseemly outbursts of enthusiasm or other inappropriate responses would probably have been held against the authors. And so a sort of clenched gentility pervades the accounts, which sometimes makes it difficult even to determine exactly what is being written about. As one patient rhapsodized, "What fairy fingers wrought those robes of fancy? How gracefully they are carried too! How well they tread the measure, keeping time harmoniously!" As much as this studied refinement veils the character of the spectacle, it reveals clearly the painfully self-conscious performativity that pervaded patients' lives behind walls. To become sane was to act in a certain way and to have the correctness of that performance certified by the authorities over a period of time. Indeed, the asylum as theater is a recurring trope in the writings of patients. In an exposé of her treatment during her time in the asylum, one ex-patient wrote that the "cure" is a matter of acting out someone else's script; any patient who tries to follow it "will find in the end that he is but a forced failure of an imitation creature, if he does not despise the system which inspires him to conceal and bury himself under these seemingly prescribed conventional subterfuges."[46] One Utica patient, responding to the literary and recreational activities at the hospital, clearly struggled to follow this script, which he identified as a code of gentility. "All persons wish to be genteel, and to appear so," he wrote. "There are various kinds and degrees of gentility: the meaning of the term is sufficiently hidden and indistinct to be expansive and capable of attenuated tenacity of signification. So, if we make knowledge of God most desirably attainable, it will the less disturb our gala enjoyments." And then, as a heartbreaking coda: "We are not so happy as we wish to be."[47] Every day, patients were expected to perform a kind of saneface minstrelsy; writing about the masking of others, they clung just as tightly to their own masks (fig. 7).

Despite the intense guardedness of the patients' writings, one occasionally gets a sense of the mask being lifted or pierced. One patient, after noting that "negro songs or melodies" are not "proper to be sung anywhere," seemed eager to get outside the asylum and reconnect with what she perceived to be the real stuff:

FIGURE 7. Performance at the New York State Lunatic Asylum, late nineteenth century. It is not clear whether the performers are patients or a visiting theatrical troupe. (Collection of New York State Archives)

> If I am wicked, I hope to be pardoned for it, and speedily made better; but . . . when in New York, near the corner of Broadway and Anthony, I should have to shut my eyes to its attractions, or, before I was fully aware, I should be within a well-known music store, [where] I should send . . . some of [the] courteous employés on an aerial ascent to the upper shelves for comic songs and negro melodies for the young sister in the West, or my tall cousin John, as I've done before.[48]

Shutting her eyes to wickedness, yet being drawn against her will: this is the record of a guilty pleasure, which her reformation as a patient is devoted to stamping out.

In addition to conflicted feelings such as these, the minstrel shows elicited certain responses that read like printed screams. In the midst of a painfully refined and florid printed dialogue between two female patients about the minstrel show, one woman refers to the performance as *"music armed to the teeth."*[49] Whatever that image calls forth, it hardly fits the model of theater as a dignified instrument of restraint, self-control, and cure. The most jarring response to the shows, however, came in a poem written by the frequent *Opal* contributor "Etta Floyd." For many years, she filled the *Opal's* pages with literary criticism, highbrow cultural commentary, and a highly melodious and usually decorous verse. It is Floyd who diagnosed the "music mania" running through the Utica wards—a disease fueled by money-driven performers quick to cash in on society's needs for novelty—the most recent of which was the fad for black or blackface performers. "Some of our best musicians," she wrote, "if naturally white, or but partially bleached, have acquired a fancy for an Ethiopian skin, imagining, perhaps, that their musical powers will be found increasing in proportion to their *personal attractions;* or, what may be more probably, supposing a greater number of auditors will be obtained by the expected pleasure of gazing upon white people converted into beauteous black ones."[50]

In contrast to the disgust she felt with commercial culture's traffic in images of blackness, Floyd depicted the asylum as a place where she could be shielded from the outside world, and be free to pursue her melancholy, solitary art. How upsetting, then, to find the whole place turned topsy-turvy by minstrels, who brought their infectious noise and its innuendos of frenzy, commercialism, sexual license, and general disorder into the poet's solitary retreat. As recorded in her poem, "The Musqueto Serenade," her encounter with the blackface minstrels set off a massive persecution and revenge fantasy in which she compares the minstrels to a swarm of attacking mosquitoes who not only whine in her ear with their "dread music," but drive her to a frenzy by biting her arm until she agrees to give them money.

> Said a lady, "Ho! Who are these minstrels I hear?
> "Such a singing and whining, it's sure very queer;
> "Yet so slyly they come, and so slyly they go,
> "That I cannot them see, or I'd give them a blow.
>
> "I am so tired of their chiming and tuning, 'tis true,
> "So you must not be frighten'd to hear great ado;
> "And beside their dread music, they're biting my arm;
> "And now tell me, my friends, how can I be calm?
>
> "They are biting me still for their songs to get pay;
> "Now their lives I will take, I most surely do say."

So this lady so fair thus on massacre bent,
Did so quickly arise with the darkest intent.

She said, "Sirs, I have pass'd upon you a decree,
"That no longer my face you dread minstrels shall see;
"Soon you'll find that your songs of the night will be hush'd
"And yourselves, it is true, irrecoverably crush'd."

The poem goes on for five more stanzas to recount how the "lady" massacres all of the mosquitoes/minstrels but one with her shoe, and this one keeps her awake all night. She constructs a muslin net to keep him out, but alas, the "biter and singer got under the net," and in the end, she is forced to declare "that those minstrels such cunning had shown / As in all her existence she ever had known."[51]

Eric Lott writes that attempts to "master" minstrelsy in the antebellum period almost inevitably wind up succumbing to its power of attraction.[52] Here Etta Floyd's rejection of the minstrel "swarm" only leads her to the state of frenzied commotion that she so deplores in popular culture. For her, the contagious disorder of the shows—in which she attempts to keep the buzzing mosquito out from under the net—becomes a figure for her own insanity; this poem records the poet's fragile sense of equipoise in a setting that she struggled to cast as a refuge from a hostile, small-minded world rather than as a prison from which she had little hope of escaping. Indeed, she stayed in the asylum until her death.

ETTA FLOYD openly registered her disgust for the "fancy for an Ethiopian skin" that minstrelsy fostered; this perhaps helped her to stabilize the unsettling mixture of attraction and repulsion, identification and disavowal, that pervaded the performances. Participation in the minstrel shows—whether acting, reporting, criticizing, or simply watching—involved mimicking lowly figures in order to exorcise the spirit of wildness, of subrationality, of disorder, that the black figures on stage were meant to represent. Outwardly white and sometimes even of respectable stock, the patients at Utica nevertheless lacked the refinement, social skills, rationality, and above all, the self-control that supposedly separated the sane from the insane, as well as the civilized from the savage or the white from the red or black. In staging a grotesque blackness, they banished from themselves that troubling interior otherness—making visible (and erasable) on the skin what was ineffable, untamable within. When the show was over, they could cast off their subrationality like a snake's skin.[53]

But such acts of miming or surrogacy always imply a certain longing, as well; blackface acts, for all their mockery, would never have seized the popular imagination were they not based on a deep if unconscious desire for black culture and black bodies. Part of what blackness signified in mid-nineteenth-century popular culture was an exemption from all the pressures of civility and modernity to which whites were subject, and which had proven crushing for so many asylum inmates. The temporal regimens of factory life, the fiscal discipline of entrepreneurship, the strictures of middle-class domesticity and sexual morality, the sobriety and spiritual vigilance demanded by Protestant theology: running afoul of these standards earned many nineteenth-century Americans a room with barred windows. But blacks' perceived constitutional incapacity to live up to white middle-class standards of behavior gave them a sort of free pass from adhering to those strictures, and this freedom was endlessly figured on the popular stage. The minstrel logic of the lazy, loose, foolish, fleshy black person was for patients an invitation to reclaim as pleasure and through play all that they were being disciplined to surmount in their asylum routines.[54]

And so for many writers, the minstrel shows provoked a shock of recognition: not the "revulsion" prescribed by physicians as a mechanism for distancing oneself from one's delusions or the "self-control" necessary to avoid excessive displays of mirth, but a kind of identification with the objects of theatrical display on the grounds of a shared incapacity to be productive citizens, a shared civil or social death. The patients were physically removed from the main currents of life and forbidden to make contact with family and friends, to vote, to write wills, to move about as they pleased. They were considered to be in need of reform, of civilization, of uplift. And in all of these senses, they saw themselves through the lens of race: if they were indeed wearing masks, then behind those masks—some sensed—was something black. One patient, for instance, published a Valentine's Day poem in typical minstrel broken dialect. In it, he poses as Jim Crow addressing a lover who has abandoned him—a poignant topic for anyone left alone in an asylum, made comical only by the author's reference to himself as "Dis Nigga."[55]

Such identifications of blackness and insanity did not originate with the patients, nor simply with the society that had confined them. According to Sander Gilman, the association of madness with blackness had its roots in the classical period, when "the melancholic was understood to have a black countenance"; it recurred periodically in Western culture as a way to associate the "other" with wildness.[56] Medieval and early modern medical

commentators reworked ancient theories of humoral imbalances by arguing
that a surfeit of black bile caused a variety of mental disturbances and was
detectable by a darkening of the skin; along these lines, Shakespeare refers
to "sable melancholy" in his *Love's Labour's Lost*.[57] Over time this coloring of
madness took on explicitly racial meanings. The English physician and poet
Sir Richard Blackmore, for instance, referred to madness (in a 1724 medical
work) as a "wild uncultivated region, an intellectual Africa, that abounds
with an endless variety of monsters and irregular minds."[58] Enlightenment
philosophers viewed the world's races and regions in a developmental frame,
in which white, European ethnicity represented rationality, progress, and
health; all others were stuck at various arrested stages of psychology, intellect, and accomplishment. According to Georges Canguilhem, such thinkers
as Monstequieu, Voltaire, and Diderot viewed "the intellectually primitive
and the intellectually puerile [as] two forms of a single infirmity," characterized by the "halting of development at an intermediate stage."[59]

By the mid-nineteenth century in the United States, concepts of blackness and madness had become so intertwined as to be nearly mutually
defining. In the eyes of psychiatry and law—as well as increasingly in
popular culture—"savage" or nonwhite races were said to share with the
insane a state of arrested or disrupted development that made both seem
like overgrown children. Because both blacks and the insane were judged
incapable of managing their own affairs in a modern democracy, both
groups were stripped of property ownership rights and were considered
in need of custody.[60] The pro-slavery ideologue George Fitzhugh, for instance, argued that blacks, like children and lunatics, could not be governed by "mere law," but must be subject to additional restraints to keep
them from crime or from coming to harm.

> Children cannot be governed by mere law; first, because they do not under-
> stand it, and secondly, because they are so much under the influence of im-
> pulse, passion and appetite, that they want sufficient self-control to be deterred
> or governed by the distant and doubtful penalties of the law. . . . Very wicked
> men must be put into penitentiaries; lunatics into asylums, and the most wild
> of them into straight jackets [*sic*], just as the most wicked of the sane are man-
> acled with irons; and idiots must have committees to govern and take care of
> them. . . . Nor will the government of mere law suffice for the individual negro.
> He is but a grown up child, and must be governed as a child, not as a lunatic
> or criminal.[61]

That last clause marks the only real distinction in Fitzhugh's text between
the rhetoric of slave-owning paternalism and the system of asylum manage-

ment, for of course the paternalism of insane asylums was meant to train disordered subjects for a life of freedom, rather than of perpetual bondage. Unlike children and lunatics, blacks could never outgrow their wildness and dependency.

The links among insanity, race, and slavery were deepened by the infamous results of the 1840 national census, the first to include demographic data concerning insanity. One finding in particular seemed to confirm the notion that blacks were in need of paternalistic care: while the rate of insanity was virtually the same for Northern and Southern whites, the rate was eleven times higher for Northern blacks than for Southern ones, and six times the rate of insanity among whites.[62] The implication was that the more freedom granted to blacks within a modern "civilized" society, the more their feeble brains cracked under the strain. Within a few years, these figures were decisively shown to be cooked—for instance, some towns in Maine reported having a lower total number of black residents than insane black residents.[63] Nevertheless, the results of the census were cited not only by advocates of slavery such as Vice President Calhoun[64] but even in print by Northern psychiatrists until as late as 1851.[65] Blacks, however, were not considered to be unusually prone to insanity—it was only their immersion in the Western world that created special conditions of risk. On the contrary, left in their natural environment, blacks and other "savages" were thought to be practically free from mental illness.[66] (This association lasted well into the twentieth century, as a 1921 article in the *American Journal of Psychiatry* makes clear: American "negroes," the author wrote, are particularly prone to a certain "psychic weakness" because they are descendant from "savages and cannibals" and are not fit to live in "an environment of higher civilization for which the biological development of the race had not made adequate preparation."[67]) Scattershot evidence seemed to bear this out. For instance, when the rebels of the slave ship *Amistad* were awaiting trial in Hartford in 1839, they made a visit to the local insane asylum and were interviewed by Amariah Brigham, then the superintendent. He asked the rebel leader Joseph Cinqué how the insane were treated in his land, and Cinqué replied that there was almost no insanity there to treat.[68]

Patient writings in the *Opal* bear traces of all of these complex linkages—they point, in other words, to the ways in which insanity was distinctly "racialized" in their thinking and feeling. Even when they did not explicitly link their situation to that of Africans or blacks, they frequently referred to themselves as "children" in need of "civilization," "uplift," and "light"—a set of what Sander Gilman calls "root metaphors" of insanity that was also shared by contemporaneous discourse about non-white races.[69] In an 1852 editorial, one patient wrote that the relations of society to the insane were like those of the "hostile parent" and "infant culprit," and that if society wanted to see the "reformation" of the child, it had to hold out hope for "reconciliation" as well as "punishment." [70] Another contributor, in a poem about the woes of slaves ("Ah, poor smitten son of Afric! [*sic*]," could easily have been writing about a patient in the asylum:

> Flows no tear from pity's fountain,
>   When from friends thou'rt severed wide?
> Cares no heart how high's the mountain
>   That from thy lov'd ones doth divide? [71]

For many patients who were permitted to publish their writing in the journal, however, the real hinge connecting their situations to those of blacks was not simply the similarity of stigmas of blackness and insanity, the presumed correspondence of the mental condition of the two groups, or the resemblance between the institutions of plantation slavery and asylum medicine, but the linkage between the reform movements that had launched both the moral treatment movement and the colonial enterprise underway in Africa. The "civilizing" missions of abolitionists, ex-slaves, and evangelists that was well underway in the "free colony" of Sierra Leone and the former U.S. colony of Liberia (by then a new republic) curiously paralleled the work of the founders of the asylum movement. [72] One strong precursor of the American asylums were the "retreats" for the insane run by Quakers, first in England in the late eighteenth century, and then in Philadelphia; and it was in 1785 that the English Quaker William Thornton lobbied the American, British, and French governments to establish a free colony in West Africa for liberated slaves, including his own. [73] Both the proposed colony and the asylums bore a heavy imprint of Quaker influence: they blended humanitarianism and a faith in the "inner light" or spiritual intuition of each individual—no matter how lowly—with an emphasis on thrift and productivity as remedies for backward or wayward peoples. [74]

These colonial enterprises were begun in what would become Sierra Leone in 1787 and Liberia in 1821. They were both originally private ventures, drawing on the interests of traders and humanitarians to establish outposts of "civilization" in Africa—beachheads from which Christianity and capital could spread across the continent. Government involvement was gradual—Liberia was never officially named a U.S. territory at any point before its independence in 1847. But a coalition of American groups, eventually coming under the banner of the American Colonization Society, continued to admin-

ister the territory, appointing leaders, establishing schools and churches, setting trade policies, and so forth. Even after Liberian independence, these
groups continued to maintain a keen interest in the new republic, raising
funds to send former slaves and "recaptives"—Africans seized in illegal slav-
ing expeditions at sea—to Liberia, and continuing their missionary work.
Their motives for doing so varied. Some abolitionists believed, following
Thomas Jefferson, that freed slaves could never integrate into American
society due to the depth of their anger and the depth of white racism; some
slave owners even supported the colony as a way to deport troublesome
slaves.[75]

The *Opal*'s pages reflect a keen interest in the fate of Liberia—especially
in the plight of former American slaves who were in positions of leadership there—and had a generally sympathetic response. In 1851, in an article
called "Africa," one patient reported that two American missionaries had
visited the asylum and spoken to patients about their work in Sierra Leone
and Liberia. The piece concluded with a short poem that, not surprisingly,
supported the mission in terms that were familiar to anyone with a connection to insane asylums:

> Afric receive to thy once wretched shore,
> Those little bands of Christian Heroes,
> Bearing a balm for all thy woes,
> A healing balm for thy keenest throes—
> And God will bless thee.[76]

"Afric" has become something like a patient, suffering "throes" and in need
of "balm." Interestingly, the Liberian enterprise itself had been imagined as
something like a mind cure for the entire race. According to the missionary
Robert Finley, Liberia should become a place where blacks' "contracted
minds will expand and their natures rise." And in the Liberian Declaration of Independence, leaders among the settlers wrote that they came "to
nourish in our hearts the flame of honourable ambition . . . and to evince to
all who despise, ridicule and oppress our race that we possess with them a
common nature; are with them susceptible of equal refinement, and capable of equal advancement in all that adorns and dignifies man."[77] The *Opal*
poem was signed, as were many pieces in the journal, simply by the word
"Asylumia." The conceit, in this context, turned the asylum into a mythical
land, somewhere between colony and nation, supporting its own culture,
with its own physical features, and burdened by its own tragic history of
deprivation and despair.

The association of institutionalization with colonization and disability with racial "otherness" was not unique to inmates of insane asylums. In some ways, the patients found themselves in a situation much like the nineteenth-century deaf, who were similarly segregated from the "normal" population in special schools and asylums, and whose self-conception sometimes mirrored the Utica patients' notion of a separate culture of Asylumia. An 1847 edition of the *American Annals of the Deaf and Dumb*, for instance, described the deaf as a "a distinct, and in some respects, strongly marked class of human beings" who "have a history peculiar to themselves"; and a deaf educator wrote in 1848 that the deaf "might almost as well have been born in benighted Asia, as in this land of ours."[78] This striking rhetorical similarity may give evidence of some cross-disability identification. Furthering this link is the fact that the *Opal* exchanged subscriptions with the editors of two deaf-mute journals—the *Deaf-Mute* and the *Radii*—and that the editor saw these journals as emanating from kindred spirits: "What meed of praise would be too extravagant for those who have 'borne the burden,' and paved the way for the glorious advancement of the children of sorrow unto perfection in comfort?"[79] (The *Opal* later complained, however, that the *Radii* had received a "legislative appropriation of three hundred dollars . . . but we do not acknowledge the like sum from the great body, for the *Opal*, nor do we expect to have the pleasure."[80]) The racial overtones of this shared disability consciousness—a metaphorical geography that maps the disabled as backwardly non-Western and therefore in need of cultural reformation and spiritual uplift—certainly bear out the disability studies scholar Lennard Davis's comment that "discussions of disability always slide into discussions of race."[81]

There is an important distinction between the deaf and insane "races," however, which may help explain the *Opal* writer's jealous reaction to his deaf counterpart's funding. Asylums for deaf-mutes in the early- to mid-nineteenth century promoted sign language (or "manual" language, as it was then called) as a means of creating what the historian of deafness Douglas Baynton calls "a cultural and linguistic community," whereas authorities behind the insane asylums were insistent on stamping out madness.[82] Some members of the deaf community exhibited a striking "racial" pride, as in the 1855 proposal of one deaf man, John J. Fluornoy, to create a deaf-only state in the western territories—a state that would eventually function like a deaf version of Liberia. ("A deaf state," he argued, "is the manifest destiny of our people. . . . It is a political independence, a State Sovereignty, at which I aim. . . . We will have a small republic of our own, under our sovereignty, and independent of all hearing interference."[83]) The notion of Asylumia as a separate state, in contrast, was self-consciously figurative and ironic, its self-deprecation bordering at times on deep abjection rather than Fluornoy's militant self-reliance. For the deaf, creation of a separate language and cultural self-sufficiency *were* the cure; in contrast, asylum writings and displays were all explicitly geared toward exhibiting the patients' triumph over their disability, rather than their embrace of it.

Despite the Utica patients' manifest needs to assimilate themselves into "normal" American culture rather than create their own self-sustaining identity, their writings about Africa point—like those of the deaf writers—to their intuition of important links between asylum care and the colonial situation. Indeed, a number of scholars interested in the psychology of colonialism have recently begun to explore connections between colonialism and psychiatry, in part by focusing on the ways in which psychiatric practice played out in colonial spaces such as Africa and India. The establishment of mental hospitals in these regions in the late nineteenth century, they have shown, shaped definitions of "European" and "native" in the new European territories by quantifying the mental attributes of each race.[84] But as patients confronted the minstrel show in Utica in the 1850s and recorded how the spectacle of racial otherness was in some sense a staging of their own situations, they contributed to an even earlier flow of ideas, associations, and practices between colonial Africa and the psychiatric scene in the West. The anthropologist Ann Laura Stoler speaks of such flows as following a "circuitous imperial route," in which some practices associated with colonial control over nonwhite races were imported and recycled in the European context, as a way to control troublesome populations at home. Official policies toward beggars, criminals, and the insane were influenced by conceptions of race developed in the colonies; techniques for controlling the one might be used in managing the other.[85] It is the emotional logic of that imperial route, as felt by the objects of reform, that some of the patients' writings on minstrelsy convey.

In an 1854 column, A.S.M. reported on the minstrel shows as a meeting of two colonized peoples—the gentle inhabitants of Asylumia and the benighted denizens of Africa. As in his article "Dialogue Between Two Southern Gentlemen and a Slave," he showed throughout his stewardship of the journal a great sensitivity to race relations, frequently seeing in the struggles of blacks a metaphor for the situation of the insane. Not surprisingly, then, he found much to ponder in the performances of the minstrels. Blackface performance, he wrote, was a commercialized rip-off of philanthropy, in which "traveling minstrels" co-opt the fascination with blackness and Africa that had permeated contemporary culture. Lately, however, even the blackface minstrels have turned to genuine philanthropy—bringing the civilizing mission back from Africa to the United States: "On several occasions . . . there have appeared here at the Asylum several companies from abroad, who were prompted by the pure spirit of philanthropy, and came to chase away the dark design of lurking sorrow,— to light up a smile in the aspect of woe; and it was well, for though insanity is a dreadful and serious evil, it may be assailed and overthrown by the lightness, hilarity and mirthful wit of these minstrels from the dark region of Africa." Prompted by these visitors, "a company from the far-off land of Asylumia, on the hither side of Ethiopia, appear[ed] in the south [evidently the south wing of the asylum]" and "during two successive evenings, did accomplish most wonderful displays."

In presenting Asylumia as a region "to the hither side of Ethiopia," A.S.M. transfers himself imaginatively from one realm of philanthropy to another, from the insane asylum in Utica to somewhere in the region of Liberia. Nonetheless, he appears to distance the Asylumians from the Ethiopians by referring to the patients as philanthropists as well as objects of charity—it is insane actors, after all, who are pictured as bringers of light. In this way, the performance marks the insane themselves as capable of lifting each other out of their debased state. And yet, this scenario is not so different from that of Liberia, where it was former slaves who did most of the missionary work, education, and institution building and who had, in 1847, achieved independence for their nation. As Amy Kaplan has written, "Colonization in the 1850s had a two-pronged ideology: to expel blacks to a separate national sphere, and to expand U.S. power through the civilizing process; black Christian settlers would become both outcasts from and agents for the American empire." [86] The comparison of blackness and insanity, then, could serve to degrade both groups and justify their expulsion, but it could also be part of an inspiring cycle of self-improvement and national pride.

Finally, in the strangest turn in A.S.M.'s piece, he expresses his hope that one day the Blackbird Minstrels of Asylumia will "delineate or caricature the habits and manners of lunas . . . ; no doubt there will be a display of the power and influence of lunacy in promoting the happiness and well-being of the human race." The array of inversions here is dizzying: an anonymous asylum inmate meditates on a troupe of insane whites imitating irrational blacks and imagines that those performers will then imitate insanity itself. Perhaps here is John Galt's "revulsive" technique on display: the insane will see their own folly more clearly if it is exhibited to them. And yet there is more: A.S.M. casts this hypothetical self-mimicry as a task not just of turning madness and blackness inside out but of uplifting the entire human race. It is the insane, he argues, who can teach the sane that our civilization has a precarious hold on refinement and cultivation: "As civilization has a great proportion of *Lunas,* it were as well to travel back to the dark paths of rudeness and barbarity, and learn to unlearn the perversion of the refined and cultivated intellect."

There is a mounting confusion in this piece. To read it is to become less and less clear about who is in need of philanthropy and who gives it, who is sane and who is not, and who is acting and whom represented. It is as if he sees madness and sanity, blackness and whiteness, self and other, as a series of masks, to which his writing only adds additional layers. The sense of a hidden self is a feature known intimately to those who have studied the colonial situation; Frantz Fanon's classic study *Black Skin, White Masks* makes clear the psychic consequences for the colonized who hide themselves behind a mask imposed upon them by their colonizers, and find their true selves lost, banished to a "zone of non-being." [87] But for A.S.M., masking seems to be a "perversion of the refined and cultivated intellect" rather than a desperate dodge of savages and lunatics. How is it that the "lunas" can uplift the entire race, rather than the other way around? It is by "unlearning the perversion of the refined and the cultivated," and by revealing that we are separated from each other—the rude and the barbarous from the polite and civilized—only by a series of masks.

THE *OPAL* contributors' wide-ranging commentaries on the minstrel shows, sometimes sardonic and sometimes playful, reveal a disparity, if not an open conflict, between the official rationale for asylum amusements (discipline, deferred gratification, self-control, and so forth) and the lived reality on the wards and in the theater (a fear of being stigmatized as psychically "black"). But it is important to remember that both the performances and the commentary emanate from a hopeful, even utopian, moment in the treatment of the insane: when it was believed that providing a sanative physical environment and a restorative cultural one would actually cure insanity and return the dispossessed to contact with society. Although at Utica the minstrel tradition continued until approximately 1890, by century's end it was staged in a very different context. Whereas during the middle of the century, the linkage of madness and blackness could generate an inspiring implication of racial/mental uplift, the last years of the minstrel shows at Utica occurred during the rise of the psychiatric eugenics movement, which, according to Robert Castel, ushered in a new era of "racialism directed against the insane."[88] Eugenics was based on the post-Darwinian premise that much of insanity was inherited and ineradicable, and that the white race was in peril of degenerating into barbarity if insanity was not eradicated.[89] Although Darwin, in his *The Descent of Man*, equated "primitive" racial cultures and people with cognitive disabilities, he was skeptical of the human ability to exert conscious control over the fate of the species; his cousin, the eugenicist Sir Francis Galton, believed that undesirable traits could be eliminated from humans through proper breeding, just as they were in dogs and horses.[90] Eliminated, rather than reformed or cured: the superintendent at Utica during these years, G. Alder Blumer, was gradually coming to endorse such eugenicist techniques as ovariotomies and vasectomies to prevent the mentally defective from passing on their taint to future generations.[91]

The reasons for this are complex. First, as new treatment paradigms, especially neurology, challenged the assumptions of the moral treatment (especially its emphasis on environmental factors in both etiology and treatment), asylums were often left only with the hardest, most intractable cases to attend to. Asylum physicians' overestimation of their own cure rates during the period of the moral treatment contributed to the problem and helped convince state legislators of the need to exercise oversight of the superintendents' management of the institutions. Consequently, many asylum superintendents like Blumer felt their power over their institutions, as well as their power to cure patients, slipping away; supporting and refining the eugenics movement was a way for them to reassert control over mental illness, even if they could not cure it. Add to this the influx of immigrant patients who brought with them newly confounding cultural problems that were often read as signs of racial inferiority, and an environment was created in which those running the asylums were attracted to ideas that explained away their own powerlessness to effect cures. Eugenics did just that. In Blumer's words—heretical for a man who had started out his career as a gentlemanly practitioner of the moral treatment—"all diseases are hereditary." To support the old moral treatment model was to court charges that one was using public funds to pamper and sustain the mentally defective. But sterilizing the insane, supporting legislation that forbade them to marry, or segregating them for life, could stand in for curing them.[92]

Under this new paradigm, the last minstrel performers at Utica could hardly have viewed their mimicry of blacks—no matter how ironically—as an opportunity to show the world "the power and influence of lunacy in promoting the happiness and well-being of the human race." In the eugenics paradigm, nonwhite races were once again compared with the insane and the "feeble-minded," but without the aim of uplifting these wayward populations. As the historian Martin Pernick has written, eugenics, "carried to the logical extreme, could make possible genocide without homicide, the bloodless extermination of unwanted characteristics." [93] Blumer shied away from extreme eugenics positions such as castration or even euthanasia for mental defectives, and he even returned to some of the moral treatment tenets once he left the state asylum in 1894 and took up the direction of the private Butler Hospital for the Insane in Providence, Rhode Island. (There, he was free from meddling state legislatures and dealt primarily with patients from wealthy families, who had no desire to hear that their bloodlines were tainted and that their relatives were irrecoverable.[94]) But the mad blackface minstrels who trod the boards during his tenure at Utica witnessed, and no doubt felt, the loss of hope that a mix of culture, medicine, and environment could cure, and that the refinement of the insane was a mark of the advancement of civilization.

———— ✳ ————

CHAPTER THREE

Bardolatry in Bedlam

Shakespeare and Early Psychiatry

THROUGH THEIR WRITING, public speaking, dramatic performances, card playing, chapel worship, and other cultural pursuits, asylum patients were expected to mold themselves into proper subjects, fit for a return to society and full citizenship. Such activities constituted the arena in which patients demonstrated their mastery of the behavioral norms established by asylum authorities and onlookers from the outside world (and in which they were sometimes detected in their failure). For doctors, monitoring and regulating the cultural lives of patients was an opportunity to convert their criticisms of nineteenth-century American life into medical practice. For them, the asylum was something of a laboratory for the purification of culture and the production of useful citizens who could live in modernity without being unstrung by its temptations, agitated rhythms, and destabilizing messages.

But what gave them the authority to establish the rules of the game? Who had given these men the right to deprive others of essential freedoms, tell them how to behave, what to read, what sort of god to pray to (or, more accurately, *not* to pray to), when and what to eat, and when they were cured? Certainly nothing in their medical training provided a basis for this type of authority: as the first generation of psychiatrists, they had no regular coursework or clinical experience that might convince the public of their expertise in these matters.[1] Although many superintendents had advanced medical training by nineteenth-century standards, a few—like Samuel Woodward, of the Worcester State Lunatic Hospital in Massachusetts—had not even been to medical school at all. Woodward learned his trade by serving as an apprentice, became interested in the treatment of the insane only when several mentally ill patients consulted him in his private practice, and did not read systematically in the works of Pinel and other European authorities on the treatment of insanity until *after* his appointment as superintendent at Worcester.[2] This lack of formal training was not necessarily a liability, given that mainstream medicine was in general disrepute. In fact, the formation of the Association of Medical Superintendents of American Asylums for the Insane (AMSAII) in 1844 was in some sense an attempt to distance asylum medicine from the rest of the medical field; some members of AMSAII even refused to join the American Medical Association when it was founded two years later.[3] But as more and more state asylums were constructed, the question of authority became ever more acute: superintendents had not only to convince family members of the afflicted of their rightful power over the patients, but they also had to convince legislators and the public at large to fund their asylums.

Despite their claims that insanity was at root a medical issue, it was not solely—or perhaps even primarily—medical expertise that asylum superintendents claimed in attempting to legitimate their authority. For all their emphasis on the modern advancement of mental science, these physicians were operating in a culture that had not yet experienced the fundamental turn toward modern science and medicine, in which approval from one's disciplinary colleagues matters more to practitioners and researchers than does the good opinion of the lay public.[4] In an 1844 article in the *Boston Medical and Surgical Journal* arguing for higher pay for asylum superintendents, one superintendent perhaps unintentionally indicated the relative priority of early psychiatrists' qualifications: "It is abominable for legislatures to demand high moral, social, literary and scientific qualifications for the medical superintendents of such institutions, and yet pay them less than a grocer's clerk gets by the year for weighing out soap and candles."[5] Moral, social, and literary attainments received higher billing than "scientific qualifications." Thorough understanding of the post-Pinelian field of asylum medicine was nice, but it could hardly guarantee the more exalted claims to cultural authority and social standing that would separate superintendents from grocery clerks. And so for recommendations, superintendents frequently turned to the one figure whose unquestioned authority in the broad field of moral goodness and literary insight might convince patients' families, state legislatures, and the public of their rightful position at the helm of their institutions. It was William Shakespeare, more than Philippe Pinel, Benjamin Rush, or Amariah Brigham, who did the most to justify the authority of the asylum superintendents.

In the first three decades of American asylum medicine, no figure was cited as an authority on insanity and mental functioning more frequently than Shakespeare. In the pages of the *American Journal of Insanity*—the official organ of the nascent psychiatric profession—no fewer than thirteen lengthy articles of Shakespearean criticism were published from 1844 to 1864, and in other psychiatric writings his name was regularly invoked in matters concerning diagnosis, nosology, and treatment. "There is scarcely a form of mental disorder," wrote Amariah Brigham in the lead article of the first issue of the *American Journal of Insanity*, that Shakespeare "has not alluded to, and pointed out the causes and method of treatment." "A very complete system of psychological medicine could be compiled from the works of Shakspeare [*sic*]," wrote A.O. Kellogg (Brigham's former assistant and later the superintendent of the Port Hope asylum, Canada West); "no textbook or treatise extant deserves to be so carefully studied by those engaged in psychological pursuits as the works of this most wonderful of men."[6]

In virtually all of these articles, the Shakespearean "system of psychological medicine" was shown to resemble almost exactly the system of moral and medical treatment that was institutionalized by the authors themselves. According to Kellogg, Shakespeare believed that madness was "a disease of the brain, and could be cured by medical means, aided by judicious care and management: all which he points out as clearly as it could be done by a modern expert."[7] Not only did a careful reading of the Bard endorse the findings of modern experts, but modern mental science provided what Kellogg called "the true key" to understanding the great works of literature, especially Shakespeare's.[8] Isaac Ray, the influential superintendent first of the Maine Insane Asylum and then the Butler Hospital, believed that just as Shakespeare could validate nineteenth-century asylum medicine, so too the advancement of medicine could shed light on the mind of Shakespeare: "The revolution in the management of the insane, that occurred toward the end of the last century, produced among its legitimate effects a better knowledge of insanity, that became visible in works of literature as well as in the current opinions of society." Longstanding problems of critical interpretation could be resolved with recourse to this new knowledge; for instance, "it is enough to state as scientific fact, that Hamlet's mental condition furnishes in abundance, the characteristic symptoms of insanity, in wonderful harmony and consistency." In this formulation, insanity and Shakespeare's "delineations" of it are collapsed into each other as givens: mental illness is simply a natural fact that Shakespeare, who worked "in the strictest accordance with the principles of human nature," could not fail to observe correctly.[9]

Ever since Samuel Johnson's account of him, Shakespeare had been granted primacy in the understanding of "human nature," a primacy that the asylum superintendents were trying to establish for themselves. And so the literary criticisms of Ray, Brigham, and Kellogg were in part a demonstration of their mastery in the cultural realm over that which they presumed to govern medically. "Human nature," wrote Brigham in his discussion of Shakespeare, "as respects the passions and emotions, is ever the same, and correct descriptions of mental phenomena, though of ancient date, are still worthy of our attention."[10] Despite Shakespeare's antiquity, when Ray and the others used the term "human nature," they were invoking an Enlightenment concept of what was distinctive and invariant in humanity—a concept that was entirely secular and mechanistic.[11] But what was radically new in their brand of "enlightened" science was the institutional authority that the asylum superintendents claimed as the logical end of such conceptions, and the social power that came with turning other humans into objects of knowledge. This authority was unusual not only within the somewhat chaotic field of medicine, but within the wider ethos of antebellum America, in that it rested with a cadre of experts with unprecedented powers to define and enforce standards of correct behavior from institutional perches that they controlled with little accountability. In this light, grabbing the mantle of the timeless genius helped to mask the novelty of their powers.

In addition to exploring why superintendents turned so obsessively to Shakespeare, this chapter will also consider what they made of him once they had hold of him. In his classic study of nineteenth-century cultural hierarchies, Lawrence Levine argues that the popularity of Shakespeare across classes in the mid-nineteenth century indicates the period's "rich shared public culture," which only later became fractured in a "struggle for power and cultural authority" between elite and popular classes.[12] The superintendents' fairly obsessive commentary on Shakespeare certainly suggests the pervasiveness of the Bard, but it should also complicate Levine's picture. The figure of Shakespeare enjoyed a secular authority that crossed classes and regions in much the same way that the biblical God did in religious settings; but just as the Bible could be used to legitimate the power of one group over another, so too could the plays of Shakespeare. His ubiquity as well as his unmatched authority therefore made him a unique instrument in the cultural wing of a battle for social control. This is especially pertinent for early psychiatry, which saw the establishment of social and cultural norms as medical issues and so could hardly ignore a figure whose overpowering cultural authority was nearly universally hailed.

The conflicts that emerge around Shakespeare in the asylum, too, look different from the "highbrow/lowbrow" split that Levine pictures. Levine writes of the gradual shift from a "people's Shakespeare" to an "elite Shakespeare," a process in which "Shakespeare was being divorced from the broader world of everyday culture" and turned, gradually, into "serious" culture that could be properly understood only by an educated and refined elite.[13] The asylum physicians certainly saw Shakespeare as a towering genius and themselves as a trained elite who had singular access to his meanings; but they did not invoke Shakespeare so much to cordon off one area of cultural activity from others as to assert their authority over the whole culture. In this sense, their use of Shakespeare was not unlike the nineteenth-century cult surrounding George Washington, a figure of national unity whose memory could be invoked to establish an extra-political authority for highly contested aims.[14] Early psychiatrists were not alone; other emerging professional classes also appealed to Shakespeare for legitimation, particularly as a new bourgeois/professional class supplanted the landed gentry who had ruled the country in the early national period. A paradoxical dialectic emerged in which doctors (and sometimes lawyers) appeared at once to be ratifying the timeless wisdom of the Bard while at the same time bending Shakespeare to their will.

THE MEDICAL reading of Shakespearean psychology by Brigham, Kellogg, and Ray was not entirely unprecedented, nor was it solely—or even predominantly—an American phenomenon. The origins of this tradition may be traced to 1778 and the writings of one Dr. Akenside, whom the New Variorum edition of *Hamlet* cites as the first physician "to assert that Hamlet's insanity is real."[15] The great American physician Benjamin Rush apologized in his 1812 book, *Medical Inquiries and Observations, upon Diseases of the Mind,* for his frequent references to classic writers, especially Shakespeare, who, Rush believed, "view the human mind in all its operations, whether natural or morbid, with a microscopic eye; and hence many things arrest their attention, which escape the notice of physicians."[16] Mostly, Rush used such citations to describe diseases, but occasionally he borrowed authors' recommendations for how to cure them. In an influential medical textbook first published in 1822, the British doctor John Mason Good used Hamlet as a template for his discussion of "melancholy attonita"—a gradual deterioration of the will that results in "an inability of firmly pursuing any laudable exertion or even purpose," and he called Shakespeare "the highest authority in every thing relating to the human mind and its affections."[17] Good inspired the more systematic 1833 work of George Farren, *Essays on the Varieties of Mania, Exhibited by the Characters of Hamlet, Ophelia, Lear, and Edgar.* Farren, a lawyer who was resident director of the Asylum Foreign and Domestic Life Assurance Company, wanted to use Shakespeare's insights into mental illness in order to "show the effect of generally-prevailing maladies on the duration of life."[18] (He did not show, however, how the fates of any particular mad Shakespearean characters helped him to compute his actuarial tables.)

From the late 1850s through the 1870s, the important British alienists John Charles Bucknill, John Conolly, and Henry Maudsley wrote extensively on Shakespeare, but several features distinguish the psychiatric image of Shakespeare on the two sides of the Atlantic. Unlike his American counterparts, Bucknill viewed his researches into Shakespeare as something of a diversion from his professional work. Whereas Kellogg's Shakespearean criticism constituted virtually his entire professional publishing output and his fellow American Brigham confessed that "we have very little to add to [Shakespeare's] method of treating the insane," Bucknill wrote that he undertook his own study of Shakespeare "to have [my] mind diverted from the routine of professional work, or of professional study."[19] Although he credited Shakespeare with "exactness of . . . psychological knowledge," Bucknill never quite claimed that the Bard had anticipated the modern understanding of insanity's forms and causes, let alone the proper methods of treating it; and as opposed to the "complete system" of nineteenth-century psychiatry that the Americans saw paralleled in Shakespeare's work, Bucknill insisted that it was unfair to judge Shakespeare through the lens of contemporary science.[20] Conolly, in a book-length study of *Hamlet*, frequently used his psychiatric expertise to unlock the medical meanings of the text. Like Bucknill, Brigham, Kellogg, and Ray, he equated *Hamlet* with "human nature"; but although he offered a few comments about the accuracy of Shakespeare's perceptions, he did not attempt to square Shakespeare with the whole system of nineteenth-century mental science.[21] Maudsley, famous for his theories of degeneration, turned to Shakespeare at several points in his career to illustrate an idea: Hamlet's malady, for instance, was the result of a "constitutional indisposition."[22] But the bardolatry of this second-generation psychiatrist went even further than that of his British and American forebears, for it led him not to ratify the medical and moral treatment movement but to question its underpinnings: "Shakespeare . . . furnishes, in the work of creative art, more valuable information [about insanity] than can be obtained from the vague and general statements with which science, in its present defective state, is constrained to content itself." [23]

Given that these British superintendents and alienists made no systematic effort to equate Shakespeare with modern psychiatric findings, it is understandable that Helen Small sees little medical purpose in their Shakespeare criticism. Instead, she views this writing solely as a "reflection on the social status — and the literary pretensions — of the authors." In demonstrating that they each had "a feeling heart and a refined sensibility — those eminently desirable qualities of the fashionable Victorian doctor," these genteel professionals evinced "a conservative desire to safeguard the gentlemanly character of physicianship from the inroads of (largely middle-class) technicians." [24] The American superintendents, in contrast, were overwhelmingly drawn from middle-class backgrounds and saw in their new professional stature a kind of social elevation and stability that few from their backgrounds could ever hope to attain. In Small's terms, their fervid Shakespearean appropriations might represent their strained attempts to prove themselves worthy of the cultural capital that was associated with their new class position; their transparently excessive literalness and inappropriate empiricism could be read as the cultural tone deafness of the upwardly mobile. [25]

This sort of explanation, however, has its limits, for Small's banishment of "social status" and "literary pretensions" from the arena of legitimate medical and professional concerns is anachronistic. In addition to the comment cited above about the importance of "moral, social [and] literary" stature in the hiring of superintendents, there were also practical considerations involving "literary pretensions" on the job. Perhaps most evident was the decisive role that psychiatrists often played as expert witnesses in legal cases involving alleged insanity. Ray, the leading authority on the medical jurisprudence of the insane, enjoined jurists to look at Shakespeare as a way of helping themselves to understand issues of criminal culpability of the insane; Shakespeare was to guide them toward proper medical interpretations, which would then be applied to the case at hand. [26]

Not only is the separation of literary knowledge, social standing, and medical authority antithetical to an understanding of the social functioning of psychiatry, but it disregards the very philosophy of practice that guided asylum medicine — a philosophy that saw social norms and cultural tendencies as medical issues. The varied "physical" and "moral" causes of insanity, as we have seen, led to a similarly mixed form of treatment, in which administering medicine was no more central than conducting schools or organizing debating societies. Psychiatric interest in Shakespeare, far from being a dilettantish display of learning, was part of a movement that swept practically all of American culture—from pathogenic yellow-covered novels and frenzied religious revivals to the socially stabilizing great works of literature and the therapeutic architecture of the asylum itself—under its medical purview.

It may seem unlikely to us that Shakespeare could have anticipated the moral treatment movement in asylum medicine, living, as he did, two and a half centuries before its advent. His was an age, the *American Journal of Insanity* often pointed out, in which insanity was generally viewed as a divine visitation, and in which only one asylum, Bethlem Royal Hospital (popularly known as Bedlam)—hardly a model for "moral treatment"—was in existence. Making matters worse, the only two of his plays to picture a doctor confronting madness end with less than resounding endorsements of protopsychiatric practice. In *King Lear,* the physician does not recommend any particular medical or moral intervention but advises Cordelia to let her raving father repose with the "foster-nurse of nature." [27] *Macbeth* is even less promising, with the hero exclaiming "Throw physic to the dogs" after the doctor confesses that in the case of Lady Macbeth, he can do nothing to "minister to a mind diseas'd." [28] Nonetheless, these articles showed a point-by-point correspondence between the Bard's "system" and the authors' own. Brigham summed up the five general Shakespearean doctrines of insanity:

1. That a well-formed brain, a good shaped head, is essential to a good mind.
2. That insanity is a disease of the brain.
3. That there is a general and partial insanity.
4. That it is a disease which can be cured by medical means.
5. That the causes are various, the most common of which he has particularly noticed. [29]

The Shakespearean criticism of Brigham, Ray, and Kellogg essentially consists of glosses on these five notions, which were cornerstones of asylum medicine's version of moral treatment. Several characters note that low foreheads mean base temperaments. [30] Lear has a "strong predisposition to insanity," which at the beginning of the play is in a state of "incubation," waiting for something to trigger it. [31] Hamlet is insane despite the fact that many of his behaviors appear rational.[32] The physician's advice to Cordelia about letting "nature" do its work through sleep and tranquility is far from an abdication of medical responsibility, but one of the profoundest insights of the moral treatment.[33] Even Stephano of *The Tempest* is allegorized as something of an asylum physician. Confronted with Caliban's madness, Stephano subdues him with methods "material" (the bottle) and "psychological" (kindness).[34]

What explains this extraordinary prevision of Shakespeare? And what explains the fact that no one before the asylum superintendents of this era was able to dig the science out of the Bard? The simplest explanation is that the superintendents simply misread the evidence. Indeed, their claims that Shakespeare's "system" was the same as their own, and that—in Kellogg's words—"many [medical] facts not known or recognized by men of his age appear to have been grasped" by Shakespeare really do appear to be incorrect, on a basic level.[35] In 1970, the psychiatrist Irving Edgar attacked this "distorted and false and . . . bardolatrous rhetoric" from two angles.[36] First, the similarities that Kellogg and others offered between their own program of treatment and Shakespeare's "delineations of insanity" were highly selective. To construct a Shakespeare preemptively hostile to the moral treatment paradigm, one could quote *Much Ado about Nothing*, where Shakespeare seems to chide those who would "fetter strong madness in a silken thread," suggesting that he favored harsh physical treatment of the insane.[37] Second, where values and ideas do seem to correspond, they can be explained by the historical resemblances between early modern and nineteenth-century views of insanity, not by Shakespeare's Nostradamus-like prognostications. The relation between skull formation and mental functioning, for instance, was hardly a recent discovery but "was common knowledge for centuries and certainly was in Shakespeare's day"; and the idea of insanity as a disease of the brain was common both to medical thinkers of the Renaissance as well as to other playwrights such as John Ford, Angus Fletcher, and John Shirley.[38] More recently, Duncan Salkeld has read nineteenth-century—and subsequent—psychiatric fascinations with Shakespeare as simply false positivism, in which "scientists" view their own conceptual apparatus as an "objective" lens, disregard historical context, and even fail to distinguish between real and fictional lives. Salkeld instead suggests that it is primarily Galenic conceptions of humoral imbalances that inform Shakespeare's representations of madness.[39]

Michael MacDonald's important work *Mystical Bedlam* can corroborate some of these criticisms: madness was indeed increasingly falling under the province of medical doctors in Shakespeare's day; both medical practitioners and "common wisdom" agreed that "madness or melancholy depended upon both physiological predisposition and environmental stress;" and the nineteenth-century concept of faculty psychology, which divided the brain into different "chambers"—so crucial to the psychiatrists' claim that one could be "partially insane"—was much like the early modern conception of the "vegetal," "sensitive," and "rational" faculties of the brain, one or more of which could become disordered. Indeed, the early modern medical approach to madness constituted a "therapeutic eclecticism" of medical, astrological, and psychological interventions—which was perhaps not as different from the mixed "moral" and "medical" programs at nineteenth-century asylums as the superintendents liked to think.[40]

If the superintendents were wrong on these counts, it still remains unclear why they were so dogged in their wrongness, what drew them to assert an ahistorical, even mystical set of connections between themselves and the Bard. A simple answer, and one that is not as farfetched as it may sound, is that far from proving Shakespeare's foresight, the similarities that the superintendents perceived were actually a matter of influence or inspiration—in other words, asylum medicine was actually a self-conscious attempt to put into practice ideas about insanity that had originated in classic literature. In *Imagining the Penitentiary*, John Bender lays out the case that the other great reform institution of the post-Enlightenment period had just such an origin. Bender's somewhat astounding claim is that "attitudes toward prison which were formulated between 1719 and 1779 in narrative literature and art—especially in prose fiction—sustained and . . . enabled the conception and construction of actual penitentiary prisons later in the eighteenth century." What the penal reformers borrowed from novels was "the underlying assumption that narrative processes can reproduce (represent) human behavior so as to recreate personality." This borrowing was possible, he maintains, because the eighteenth-century public sphere was structured in such a way as to allow discourse to flow easily "from one field of interest to another and from one social stratum to another."[41]

Extravagant though Bender's claim may be, the evidence he presents of particular literary borrowings is plausible. In some ways, the originators of the moral treatment movement in psychiatric practice seem to have borrowed similarly from the literary field. Philippe Pinel, the legendary founder of the movement in France, claimed to have based his philosophy and practice in part on readings in classic Greek literature; one of his most important followers added as a formative text Samuel Richardson's

Sir Charles Grandison, in which a physician cures a case of insanity through psychological interventions.[42] And, as Elaine Showalter has written, "superintendents of Victorian lunatic asylums . . . turned to [Shakespeare's] dramas for models of mental aberration that could be applied to their clinical practice." Showalter notes the tendency of British superintendents in the mid-nineteenth century to invoke Ophelia and Hamlet in describing common conditions among their patients; American superintendents made similar observations.[43]

One very practical borrowing from Shakespeare came as far back as 1828, when the London physician Sir Henry Halford devised a "test" of insanity that was derived specifically from Shakespeare. When faced with a man "in a state of mental derangement" who appears to be in a lucid interval but wants to revise his will in a way that is certain to bring litigation after his death, Halford concocted an application of Hamlet's bedroom scene with his mother, in which the prince defends his apparently wild speech by saying:

> bring me to the test,
> And I the matter will reword,—which madness
> Would gambol from.[44]

Remembering this scene, Halford asked his patient to reword his will. The patient, in responding to the doctor's questions, got many of the figures and names wrong, or "gamboled" from the matter, and so the new will was declared invalid.[45] "Hamlet's test," as it came to be known, became a common maneuver in the medical jurisprudence of insanity, although it was a controversial one—with Kellogg, Ray, Bucknill, and Conolly all considering seriously its applicability and its limits.[46]

Such scattered borrowings are real enough, but this is not the main story that the physicians told about the correspondence between Shakespeare and nineteenth-century psychiatry. It was not that they read around in Shakespeare until they found an idea worth putting into practice, but that a careful examination of Shakespeare's works validated nearly every aspect of the system they had constructed independently of him. How had this happened? One explanation that presented itself was that Shakespeare had made a special scientific study of insanity, and his results were simply duplicated by independent researchers. At about this time, lawyers in both England and the United States were arguing that Shakespeare's great legal knowledge suggested that he had studied law or worked in a law office.[47] It might similarly be presumed, wrote Kellogg, that his extraordinary understanding of "insanity in all its forms" would indicate that he had studied patients at Bethlem Hospital.[48]

Yet physicians' claims were even more forceful than lawyers': Shakespearean substantiation of their ideas and practices was not a case of validation from a gifted fellow practitioner, but a blessing from a god in the machine. It was precisely *because* Shakespeare had no formal training in psychological medicine or institutional experience with the insane that his proleptic approval was so forceful.[49] Shakespeare's observations were all the more wondrous because they were the result not of his practical experience but of his singular genius, against which there was no appeal. His genius consisted largely of an ability to predict, without any awareness that he was doing so, the findings of nineteenth-century mental and medical science. "Whether Shakespeare himself was conscious of what he was producing, matters little," wrote Kellogg.[50] "The accuracy of his pathology," he continues, "has stood the test of experimental science for upwards of two centuries." [51] And yet it was only *through* the development of experimental science in the nineteenth century that this dimension of Shakespeare's genius could be appreciated. Accordingly, modern medical practitioners were the best judges of Shakespeare's treatment of insanity and, indeed, of his comprehension of the entire field of "human nature," which is, as Brigham wrote, "ever the same." [52]

This was a dynamic common to hubristic nineteenth-century readings of Shakespeare. Ralph Waldo Emerson, in his celebrated essay "Shakspeare; Or, the Poet" (1850), wrote that "it was not until the nineteenth century, whose speculative genius is a sort of living Hamlet, that the tragedy of Hamlet could find such wondering readers." But apart from this shared sense of the present as the long-deferred moment at which the veil over Shakespeare is lifted, Emerson's romantic vision of the nineteenth century has little in common with the positivism of the asylum superintendents. Shakespeare is for Emerson a populist genius, who speaks to "the Shakspeare in us" rather than to the elite few who by virtue of special training can understand him. And rather than simply leaping out of his time and speaking directly to the nineteenth century, he has a "ground in popular tradition," and he has "a heart in unison with his time and country." However, Emerson's notion of a nineteenth-century revelation of Shakespearean truths similarly depends on "science" as the field that both elevates Shakespeare and allows modern man to understand him, for Shakespeare's greatest accomplishment was to give "to the science of mind a new and larger subject than had ever existed, and planted the standard of humanity some furlongs forward into Chaos." [53]

The "science of mind"—how the mind works, its relation to the body, that relation's determination by environmental and biological factors—this was the very essence of human nature that psychiatry was purporting to turn into its field of expertise. But the notion of a group of experts asserting their authority over that which was by definition universal, or "ever the same," and turning it into a "science" put the nascent profession on the defensive. What gave them the right to define normality, to confine abnormality, to tell others what sorts of behaviors and phenomena were dangerous or healthy? This was especially problematic in early-nineteenth-century America (as in France), where the medical profession operated in a culture deeply suspicious of elite professional organizations that controlled entry into their own ranks through licensing boards, exclusive training programs, and the like.[54] As sociologist Paul Starr has written, the egalitarian rhetoric of the Jacksonian period, combined with a post-Enlightenment distrust of elite groups' monopolies over the professions, created a double bind for medical practitioners. In Starr's words, "science shares with the democratic temper an antagonism to all that is obscure, vague, occult, and inaccessible, but it also gives rise to complexity and specialization, which then remove knowledge from the reach of lay understanding."[55] In addition, the United States had a weak central government and few institutions to regulate entry into the medical and other professions; medical school was not even a requirement for practice, and no professional organizations controlled licensing. American medical practitioners, therefore, had a particularly difficult time asserting their authority against a wave of popular resistance to elitism. One approach that many physicians of the period used to legitimate their authority was to claim that they were not really experts at all—their treatments were grounded in homeopathic and folk remedies. The physicians simply looked to nature or to the community and sifted the various treatments they found there.[56]

Asylum medicine had a set of problems and advantages somewhat different from other forms of medical practice. Many physicians were drawn to this emerging field because it offered a kind of professional security and social prestige that traditional forms of medicine did not. At a time when most physicians were constantly scrambling to line up patients, making exhausting rounds of house calls, and still finding it difficult to distinguish themselves from charlatans, asylum medicine offered unmatched job benefits. A centralized site for practice with a stable client base; a guaranteed salary, often secured through state funding and generous private behests; absolute authority over a large staff, not to mention over the lives of hundreds of patients; and a secure bully pulpit from which to voice one's vision of the good life and how to avoid the disastrous—these features of asylum superintendence were unmatched in any other subfield of medicine, indeed, in any profession at all.[57] This unprecedented social authority, however, aroused popular suspicions that the scope of superintendents' power was unwarranted, or worse, part of conspiracy to undo prized American freedoms. Virtually coincident with the rise of the asylum was the rise of the asylum exposé in popular literature (see chapter 6), in which physicians' claims to expertise, benevolence, and extraordinary success were shown to cover up random experimentation with drugs, mad power plays, spectacular physical abuse, and the pathologization of dissent from the asylum regime.[58]

What the superintendents needed, then, was what Starr calls "cultural authority"—that is, control not just over other people's actions, but over the "meaning of things."[59] More particularly, they needed a claim to authority that did not imply elitism; they needed a form of ostensibly natural legitimization that would appear to have originated outside themselves and their interests and would be universally recognized. And this is what they sought in Shakespeare. Ray indicated this legitimating and naturalizing function in an article in the *American Journal of Insanity* on the steps an asylum superintendent should take in order to become an expert medical witness in a court of law. Medical books and abstract philosophy were of limited value and should never be appealed to on the witness stand. Primary education for expert witnesses, he wrote, should be grounded in Shakespeare and Molière, and other "immortal works which represent men in the concrete; living, acting, speaking men, displaying the affections and passions, the manners and motives of actual men." Such literary training is second only to "personal observations and study of mental phenomena as strikingly exhibited in real life."[60] Shakespeare, then, has value because his fictions are nearly on a par with "real life." In the words of Kellogg, his authority came from having looked "into the volume of nature with a glance deeper and more comprehensive than that of any other mortal not divinely inspired."[61] Moreover, it was a democratic type of authority that the psychiatrists found in Shakespeare. Unlike lawyers who were claiming Shakespeare as one of their own elite group, asylum superintendents contented themselves "with regarding him as the common property of all thinkers in each and every department of literary effort and scientific research."[62] Shakespeare's authority, then, derives from "nature" and observation of "real life"; its power is "immortal," and any practices and theories deriving from it are far from elitist, but rather, are the "common property" of all.

This strand of asylum superintendents' writings on Shakespeare is consistent with Levine's claim that throughout much of the nineteenth century in America, Shakespeare was not considered a part of elite culture but was performed and received as an "integral part" of popular culture.[63] And yet, to assert the correctness of one set of practices and ideas based on his authority was to assert cultural authority *over* Shakespeare (and human nature) and to reintroduce the problem of an elite possession of knowledge. Shakespeare might have been figured as an antielitist authority, but wouldn't claiming expertise over Shakespearean meanings imply the same sort of elitism his name was meant to ward off? This is the problem physicians encountered when they tried to defend against competing interpretations of Shakespeare—or, to be more exact, when they tried to dismiss mere literary criticism in favor of a scientific approach to Shakespeare's art. Dismissing the amateurish psychological readings of Shakespeare by Goethe and Schiller, who are not familiar with the medical concept of partial insanity, Kellogg wrote:

> In the plenitude of his knowledge—a knowledge derived not from books and the accumulated experience of others, but from the closest observation of what he must have seen in actual life,—[Shakespeare] recognized what none of his critics not conversant with medical psychology in its present advanced state, seem to have any conception of; namely, that there are cases of melancholic madness, of a delicate shade, in which the reasoning faculties, the intellect proper, so far from being overcome or even disordered, may, on the other hand, be rendered more active and vigorous, while the will, the moral feelings, the sentiments and affections, are the faculties which seem alone to suffer from the stroke of disease.[64]

We are presented with a closed circle, then: only Shakespeare can intuitively understand the subtle workings of the mind without the aid of mental science, and only medical practitioners can understand the mind of Shakespeare. But if it takes a genius like Shakespeare to understand the workings of the mind, and there have been no geniuses like him since, then how can anyone understand Shakespeare? And how has the science that so closely resembles his notions of the mind come into being? On this the asylum superintendents were silent, but some awareness of the problem occasionally haunts their writings, as when Kellogg explains what appear to be mistakes in Shakespeare's representations of madness. The playwright's "knowledge of the human heart and mind . . . was so accurate that he never makes a mistake, and when he appears to we should strongly suspect that we do not understand him, and wait humbly and labor patiently for a more accurate knowledge of his purposes and intentions."[65] Psychiatric wisdom is only an approximation of Shakespeare's wisdom, he appears to say. On closer inspection, however, this apparent humility cedes no ground of psychiatric infallibility. On matters of "human heart and mind," Shakespeare is correct, and we are correct; any discrepancy is merely a matter of our not understanding him. There is no danger in the formulation that Shakespeare will ever undercut any aspect of the asylum program, for the way to get past the apparent mistakes is not to reevaluate one's science but to dig deeper in Shakespeare until he no longer fails to contradict us.

The Shakespeare who appears so frequently in a legitimating role in the writings of the early psychiatric movement was really a set of texts poached to fill a void in institutional authority. This void was shaped by the asylum's precarious position as a carceral institution in a freedom-loving republic, by its exercise of profound social authority in a society suspicious of concentrated power, and by its standing as a specialized medical subfield in a post-Enlightenment milieu that demanded that all knowledge be stripped of jargon and other mystification. The psychiatric appeal to Shakespeare was an appeal to a secular god who could gloss over some of these contradictions.

THE FOREGOING analysis, I hope, sheds light on how "Shakespeare" functioned to establish cultural authority for the practitioners of asylum medicine, but it does little to tell why. Since alternate readings of Shakespeare that were less than congenial for appropriation by advocates of the asylum movement were readily available (and since most previous critics seem to have gotten him so disastrously wrong), why select *him* as the legitimating or licensing authority for asylum medicine?

Part of the answer has to do with Shakespeare's unrivaled stature as the all-purpose cultural authority during the Victorian period. The most obvious rival to confer cultural legitimacy on social practices was the Bible, but Gary Taylor has shown that in Britain and America, Shakespeare began to replace—or at least approach—the Bible as the primary icon of modern civilization.[66] This is because the scientific age needed a new authority that would stand in place of received religion. In this light, Shakespeare was the perfect Bible surrogate for the American asylum, which was born in a period of religious turbulence, and which tried to substitute itself for religion (or at least to subsume religion) as a regulator of morality and correct behavior. Superintendents were by and large devoted Christians, but they warned of the dire mental health consequences of religious excitement, and they carefully regulated the religious worship of patients.[67] The Shakespeare who is appropriated—or really constructed—by the asylum superintendents is a thoroughgoing rationalist, one who proceeds by empirical means, a commonsense proto-Enlightenment authority. This construction yields some moments of unintentional comedy in the superintendents' criticism, as when Kellogg coolly analyzes the psychological effects of Hamlet's encounter with ghost: "Here enters the pathological element into his mind and disposition, and the working of the leaven of diseases is soon apparent . . . . Though some faculties of his great spirit seem comparatively untouched, others, as we shall see, are completely paralyzed." [68] The effects of the meeting are thoroughly rationalized, but Kellogg never considers that ghosts themselves are supernatural.

And yet this modern or rational Shakespeare had a flip side: the nostalgic, antimodern purveyor of timeless verities, one who could stand as a counterweight to all the damage that modernity had wrought. The nineteenth-century notion of literary "genius," according to Raymond Williams, stood as the dialectical opposite to the mechanization, alienation, and atomization of the industrial age of capital. [69] If capital's effects were to isolate citizens and tear them away from nature, literary insight was universal and proceeded directly from nature. As the nearly universally recognized world's leading genius, Shakespeare, "nature's poet," helped hold down a place for literature apart from the economic field. And in America, the fluidity of social relations under early capitalism was made all the more disorienting because of the absence of distinct social hierarchies and the lack of a sense of cultural rootedness in tradition. Perhaps this accounts for the peculiar form of deification of Shakespeare in America, in which , Michael Bristol has written, "More so probably than in Britain, the Bard has been identified with general universal human interests, or to put it another way, with social and cultural goodness." [70] The Shakespeare who can do no wrong, who can cut past the confusion of modernity and social flux, is himself a product, Bristol argues, of modernity and social flux.

So too was early psychiatry, which conceived of modern life as posing new threats to mental health. It was a common sentiment in early psychiatric writing that advances in civilization caused increased mental stress and thus, if not checked, upsurges in insanity. "Primitive" peoples, the superintendents argued over and over, were far less subject to insanity than were Europeans and especially Americans (see chapter 2). The strain of increased mental activity that accompanied the advent of democracy, the dangers and excitement of living in cities, the ambitions fostered by social mobility and democratic culture, the artificiality of life as lived by the wealthy, and the taxation placed on young minds by early education—all of these factors explained the insanity boom in the most advanced nations.[71] As Edward Jarvis put it, "Insanity is . . . a part of the price which we pay for civilization. The causes of the one increase with the developments and results of the other."[72] It was an unresolved contradiction, of course, that human nature was "ever the same" and yet mental illness could be on the rise. But the pastoral asylum, with its removal from the chaotic buzz of the city, emphasized restoring a premodern stability to social relations: the superintendent was the kindly father or feudal lord, and his wards were so many children in need of moral instruction.[73]

The asylum also posed as the defense against dangerous cultural forms infecting the modern era. Advances in technology led to the production of cheap literature, which appealed through sensationalism to working-class readers in need of a quick fix of excitement, or to bored women who were the chief consumers of cultural products. Novel reading was often listed in annual reports as a cause of insanity, and Ray wrote a tract on the dangers of popular literature to vulnerable children and workers.[74] An important role of the paternalistic superintendent was to ward off such threats by supervising patients' cultural tendencies—for instance, selecting only useful and appropriate material for the libraries. Shakespeare's timeless wisdom and lofty themes were the perfect counterpoint to all the confusion of modern life and modern culture; his reputation was a bastion of stability amidst the chaos of the market revolution. And the image of Shakespeare as unassailable authority mirrored the superintendents' own position (at least in theory) within the asylum: the authority who will brook no challenge, the father among a race of wayward children, the sage who can speak to the ills of the modern age without being poisoned by them.

The superintendents turned to Shakespeare, then, because his work was a traditional font of wisdom that would anchor the novelty of their authority (some would say, their authoritarianism) in received wisdom, and because Shakespeare himself was a premodern visionary who could intuit all the progress that lay in front of him, without being touched by the corruption that attended that progress. And yet the force of the appeal to Shakespeare betrays a weakness in their approach. As a newly established professional elite, psychiatry desperately needed to prove itself in order to gain not just the validation of external authorities but the broad consent of the public. Families of patients and prospective patients constantly needed to be convinced of the efficacy of asylum care, and state legislatures needed to be persuaded to find money to fund them. But the conception of mental functioning that underlay the moral treatment movement was so capacious—encompassing such a wide range of medical and "moral" phenomena—as to include virtually the entirety of human experience, in its physical, social, and cultural dimensions.[75] And so psychiatry had to draw on and reshape broad cultural forces in order both to achieve social authority and to bring patients back into a normative relation to their social world. As asylum superintendents set for themselves the impossible task of purifying nineteenth-century culture on medical grounds, they had no specialized language or even conceptual apparatus to shield themselves from the critics, for they operated in a culture that had not yet carved up knowledge and discourse into discrete categories of expertise. Some patients seized upon this weakness, and again Shakespeare is part of the story.

ALTHOUGH MOST asylums had stages on which a lively mixture of amusements popular on the outside were presented by and for patients, no records found to date indicate a performance of Shakespeare in an American asylum to match the one at Fisherton House Asylum in England in 1857. (There, according to Showalter, "an actor's recitation of the murder scene from *Hamlet*—not a wise choice—upset the inmates, especially one who had cut off his doctor's head and kicked it about the garden."[76]) In a time when stage performances of Shakespeare were extraordinarily popular—constituting, according to Taylor, twenty to twenty-five percent of all antebellum stage plays—the psychiatric appropriation of Shakespeare in the United States was entirely a print phenomenon.[77] Levine's portrait of Shakespearean performance in a boisterous popular milieu (complete with catcalls and hurled vegetables) suggests some of the dangers of staging his plays in asylums, in which entertainments were rigidly policed by the authorities. Nonetheless, if the even rowdier blackface minstrel shows could be performed on asylum stages, then why not Shakespeare, with whom the superintendents were so obsessed? It is always difficult to interpret an absence, but it appears that the superintendents were so intent on protecting their image of Shakespeare—keeping him on the side of science, order, rationality, and good taste—that they feared putting him on stage, where he might be open to the alternative meanings of insane actors and audiences. In an age of popular staged Shakespeare, better to keep him contained in the more tightly controlled realm of print.

There are, however, a few surviving accounts of patients reading and thinking about Shakespeare. Several patients writing in the *Opal* cite Shakespeare in much the same way that their doctors do. A.S.M., the longstanding editor, reports that a judge has written to him asking for an appropriate definition of insanity. The editor defers to his superintendent on this matter, but, like Ray, instructs the judge to have a look at *Hamlet* for edification.[78] Such responses are in keeping with the *Opal's* function as a house organ. Given the superintendents' major investment in enlisting Shakespeare into their struggle for legitimation, patients writing in this "public transcript" of asylum life had little choice but to affirm their line of analysis. Occasionally, however, the *Opal* reveals a glimmer of what James Scott calls the "hidden transcript"—that heavily veiled critique of power disguised by carefully maintained "innocuous understandings of their conduct."[79] One writer, for instance, opines that Shakespeare's influence might be too elevated in the insane asylum and in the culture at large: "The private study of Shakespeare will, no doubt, expand the mind, and his perfect characters afford food for contemplation in the hour of retirement, but to our eye they always appeared a little too natural." Perhaps taking a swipe at the secularism and naturalism of the superintendents, the patient writes, "If we can learn more by studying the Bard than the Bible, or more virtue by going to the theatre than going to Church, priests had better become actors."[80]

The author's tentative and indirect rebuke of the authorities is something like what Scott calls "grumbling"—a purposely vague form of criticism that stops just short of insubordination.[81] But beyond the public transcript—beyond the closed world of the asylum—such criticism can be more direct. By far the most extended critique of the superintendents' appropriation of Shakespeare comes from Mrs. George Lunt, a former patient at an unnamed private institution. In an 1871 memoir of her asylum stay called *Behind the Bars*, Lunt sought to reform asylum practices primarily by limiting the power of superintendents, whose rule she depicted as "the condensation and epitome of all the governments ever swayed by tyrants or distorted by despots."[82] This comparison of superintendents to tyrants is a familiar gesture in asylum exposés, but Lunt differs crucially from most of her fellow memoirists in her approach, especially in her self-representation. Whereas most asylum exposés recount in shocking detail the physical and psychological abuse of the writer while in confinement, Lunt mentions few such incidents.[83] She tends instead to abstract her own experience and to seek the broader meanings of incarceration generally: "No amelioration of the condition of the insane can be effected by efforts which come from a mere sense of personal affront, rather than philanthropic aims. . . . The only way to look at the question is in a broad light, putting self out of sight, except as it may aid the mind to remember the sufferings of others."[84] Her memoir, accordingly, has an impersonal, even lofty tone; she spends more time reflecting on literature than on her own subjection in the asylum. As her publisher wrote, this quality was meant to make the "repellent" subject under consideration "of extraordinary general interest by agreeable literary allusion, and not a little of the charm and value of philosophical remark." [85]

In keeping with this elevated stance, Lunt portrays herself as the social and intellectual superior of those who had held power over her at the asylum. Here, she writes, "behind these mortared walls and iron bars, men of thought, of culture, of social caliber, of business capacity, are doomed to live. Here, women of intelligence, spirit, of refinement, with homes, with families . . . are left to stagnate." One of the greatest embarrassments that can befall such a patient is to encounter an asylum trustee whom she has known and met on equal footing before her confinement. And yet she is embarrassed also for the trustees, who find themselves lectured to by "inferior" physicians in "a dogmatic, impertinent style, at which the patient, if not the gentleman visitor, rebelled" [86] The superiority of patients and trustees to physicians is clearest to her in the speech and cultural literacy of her captors.

> The patient, it is easy to suppose, may be far beyond the master in intellect, in literary attainments, and in scholarly accomplishments, however these may have become untuned by disease; when the man is well again, his thought, his argument, his conclusions, his culture, his scholarly range of information, may be all a learned puzzle to the physician, who, howsoever accomplished in his profession, may be neither scholar, critic, nor philosopher; to him a logical aphorism, a classical quotation, a clever repartee, a broadcast reflection, may be blindly set down in his inquisitorial index book as the vagrant fancies and sophistries of a madman. [87]

Which brings her, of course, to Shakespeare. Although she does not refer directly to the *American Journal of Insanity* series on the Bard, she seems to have read it closely, and in a twenty-five-page alternative reading of Shakespeare she dismantles its presuppositions. Lunt shares with Brigham, Kellogg, and Ray the sense that Shakespeare "was the finest character delineator of madness and great mental conflicts the world has ever known." And she refers to him repeatedly not only as a "great poet" but as a physician and philosopher. Here, though, the similarity ends. Shakespeare did not believe, as the superintendents did, that the mind could be explained "by purely physical laws and calculations"; instead, his works consist of a set of "ideal studies" that "seem to come, like breaths and images from another world." Theories of mental functioning and insanity derived from actual cases may be "corroborated by analogy" with these Shakespearean ideal forms, but one would be foolish, she implies, to drag those ideals down to the level of the actual, to validate *him* by the weak tools that pass for science.[88]

What is needed for proper appreciation is the refinement and subtlety of mind that Shakespeare and his characters possess. Men and women "of thought, of culture, of social caliber" may be up to the task, but the ill-bred, materialist social climbers who run the asylums decidedly are not.[89] Whereas Kellogg had seen the reality of Hamlet's mental illness as the "true key" to unlocking the play's meaning, Lunt shows that Kellogg has merely demonstrated his own intellectual inferiority to the Dane. He is on a par, instead, with those who accuse Hamlet within the play itself:

> Hamlet was *neither witless nor mad;* for it is apparent in his case, that the opinions with regard to his insanity have been drawn rather from attempted perversions of his mood by other characters in the drama, than from his own conduct, however erratic. The queen, his mother, his uncle, Polonius, and all who surround him fix this stigma upon him, for reasons which the details of the play make evident. It cannot, it is true, enter into their limited minds to conceive of a soul with elements so fine as his; their grosser nature can grasp at nothing beyond the actual present, and being at odds with him, and fearing his moods and clouds of action, they fasten this excuse of madness upon him to cloak their own guiltiness and monstrosities.[90]

Hamlet's "stigma" is thus the mark of a superfine mind misunderstood by his social and intellectual inferiors—the delusional "doctors" who are really no better than the grocery clerks from whom they try to distinguish themselves. In her abstract and indirect manner, "putting self out of sight," Lunt is of course writing about herself through Hamlet, using the ideal to corroborate "the actual present." Like so many avatars of Polonius, the superintendents can never fathom the workings of Hamlet's mind; nor can they understand Lunt herself.

While superintendents had used Shakespeare in an effort to ground their authority in a nonelite common culture, Lunt is arguing that their commonness is exactly the problem. She shifts the grounds of Shakespeare appreciation from common sense to refined sensibility; understanding the great poet and the stigma known as insanity does not require trained minds looking to nature, but elevated sensibilities confronting each other in the ether of the ideal. The superintendents appeal to Shakespeare as the equivalent of nature's god; she appeals to him as the most prized—and forbidding—piece of cultural capital.

Lunt's self-positioning as a dispossessed member of the cultural elite—a neo-aristocrat brought low by the ascending professional class of psychiatrists—is especially poignant if one considers the ways her gender and her supposed insanity placed her at a rhetorical disadvantage in responding to the doctors. She turns to Shakespeare in part—one imagines—because a strictly medical avenue for dissent is closed to her. As women were systematically excluded from the healing arts—and especially within the intensely masculine and patriarchal realm of psychiatry—their voices were doubly silenced: once as mad, once again as female.[91] Showalter claims that in the mid-nineteenth century, women began to represent the majority of asylum patients and were presumed to have a special susceptibility to insanity because of the emotionally and intellectually destabilizing effects of their reproductive systems.[92] This assertion has been refuted by historians Andrew Scull and Nancy Tomes. Scull argues that female asylum patients never outnumbered males by more than a few percentage points, which can be explained by women's relative longevity and by physicians' tendency to keep female patients longer; Tomes faults Showalter for failing to take into account the special causes and manifestations of insanity in *male* patients.[93] While these are important criticisms, Showalter's point can still stand in a broader sense: even male patients can be said to have been feminized by what she calls the "female malady"—they were dispossessed of agency for their actions, stripped of political rights and domestic authority, made to submit absolutely to the will of the physician. In this context, Lunt's talking back through Shakespeare is a refiguring of the grounds of authority, shifting it from the gendered dimension of male doctor and female or feminized patient to the class-based question of cultural literacy.

The surprising class dynamics of the patient resisting her doctors' social authority from above rather than from below should not obscure another dynamic at work here. Curiously, while Lunt asserts that Shakespeare can be appreciated only by the finer minds of "men of thought, of culture, of social caliber" and "women of intelligence, spirit, of refinement," the force of her argument depends on Shakespeare's centrality in the common culture. Lunt resembles the superintendents most in assuming that Shakespeare is the "true key" to understanding the workings of the mind. But in appealing to Shakespeare, she employs a tactic familiar to the oppressed, even the enslaved, in talking back to their oppressors. Eugene Genovese has written of slaves' Christian faith that "no matter how obedient—how Uncle Tomish—Christianity made a slave, it also drove deep into his soul an awareness of the moral limits of submission, for it placed a master above his own master and thereby dissolved the moral and ideological ground on which the very principle of absolute human lordship must rest."[94] If Shakespeare was the new Bible for the rationalist age, the case of Lunt resembles that of the slave looking for the key to her liberation in scripture, where the master has found a justification for her enslavement.

——— ✳ ———

CHAPTER FOUR

Emerson's Close Encounters
with Madness

WHAT WOULD the transcendentalist movement look like if we posited the insane asylum—rather than the university, the church, or the slave system— as the central institution against which America's first homegrown group of public intellectuals took shape? The question has at first an intellectual component: how did this community of thinkers and activists, who defined themselves by their reaction against rationalism in mainstream Unitarian thought and their commitment to individual liberties, respond to the emergence of a new institution with broad powers to rescind those liberties in the name of bourgeois codes of rational conduct? But the question also has a surprisingly material and even intimate side: throughout the transcendentalist movement's history, key members faced the specter of institutionalization in asylums for their loved ones, followers, and even themselves.

The relation between transcendentalism and early American psychiatry can come into focus through reexamination of an episode that is familiar in American literary history, but the relevance of which to the social construction of madness has not yet been studied. This is the story of Jones Very, a visionary young poet and essayist who had attracted the attention of leaders in the transcendentalist movement—most notably Ralph Waldo Emerson— in part by running afoul of the academic and religious authorities against whom the transcendentalists themselves were rebelling. The height of Very's most creative period was the fall of 1838, when he produced a torrent of religious sonnets that are still anthologized today. At the same time, however, the anti-transcendentalists succeeded in getting him committed to McLean Asylum for the Insane, one of the oldest and best-respected private asylums

in the country, and one that served as a model for the ambitious state institutions that were just then coming into being.[1] Word quickly spread that
Very had been sent over the edge by transcendentalist ideas, and the social
conservatives responsible for his incarceration used him as a proxy in their
war against Emerson's spreading influence. Very stayed at McLean only a
month, and little of what happened to him while he was there can be recon-
structed, but from the swirling responses surrounding his supposed mental
breakdown and institutionalization, we can glimpse a whole network of
social, intellectual, and institutional relations that emanated from the clash
of early American psychiatry, academic Unitarianism, and New England's
intellectual avant-garde. In particular, we can see some of these groups'
shared assumptions about the threat to social stability (sometimes a psychic threat) posed by modernity and democracy—a linkage that marks each
of these disparate movements as responding to the main features of Romantic thought. And most poignantly, the story reveals the ultimate acqui-
escence of the transcendentalists, and especially of Emerson, to psychiatric
authority over one of their own number. This accommodation does not fit
easily with their typical group portrait, which shows them heroically valu-
ing eccentricity, intuition, and nonconformism as tools to liberate individuals from the powerful institutional structures that restricted their thought
and behavior. Instead, Emerson's tacit acceptance of Very's forced confinement suggests that, at a formative point of his career, he saw the insane
asylum as a restraint that formed the boundary between healthy individualism and social deviance: a curb placed on the individual will when that will
could not restrain itself.

An orthodox Foucauldian reading of this incident would see Emerson
resisting but ultimately bowing to the asylum movement's "power of normalization" and ceding to its "authority responsible for the control of abnormal individuals."[2] Emerson's famous injunction, "Whosoever would be
a man must be a non-conformist" would in this light be an empty plea for
abstract individualism; when "non-conformists" are labeled as "abnormal,"
they are locked away under the name of public hygiene.[3] While this reading has its points, it depends on a picture of McLean Asylum that Emerson
and the other actors in our story could never have seen—a picture in which
"asylums" are squarely on the side of social order and the state. While this
became increasingly true in the 1840s and 50s, it was by no means clear
in 1838—and even less so for an elite private institution like McLean. The
restrictions on personal liberty experienced by patients at McLean were effected with only minimal government involvement, and even state asylums

could still plausibly be presented as forming an institutional bulwark of liberty that offered certain freedoms—from neglect, from physical abuse, from despair—that the insane so often suffered in the early nineteenth century. Why Emerson and company chose to accept this image is part of the drama.

Rather than clearly confirming or overturning the "social control" reading of asylum history, then, the story can suggest something of the ragged constellation of forces that lined up, sometimes grudgingly, behind the new asylum movement.[4] One reason that Emerson supported the psychiatric regime at McLean was that transcendentalism and American institutional psychiatry developed out of the same intellectual milieu. Their shared interests in restoring vigor and mental well-being to a modernizing society reflects their common romantic nostalgia for a world of social and spiritual harmony that they felt had been ruptured by advances in capitalism, urbanization, and the social mobility that attended them.[5] But the two movements did not relate to each other solely in intellectual terms: their interactions were shot through with power dynamics and uncomfortable personal, professional, and institutional relationships as well. At the time of the Jones Very affair, Emerson had been entangled with the politics of McLean Asylum for over a decade, and some of his Unitarian foes were at the forefront of the asylum movement. When this entanglement is unraveled, it will show the key actors and social forces of the Jones Very episode—Emerson and his circle, Dr. Luther Bell and the emerging psychiatric establishment, and the Unitarian power structures of Harvard and Salem—all jostling for position within a shared social and intellectual space. Very's confinement caused discomfort all around, but the Unitarians used the case to mount an aggressive challenge to the transcendentalists, who were ultimately forced into a defensive rearticulation of their values.

ON JULY 15, 1838, Emerson came to Harvard Divinity School, his alma mater, to deliver what would later be known as the "Divinity School Address," one of the most famous public challenges to an entrenched religious authority in American history. A lapsed Unitarian minister, Emerson was entering the stronghold of Unitarian thought, which was the intellectual and spiritual backbone of Boston's elite social classes.[6] Unitarianism had originated as a liberal reaction to Puritanism, an attempt to reconcile Enlightenment rationality with Christian scripture. There was nothing in the Christian religion, Unitarians taught, that was incompatible with science; therefore rational, scientific inquiry could only lead to a glorification of

God. In fact, according to William Ellery Channing, the most famous Unitarian preacher of his day and an inspiration for early transcendentalism, "God is another name for human intelligence, raised above all error and imperfection, and extended to all possible truth."[7] A corollary of this belief in the resemblance of God to man was the belief in the divine imperative to reform human character; this marked a clean break between Unitarian "rational Christianity" and the beliefs of their Puritan forebears (along with the Calvinists who still held sway in places like Princeton and Amherst) in the innate depravity of man and the unbridgeable gulf between God and His creations. The Unitarian establishment at Harvard saw themselves as enlightened champions of progress, and this found them favor among the new bourgeoisie of Boston, whose wealth and standing increasingly came from the manipulation of technology.[8] Unitarian congregants—along with Quakers—were also at the vanguard of the era's most important social reform movements, including the asylum movement and prison reform; the reformers enacted in a secular key the Unitarian belief in the powers of the enlightened mind to remake the world in God's image.[9]

But once the Unitarians had achieved institutional authority at Harvard and in the most powerful churches of the area, they increasingly defended their elite position and their once-upstart creed from social and intellectual challenges. There was a limit, after all, to their endorsement of Enlightenment skepticism, in that it could never turn on Christian revelation itself. Earlier in the year, the Unitarian establishment had helped secure the conviction of the atheistic Abner Kneeland, leader of the Society of Free Enquirers, for "scandalous, impious, obscene, blasphemous, and profane libel of and concerning God," the last such conviction in Massachusetts history. The case split the Unitarian movement, with liberals like Channing, George Ripley, and Emerson—who had not yet entirely broken with Unitarianism—coming to Kneeland's defense, and conservatives, many of them ensconced at Harvard, applauding the conviction.[10] At issue in the case was not just Kneeland's questioning of religious faith, but his sexual morality as well. Kneeland had initially run afoul of authorities by publishing in his journal material that was considered obscene, particularly his philosophical defenses of birth control and free love; he even arranged to sell a scandalous tome that graphically discussed the proper techniques for postcoital contraceptive douching. This activity was considered to be a threat to social order because, in the words of historian Helen Lefkowitz Horowitz, it would give readers "a means of engaging in sexual intercourse without enduring the consequences of pregnancy."[11] The Unitarians who opposed Kneeland had themselves been tarred with the charge of radicalism, even Jacobinism; as they consolidated power, they forcefully rejected those charges, in part by deflecting them onto free-thinkers like Kneeland.

Within Harvard itself, the Unitarian establishment was facing new challenges. As the Unitarians opened up the curriculum to more and more types of secular inquiry, they inadvertently encouraged students to stray from their theological teachings and unquestioned institutional authority. The student philanthropic society, for instance, scandalously wanted to invite abolitionists, considered at this point by virtually the entire social elite of Boston to be disreputable troublemakers, to speak on campus. And the freshman class of 1833 (of which Jones Very was a member) rioted over a tutor's allegedly unfair treatment of a student and the administration's ham-handed resolution of the matter. Furniture was thrown, windows broken, property desecrated, and the majority of the class was dismissed for three months.[12]

Finally, in matters of theology, the Unitarians were riven by debates about the "doctrine of miracles." Following John Locke's *Discourse of Miracles,* mainstream Unitarians believed that intuitive truths were those belonging to inductive logic, such as those derived from geometry. But other truths could come to humans through revelation, which gave access to a world beyond the senses. To establish these truths, Locke argued, we need "credentials," or miracles, whose existence could be detected through rational means. (Something was a miracle if it could be proved to exist but could not be explained by the laws of nature.) According to Locke and his Unitarian followers, those who denied the existence of miracles were either unbelievers or "enthusiasts." This latter group claimed to receive divine truth directly rather than through evidence of miracles. Because their beliefs were unverifiable, they could even be evidence of insanity, or "conceits of a warmed or overweening brain."[13] Adherence to the doctrine of miracles became a litmus test for true believers in the rational Christianity of Harvard; the more conservative faculty protested loudly when any dissenting voices were allowed to publish in official church and Divinity School organs.[14]

In this tense atmosphere, Harvard authorities were on high alert when the students invited Emerson, who had formally renounced his Unitarian pulpit five years earlier, to speak at their commencement. Initially inspired by the Unitarians' freedom from creeds and rejection of Calvinist notions of human depravity, Emerson increasingly viewed the "rational" part of rational Protestantism to be a barrier to faith. For him, it was not simply that man *resembled* God in his intelligence, but that man *was* God, or at least that man was an aspect of God—and as such was so vast as to be unknow-able to himself.[15] As he explained to his former congregation on a return visit, he had renounced the pulpit because he could not countenance the idea that one man should teach others spiritual truths that should properly be found within each: "Man begins to hear a voice," he said, "that fills the heavens and the earth, saying, that God is within him, that *there* is the celes-tial host."[16] Although this doctrine rejected the mediating structures of the church and the external "proofs" of miracles, it was actually more strictly spiritual than the Unitarian belief. If God was inside, rather than outside, his existence and teachings could never be proven by the cold rationality of empirical science or the formal creeds of institutional religion; instead, knowledge of the divine required the white hot discipline of faith, albeit an inner-directed faith.

On that summer day in 1838, Emerson informed the students that their teachers were actually holding them back from perceiving the highest truth. In passionate oratory, he denounced the "defects" of "historical Christian-ity": that its focus on "the *person* of Jesus" obscures the holiness of each individual's soul; and that its conception of "revelation as somewhat long ago given and done" presents a desiccated religion, "as if God were dead."[17] This was a direct attack on Unitarian practice. Because the Unitarians be-lieved that testimony from the Bible about Jesus' performance of miracles needed to be tested empirically, studies of the historical Jesus were central to their theology.[18] Sounding like one of Locke's mentally unbalanced "en-thusiasts" who reject even the notion of evidence, Emerson admonished his auditors to "go alone" and preach God's will as it was revealed to them, "without mediator or veil." He encouraged them to cast off the teachings of authority and consider themselves prophets, for "the need was never greater of new revelation than now. . . . Yourself a newborn bard of the Holy Ghost,—cast behind you all conformity, and acquaint men at first hand with Deity."[19]

Predictably, the students were enthralled, and the authorities were not amused. The liberal Unitarian minister Convers Francis later reported that after the "Address," Harvard divinity students were taught to "abhor and abominate R.W. Emerson as a sort of mad dog"; and Emerson's uncle Samuel Ripley begged him not to publish it because he would be "classed with Kneeland, Paine, &c."[20] Andrews Norton, sometimes referred to as the "Unitarian pope," had recently left his post at the Divinity School in part out of outrage at what he perceived as the dilution of Unitarian doctrine in the curriculum.[21] In a wonderful fulmination published in the *Boston Daily*

Advertiser, Norton suggests the inseparability of the Unitarians' theology from their social position, as well as the threat posed by the transcendentalist young Turks to Unitarian authority.

> They [European romantics and American transcendentalists] announce themselves as the prophets and priests of a new future, in which all is to be changed, all old opinions done away, and all present forms of society abolished. But by what process this joyful revolution is to be effected as are not told; nor how human happiness and virtue is to be saved from the universal wreck, and regenerated in the Medea's caldron. . . . The state of things described might seem a matter of no great concern, a mere insurrection of folly, a sort of Jack Cade rebellion; which in the nature of things must soon be put down, if those engaged in it were not gathering confidence from neglect, and had not proceeded to attack principles which are the foundation of human society and human happiness.[22]

Turning his fire on Emerson's "Address," he wrote that the fact of its being delivered at the Divinity Hall Chapel was cause for alarm.

> No one can doubt for a moment of the disgust and strong disapprobation with which it must have been heard by the highly respectable officers of that Institution. They must have felt it not only as an insult to religion, but as personal insult to themselves. . . . The preacher was invited to occupy the place he did, not by the officers of the Divinity College, but by the members of the graduating class. These gentlemen, therefore, have become accessories, perhaps innocent accessories, to the commission of a great offence; and the public must be desirous of learning what exculpation or excuse they can offer.[23]

Innocent accessory or not, one of those students was made to pay for Emerson's incitement to demolish the social order. This was Jones Very. And the means of his punishment was to place him in an insane asylum.

A NATIVE of Salem, Massachusetts, Jones Very was the son of a poor but fiercely proud mother, Lydia Very, and her first cousin, a sea captain whom his son would barely come to know. The two lived together in a noncontractual marriage, which accorded with Mrs. Very's atheism and attraction to the ideals of Frances Wright, the notorious free-thinker who advocated the abandonment of marriage as an institution. She was viewed by townspeople as a "tiger of a woman," and "almost a maniac" in defense of her beliefs (or unbeliefs).[24] In 1833, at the age of twenty, her son Jones entered Harvard on a scholarship, threw himself into his studies, immersed himself in the Unitarian faith, and eventually graduated second in his class.

His undergraduate tenure was not without turbulence, however, for he was one of the riotous cohort that was "denounced on its graduation as unfortunate" for the "awful rebellion" that had occurred in 1833.[25] Very did not actively participate in these riots but he did sign a class petition protesting the college's "system of rank."[26] Whatever his feelings about the administration, however, they did not prevent him from returning to Harvard after his graduation in 1836. For the next two years, he was employed by the university as a tutor in Greek, and he pursued studies as an "unclassified" or unofficial student in the Divinity School. But reflecting students' discontent with their rigid, rationalist education, he began to read widely in the European romanticism of Carlyle, Goethe, and Burke. In September 1836, he purchased a fateful copy of Emerson's *Nature*. In particular, he was drawn to the idea that one should seek God in nature—and within oneself—rather than through custom or ritual.[27]

At Harvard, Very developed an unorthodox teaching style, which endeared him to students but could hardly have pleased the administration. In a course on Greek, he would rhapsodize on Shakespeare, Milton, and divinity; and he encouraged conversation instead of lecture and rote learning in his classes (much as the transcendentalist pedagogues Bronson Alcott and Elizabeth Palmer Peabody were doing in their Temple School). He took long walks with his students and visited them in their apartments to discuss lofty matters. Several students grew quite devoted to him; Alcott would later write that "his influence at Cambridge on the best young men was very fine."[28] But some of his notions and behaviors were troubling to students. Very renounced any interest in women, declaring this a "sacrifice of Beauty" in the name of ascetic discipline; one student wrote home that Very was often ridiculed for being "overcome by monkish austerity & self-denial."[29]

Very was publishing poems reflecting some of his ideas, and these caught the attention of the managers of the Salem Lyceum, who invited him to lecture. There he came into contact with Emerson's widening circle of intellectuals, who were fascinated. In April 1838, just three months before Emerson's electrifying "Address," Very found himself lecturing before Emerson at the Concord Lyceum and dining with the great man afterward. For the most part, Very talked and Emerson intently listened. He spoke about dramatic and epic poetry, romanticism and classicism, Shakespeare and Jesus, and mostly, through all of this, himself. Shakespeare, he told Emerson, was one of God's great "natural" creations, but he lacked only that which Very himself was on the verge of discovering, which is a self-consciousness of his inhabitation by God. Very felt a "perfect [spiritual] union and relationship" with Shakespeare; therefore, proper interpretation of Shakespeare's plays could be reached by looking within himself.[30] Very's comments (later published in an essay) prefigure certain of Emerson's own ideas; indeed, the notion of the poet's access to a transpersonal soul is a major strand throughout his writing, which Sharon Cameron has called "Emerson's impersonal."[31] There is certainly an aspect of this in the "Divinity School Address," as when he says that the preacher's task—much like that of Very's confronting the divine Shakespeare within him—is "to live with the privilege of the immeasurable mind."[32] In fact, several critics have suggested that Emerson had Very directly in mind when he composed his "Address."[33] Emerson was preaching, but he was also responding to the sermon Very had delivered to him.

Not long after hearing Emerson's call for "a new revelation," Very began acting even more strangely. In his Greek class, he told students that their bodies were simply vessels for a timeless struggle between God and Satan, that he himself had been visited by two "consciousnesses" not his own, which led him to declare to all that "the coming of Christ was at hand." Later, he would write that these "changes" were a symptom of his "new birth," and that he was directed by "the voice of John in the wilderness of my heart, and that the purification I experienced, in obeying him in cutting down the corrupt ties and preparing the way for the one who came after was that of his baptism of water."[34] One night, he broke into the study of Professor Henry Ware, Jr., a friend of Emerson's who had been shocked by the "Address." Ware, as it happened, was in the process of drafting a rebuttal of Emerson's doctrine ("It is a virtual denial of God, and a consequent overthrow of worship and devotion;—it injures happiness by taking from the affections their highest object, and virtue by enfeebling the sense of responsibility," and so forth).[35] According to a student who wrote about the confrontation in his diary, Very and Ware argued over an interpretation of the section of the book of Matthew in which Jesus predicts that Judas will betray him, and Very refused to yield to the professor because "a revelation had been made to him, and that what he said was eternal truth—that he had fully given up his own will, and now only did the will of the Father—that it was the father who was speaking thro' him. He thinks himself divinely inspired, and that Christ's second coming is in him."[36]

The next day, Very went back to class and used language so wild that several of his students wrote home, distraught over their beloved tutor's apparent descent into madness. As a scandal brewed, he was quickly relieved of his duties at Harvard by the president, Josiah Quincy, who was ever alert to the possibilities of student disorder—especially in the wake of the students' scandalous behavior in recent years. Very's brother Washington was summoned to take the tutor home to Salem. Jones's first impulse—or directive from God—was to visit Emerson at Concord and hand-deliver the essay he had been writing on Shakespeare; but his brother allowed him only to send it to him, along with an accompanying letter.[37] The next day, back in Salem, he heeded God's call again, this time to spread his message door-to-door. One of his first visits was to Elizabeth Palmer Peabody, an important member of the Transcendental Club who had arranged the initial meeting between Emerson and Very. After he informed her that he had come to "baptize" her "with the Holy Ghost and with fire," he asked her how she felt. "I feel no change," she said, to which he responded, "But you will . . . I am the Second Coming." He proceeded to the homes of several local ministers. According to Peabody, first was John Brazer, minister of the church that Very had been attending, who, in true Unitarian fashion, asked him for empirical proof of "the *miracles* that tested his mission. Very said 'this revelation would not have miracles.' 'Then,' said Mr. B, [in perfect Lockean fashion] 'I must say to you—you are laboring under hallucination.'"[38] Next came a Baptist minister, who threw him out of the house, and then the Unitarian Charles Wentworth Upham, who, according to Peabody, informed Very "that he should see that he be sent to the Insane Asylum." Later that night Mrs. Very confronted Upham—or perhaps he confronted her first—and she "declared that Mr. Very should *not* be carried to the Insane Hospital. She said that if there was anything in him that seemed insane it was caused by the brutal manner in which he had been treated." Peabody, genuinely concerned about Very's state of mind (but also feeling the heat that Upham and Brazer were bringing to her circle) convinced Very's brother to take him to McLean, where—despite maternal resistance—he was soon committed.[39]

Brazer and Upham were confirmed anti-transcendentalists, both of whom had supported Andrews Norton in his battle to tamp down on dissident views published in church organs. Upham in particular had been spoiling for a fight with Emerson since the publication of *Nature*, which he found to be an infidel text.[40] Both men saw in Very's behavior another chance to lash out at Emerson (who had been a classmate and a former friend of Upham's), whom they publicly blamed for Very's collapse.[41] Their campaign to smear transcendentalists caught on: a number of letters among the literati around Boston repeated the idea that Very had been "blown up by Emerson" and that "he is quite intimate with Emerson and the other

Spiritualists, or supernaturalists, or whatever they are called, or may be pleased to call themselves." [42]

In an instant, the literary, philosophical, academic, and religious establishments of greater Boston came crashing down on Jones Very's head. Because of the infighting among the Unitarians, Brazer and Upham's animosity toward Very has generally been explained by the divisions within the church that eventually led to the secession of the transcendentalists. [43] But what has not been explained, in part because it seems so natural, is how and why they sent Very to an insane asylum, and what role institutional psychiatry played in the environment that gave rise to the schism. Even Very's extraordinarily sympathetic biographer, Edwin Gittleman, passes over this question with the cryptic comment: "Very allowed his enemies no alternative to having him placed in an institution for the insane." [44]

How did committing a false prophet to an insane asylum come to seem such an obvious course of action among the religious establishment of greater Boston? One part of the answer comes from the historical linkage of Unitarianism and the reform movements that helped establish and support institutional psychiatry in its formative years. The great reformer Dorothea Dix, whose detailed reports to state legislatures on the deplorable conditions of the insane were crucial in the effort to secure public financing for asylums, was a devout Unitarian who considered William Ellery Channing her mentor. [45] And the Rev. Robert C. Waterston — a close friend of Very's at Divinity School — wrote a pamphlet on insanity in order to aid Dix in her efforts with the Massachusetts legislature. Singling out McLean as the model for a benevolent institution, he wrote that "this magnificent Charity, this philanthropic Asylum for suffering humanity, may well be considered as one of the chief glories of New England. Every citizen of Massachusetts may kindle with holy joy as he contemplates its wide-spread influence." [46] The psychiatric boosterism of these Unitarians stemmed, according to historian Norman Dain, from their rejection of the concept of depravity, their church's emphasis on brotherly love and humanitarian works, and their faith in science and progress. These beliefs allowed them, in Dain's words, "to accept the concept of somatic pathology and to sanction medical treatment of insanity." [47] In addition, their rejection of religious enthusiasm made Jones Very a perfect target for their humanitarian intervention.

A darker possibility comes into view when we more precisely locate the scene of Very's undoing in Salem, where nonbelievers had, two centuries earlier, been tried as witches. Many Unitarians flirted with the idea that mental illness, rather than sin or Satan, caused irreligious behavior. [48] And so one might be tempted to say that for the Unitarians, psychiatry replaced witch-hunting as the proper mechanism by which to rid a community of troublesome dissenters. But their writings on the matter defend against this idea. Upham himself had been fascinated with the historical lessons of the witch trials at least since 1831, when he delivered a series of lectures later published under the title *Lectures on Witchcraft*. At least one of the accused witches, he argued, was "subject to a species of mental derangement of which sadness and melancholy were the prevailing characteristics,"[49] but most of his neo-psychiatric language — delusion, frenzy, derangement — was used to describe the mental aberrations of the accusers rather than the accused. Above all, his is a tract of caution, urging religious leaders "to check the prevalence of fanaticism, to accelerate the decay of superstition, to prevent an unrestrained exercise of imagination and passion in the individual or in societies of men, and to establish the effectual dominion of true religion and sound philosophy."[50] The lesson he learned from the witch trials, then, was not that dissent should be tolerated; instead, this sad episode taught him "useful lessons to guide and influence [the religious leader] with reference to the cultivation and government of his own moral and intellectual faculties and to the obligations that press upon him as a member of society to do what he may to enlighten, rectify, and control public sentiment."[51]

Seven years after Upham delivered these lectures, he convinced himself that Salem's new dissenter was not a witch in need of hanging or execution but a poor mad soul in need of medical and moral treatment. The chief danger, however, was not that such a soul might be unjustly persecuted, but that Very himself might inflame the community: committing him to McLean would be a judicious measure to "control public sentiment." At a time when Abner Kneeland himself was lauding Emerson as a fellow "free enquirer," here came knocking on Upham's door the bastard son of a free-thinker and the apparent intellectual disciple of the mad-dog Emerson.[52] Very had drunk from a witches' brew of anti-establishmentarianism. For together, transcendentalists and free-thinkers endangered the very pillars of civilization: faith in God, church, and rationality; respect for authority; and sexual probity.

A crude and sweeping version of the psychiatry-as–witch hunt argument was made by Thomas Szasz, who wrote in 1970 of "the transformation of a religious ideology into a scientific one: medicine replaced theology; the alienist, the inquisitor; and the insane, the witch."[53] This monochromatic polemic can hardly explain the complex forces that brought asylums into such prominence in the nineteenth century. But one young Salem writer who knew Jones Very well and would himself, years later, be tormented by Upham played frequently with the idea of psychiatry as a modern-day version of an ancient theological inquisition, an association that would culminate in an important plot thread in one of the classics of nineteenth-century fiction. Nathaniel Hawthorne first met Jones Very at his future sister-in-law Peabody's home in 1837, and Very soon began to call on him at his home. Hawthorne jotted morosely about him in a number of journal entries, particularly complaining about Very's tendency to overstay his welcome at his home, about Very's attempts to baptize or convert him, and about his sense that Very "wants a brother" (which was also Melville's unfortunate reaction to Hawthorne); but Peabody remarked that eventually a "strange intimacy" developed between them.[54] Hawthorne, it seems, recognized in Very a type of persecuted eccentric that he had written about in an 1833 tale called "The Story Teller"; he mentioned Very as a misunderstood genius in another; and he wrote in yet a third about a delicate young poet just returned from an insane asylum.[55]

Years later he would return to the Very/Upham scenario again, in a way that eerily collapsed the distance between Very's supporters and his persecutors. Hawthorne had been influenced by Upham's study of the witch trials in the crafting of his fiction, but in 1849, he found himself on the receiving end of one of the minister's abuses of power. Upham—his need to torment major figures of the American literary renaissance apparently not yet satiated—was now a Whig congressman from Salem, and he arranged the firing of the Democrat Hawthorne from his post as surveyor of the Salem Custom House. This was, of course, the impetus behind the famous "Custom House" preface to *The Scarlet Letter* (1850), in which Hawthorne refers to himself as a "decapitated surveyor." The headless author would, however, exact his literary revenge on Upham less than two years later with the publication of *The House of the Seven Gables* (1851). Here, Judge Jaffrey Pyncheon—the nineteenth-century descendant of witch-hunters—threatens to confine his cousin Clifford in an insane asylum for blocking his acquisition of property. Judge Pyncheon, who dies a grisly death at the end of the novel, choking on his own cursed blood, is modeled on none other than Upham. The sensitive aesthete Clifford is finally free of the specter of the asylum, where he would no doubt have become the latest of the witch-hunter's victims.

HAWTHORNE'S FANCIFUL reworking of the Jones Very story, in which incarceration at an asylum is the culmination of a modern-day witch hunt,

FIGURE 8. McLean Asylum for the Insane, Somerville, Massachusetts, 1846. The asylum was renamed McLean Hospital in 1892 and was relocated to Belmont, Massachusetts, in 1895.

should not allow us to conceive of McLean as a Gothic chamber of horrors. "Social control" theorists like Foucault and Szasz have neglected to convey, among other things, the sheer grandeur of such institutions. Established in 1818 by private subscriptions and some state funding, McLean was regarded as the most exclusive asylum in the country.[56] Situated on "a beautiful promontory" in rural Charlestown, it was close enough to Boston and Cambridge to facilitate frequent patient outings to a wide range of cultural and religious institutions[57] (fig. 8). According to physician Edward Jarvis—who will figure shortly in the story—"from its great wealth, its magnificent and convenient architectural arrangements, and the abundant means of amusement and occupation, this may be considered as the best adapted to its noble purpose of all the asylums in our country"[58] (fig. 9). The asylum had a working farm, a garden, a nursery, a woodwork room, a bowling alley, a billiard table for each sex, chess, cards, checkers, newspapers, drawing and surveying materials, a library, six horses, carriages, musical instruments, and other "means of labor and amusement."[59] The roughly 130 patients were housed in "families" of 10 or 12, which were grouped according to "the nature and development of their derangement."[60] Each patient had a sitting room, a sleeping and dining apartment, and a bathing room, and met regularly with his or her "family" for regular cultural and social activities. Prominent among these were religious services in each wing on Sunday evenings, "during which the physician read a sermon to those who were well enough and desired to attend"; others were encouraged to attend services at

FIGURE 9. Entrance hall of McLean Asylum, late nineteenth century

local churches of their denomination.[61] Finally, the institution prided itself on renouncing physical restraints for its patients, except in extreme cases, so that the "strong rooms" were used only three to four times a year.[62]

One of the mysteries surrounding Very's stay at McLean is who paid for it. The charge of $3.50 per week was certainly more than Very's mother could have absorbed; even if she could have paid, a woman as strong-willed as she would hardly have consented to pay for what she considered to be the wrongful confinement of her son. McLean had always subsidized a number of impoverished patients, but ever since the state asylum had opened in Worcester in 1833, McLean's administration was increasingly rejecting paupers and others who were objectionable to an elite clientele.[63] One possibility is that the expense was borne by Upham and Brazer, maybe even with the help of their congregations. Perhaps they avoided the protests of transcendentalists and others sympathetic to Very by sending him to McLean rather than Worcester, where—despite the utopian rhetoric surrounding its conditions and cure rate—over fifty percent of the patients had been transferred from jails, almshouses, and houses of correction. In the first year of its operation alone, eight admitted patients were convicted murderers.[64]

At McLean, Very was placed under the care of the superintendent, Dr. Luther Bell, who allowed him to roam the grounds, lecture patients on literature, and continue with his writing.[65] A subsequent letter to a friend records that although his religious views were unchanged, a kind of "peace" broke out between his warring consciousnesses, which had learned to coexist amicably within him.[66] Little else can be definitively recovered of his perspective on his stay at McLean, since patient records there are still kept confidential and since most of Very's writing from the period views all earthly phenomena as a pale shadow of a deeper spiritual reality. Certainly Bell did not cause the voice of God to cease speaking through his patient, for the months during and after his stay at McLean witnessed a steady outpouring of essays and poems that continued in the ecstatic voice of the previous year. And the general outlines of McLean sketched above—notably the institution's elite standing in the field of asylum medicine, its opulence and physical beauty, its emphasis on humane treatment and encouragement of patients' creativity—all suggest that a stay there for a relatively impecunious scholar and poet might have been something of a respite from the personal tumult Very was experiencing in the fall of 1838. In addition, as an ascetic committed to conquering his own sexual impulses, he may well have found reinforcement in the strict sex segregation of the asylum wards and the heavy surveillance that attended all contact between the sexes.[67]

The concern with regulating patients' sexual urges was due in large measure to Dr. Bell's highly developed theories about the mental health risks of sexual excitement and masturbation. (He proposed, among other things, a special masturbators' ward in larger asylums, where offenders would be placed under the "unceasing surveillance of a conscientiously vigilant and active attendant, whose eye, during the hours of waking, shall never be off his charge, and at night shall either sleep with him . . . or else use a mode of securing the patient from any possibility of effecting his purpose at night, by confining him with straps in his bed." [68])

Bell released Very after a month, concluding that although he was indeed insane, he was not a threat to the community and should be returned to the care of his mother. Back in Salem, the rumor spread that Bell had cured him of a digestive disorder, but Elizabeth Palmer Peabody maintained that he was "as crazy as ever," and she reported that he continued both to sermonize and to write beautiful poetry. She wrote to Emerson, telling him to expect another visit from Very; and she warned him of the trap that such a visit would lay for him. Brazer was still hounding Very, demanding that he provide "miracles to prove his mission or [yield] the point that he is insane. Since he has come home [Brazer] has been telling him that *you* (from whom Mr. B . . . affects to believe all the thing comes) are now universally acknowledged to be & denounced as an atheist—& measures are taking!! to prevent you from having any more audience to corrupt. . . . But the result is—that Mr. Very thinks you *and he* are persecuted—& he goes expecting full sympathy." [69] Mary Peabody, writing to her sister Elizabeth, amplified the threat to both Very and Emerson: Very was threatened with being sent "somewhere where they could not hear him or let him be heard"; as for Emerson, "if they could prove the charge of blasphemy against him they would deprive him of his liberty as they had done to A[bner] K[neeland]." Mary replied to Very that if he and his mother remained steadfast, and perhaps if he applied leeches to his head, he could resist "the wolves & bears." [70] Elizabeth advised him to "take medicine and obey his friends—because if it is truth he utters—medicine will not purge it away." And to Emerson she counseled "I would not—if I were you—stretch your charity so far as to invite him to stay in the house—or if he comes late & you have to—in charity—limit your invitation—else you may not easily get rid of him." [71]

Nonetheless, when Very visited Emerson he was welcomed for five days of intense conversation that left a lasting impression on the older man. In Emerson's notebooks, he records his impressions of a man who presented a dark mirror of his own thoughts, offering an almost apocalyptic vision of the institutions that transcendentalists were criticizing in a more hopeful mood: "His poison accuses society as much as society names it false & morbid, & much of his discourse concerning society, the church, & the college was perfectly just." [72] Very's unrelenting attack was almost unbearable: "J[ones] V[ery] says it is with him a day of hate; that he discerns the bad element in every person whom he meets which repels him: he even shrinks a little to give the hand . . . The institutions[,] the cities which men have built the world over, look to him like a huge blot of ink." [73] Even Emerson came under attack for not renouncing his own will and passively obeying the dictates of the God he knew was inside him: "He thinks me covetous in my hold of truth, of seeing truth separate, & of receiving or taking it instead of merely obeying." A chill passed over Emerson at the end of the visit. "In dismissing him," he wrote, "I seem to have discharged an arrow into the heart of society. Wherever that young enthusiast goes he will astonish & disconcert men by dividing for them the cloud that covers the profound gulf that is man." [74]

In a way, Emerson did indeed help to discharge that arrow into society. By 1839, he had arranged for the publication of Very's first collection of essays and verse (including the essay on Shakespeare), and he sent off copies to admired friends. Much to Emerson's credit, as he and his circle were still being blamed for Very's collapse, he stood by Very both privately and publicly. But on the crucial question of Very's forcible committal to McLean, Emerson never protested—this at a time when Brazer was threatening once again to make of Very, and perhaps Emerson, a second Abner Kneeland. Even his defenses of Very's sanity were equivocal; as he wrote of him in the essay "Friendship": "To stand in true relations with men in a false age is worth a fit of insanity, is it not?" [75]

And the publication, ostensibly a tribute to Very's literary power, can also be read as an attempt to control the wildness of Very's vision, to sanitize him for public display. First of all, Emerson did not allow his name to be printed anywhere in the volume. And then he edited out many of the most rapturous and messianic of Very's writings, as if to exorcise a spiritual force he himself had helped unleash in his supposed disciple. (One poem left out, for instance, begins "Thou wilt be near me Father, when I fail, / For Thou has called me now to be thy son." [76]) Emerson even considered including a "psychological biography" of Very at the outset of the volume, which would have blunted the pronouncement of Very's genius by presenting him as a literary curiosity. Very of course objected to the editorial changes, insisting that the work could not be altered since it was not properly his own writing that he had entrusted to Emerson, but that of God. Emerson's famous (but perhaps apocryphal) reply perfectly compresses his desire to control the force that he was releasing to the public: "Cannot the spirit parse & spell?" [77] Making matters worse, although Emerson's first recorded response to the sonnets, in an 1838 letter to Very, had been "I love them and read them to all who have ears to hear," [78] after the book appeared in 1839, Emerson contributed an unsigned and extraordinarily patronizing review to the *Dial.* He considered the "genius of this little book" to be "religious," but the poems themselves had "no pretension to literary merit." He did allow that the poems—though "monotonous"—were "almost as pure as the sounds of Surrounding Nature"; but he also reminded readers that the author had been "taxed with absurdity or even with insanity." [79]

Why did Emerson not defend his friend more vigorously? If Emerson could attack in broad daylight Harvard Divinity School for shackling religion and repressing the ecstatic insight of the unmoored soul, why did he not even question the logic of the asylum that imprisoned—even briefly, and within a gilded cage—a young friend who seemed to have been liberated by his words? The standard reading of this incident in the critical literature on transcendentalism is that Very put Emerson in the awkward position of facing one who took his own ideas to their literal extremes. [80] His arm's-length tribute to Very is consistent with a pattern that later saw him embrace the rebel John Brown as the embodiment of transcendentalist "pure idealism," but also to pronounce him "precisely what lawyers call crazy, being governed by ideas, & not by external circumstance." [81] But his reluctance to see—or his fear of seeing—his own ideals realized is not the only source of Emerson's awkwardness. In his concern that Very's unbridled vision might reflect badly on him, he seems to be reacting to the spreading stain of insanity that was being used, through Very, to denounce his own work and influence. To champion Very as the voice of sanity was to risk seeming mad himself; but to acknowledge his mental collapse was to risk being blamed for it. In pronouncing Very a genius but exercising a custodial role over his output that was in some ways akin to that of the asylum keepers, he chose an awkward middle road. The other transcendentalists, in one way or another, went down the same path.

EMERSON'S FEAR of stigmatization was intensified by his family history. In 1828, when Emerson himself had just left Harvard Divinity School and was seeking a position as a pastor, his beloved older brother Edward Bliss Emerson began to succumb to "fainting fits, & delirium" and was generally "affected strangely in his mind." [82] Waldo consulted an old family friend, Dr. Edward Jarvis, who took a special interest in mental illness, and together they decided to send Edward to McLean. Emerson's own involvement in this course of action was anything but passive, as his journal entries attest. Just before Edward's committal, Emerson wrote of Edward's behavior, "If it continue, it will become necessary to send him to *Charlestown*. For besides the state of feeling produced by watching him being unutterably wretched & ruinous to infirm health—it removes me from employment the profits of which are only more necessary to me on account of this calamity." [83] Although his concern for Edward's mental health was no doubt genuine—he had been acting strangely and morbidly for at least three years, and even their mother agreed that "the Hospital" might be "a dismal necessity"—here he confessed to his own diary a concern for profits and career advancement as primary reasons to commit his brother to McLean. And it was not easy to do so. Dr. Jarvis came with the two brothers to the asylum, and when Edward was presented before Dr. Rufus Wyman (then the superintendent), "Dr. Wyman objected very strongly to taking him saying it was a very peculiar & important case & ought to be dealt with alone under private care." But Jarvis and Emerson went over Wyman's head: "We had obtained leave of the board & we made him see the impossibility of doing anything else & he grants the only great privilege they can, that of entire seclusion from all other patients." [84]

These rather extraordinary exertions were not the only ones Emerson made regarding the management and even politics of McLean. In fact, one reason for Bell's reluctance to admit Edward was the presence of other Emerson family members in McLean, one of whom was held there largely at Emerson's will. His younger brother Robert (usually known as Bulkeley)—described by one Emerson biographer as "mentally retarded and emotionally unstable" and by another as suffering from advanced Tourette's syndrome—was himself already a patient at McLean when Edward arrived. [85] Bulkeley bounced from boarding at McLean to area farms or with relatives until he died in 1858; through all of this, Emerson and his oldest brother William paid for and made decisions about his care. According to Jarvis, the fact that Edward had a brother as well as an "uncle" (apparently a collateral relation) at the asylum was one reason for Dr. Wyman's reluctance to admit him: encountering these other family members "would doubtless make him worse." [86] And in possible recompense for all of Dr. Jarvis's efforts on behalf of Edward Bliss Emerson's committal, Emerson wrote a letter of recommendation to a McLean board member on behalf of Jarvis's unsuccessful bid to become superintendent of the asylum in 1836, two years before the Jones Very affair.[87]

We are not taught to think of Emerson as a key, or even minor, figure in the legitimization of institutional psychiatry as a discipline. Perhaps it is a stretch to do so. But the sequence of events leading to Jones Very's commitment and Emerson's timorous response to it may be as significant as many of the practical measures taken to establish the legitimacy of the new profession. Historians of psychiatry agree that the rise of the asylum in the United States met with little or no organized intellectual resistance, or even serious debate, until decades later, when dozens of state-run asylums had been constructed (drawing on the model of McLean and a handful of other private asylums), and tens of thousands of unfortunate persons—the maladjusted, the drunken, the visionary, the drug-addled, the brain-damaged, the promiscuous, the self-polluting, the lazy, the depressed, the raving, and the violent—had passed through their doors.[88] If an intellectual figure existed who might have been counted on to raise key questions about the emergence of this institution with unprecedented powers to rescind the liberties of individuals and to enforce bourgeois norms of behavior on noncompliant, vulnerable subjects, Emerson would have to be near the top of the list. His philosophical valuation of impulse, intuition, and nonlinear thinking would seem to mark him as the natural enemy of the asylum movement's systematic attempts to reprogram deviant minds through carefully controlled environmental and medical means. Finally, his organicism, his hostility toward professionalization and the fragmentation of social life (as set forth in essays like "The American Scholar") stand in implicit contrast to psychiatrists' attempts to define their practice as a highly autonomous specialty within an increasingly professionalized medical community.[89] In actively seeking their help in family matters and acquiescing in the case of Very, was Emerson not acknowledging their legitimate authority over the human behaviors and patterns of mind that he wanted to liberate from oppressive institutions?

One must take into account the elite status of McLean to make full sense of Emerson's involvement with the institution. There the utopian dreams of antebellum psychiatry were less likely to be punctured by cries of abused or violent patients than in the new state institutions, and there sensitive souls like Edward Bliss Emerson and Jones Very could feel personally attended to, rather than caught up in some vast institutional machine.[90] Even so, Luther Bell and his predecessor Rufus Wyman were as committed as any asylum superintendents to enforcing the codes of normality that

Emerson at least abstractly railed against. As one patient of the time put it, "I understood that some persons had been kept in the Hospital from three to fourteen years, and was told that I must be easy in order to ever regain my liberty. I therefore found that an apparent contentment with my situation would be the most effectual means to obtain my discharge."[91] In this Goffman-like comment, the patient presents life at McLean as a charade in which patients are pronounced cured as soon as they appear to accept their keepers' version of proper conduct.[92]

And so it would be easy to accuse Emerson of hypocrisy. But given his family's psychiatric history—what he referred to as their "constitutional calamity"—he must occasionally have feared for his own mental well-being.[93] These fears were no doubt activated in a climate in which his opponents demonstrated their readiness to use institutional confinement as a way to control their enemies, and in which Unitarians were taught to regard Emerson as a "mad dog."[94] The charge stung. In the poisonous atmosphere following the "Divinity School Address" and the Jones Very fallout, Emerson was initially reluctant to return to the lecture circuit.[95] Given all this, Emerson's silence in regard to Very's confinement looks more like caution, or even fear, than callousness.

Beyond this, there are important intellectual grounds for Emerson's acceptance of psychiatric authority. Both transcendentalism and the asylum movement were born in the moment of what Michael Löwy and Robert Sayre call a romantic "critique of modernity . . . in the name of values and ideals drawn from the precapitalist, preindustrial past."[96] Both movements responded in surprisingly similar ways to some of the key developments of nineteenth-century life: the social dislocation that came with mass migrations from farms and villages to modern metropolises; the loss of contact with nature that attended such a shift; the threat to traditional values posed by the rise of wage labor and consumerism; the fragmentation of social life that arose with the emergence of early capitalism; the loss of spiritual values in a society that began to worship technology. The transcendentalist critique of specialization, entrenched institutional and professional authority, rational instrumentality, and the valuation of technological progress gave birth to all sorts of experiments in anti- or extra-capitalist movements that would restore the harmony of the individual within a social whole (as in Brook Farm) or within the natural world (as in Thoreau's *Walden*), as well as to strands of Emerson's writing in which he laments the tendency of "empirical science" to "bereave the student of the manly contemplation of the whole."[97] Although the transcendentalists differed from one another in terms of their responses to the market economy—with Orestes Brownson coming close to calling for open class warfare and Emerson and Thoreau seeking only to reform or spiritualize the capitalist system rather than overturn it[98]—they all found the materialism, artificiality, social fragmentation, and amorality of market principles to be opposed to the "higher laws" of the soul. What they sought was to restore individual wholeness, which they romantically linked to childhood, "savage" or precivilized tribes: a precapitalist and premodern state of being that Emerson referred to as the "aboriginal self."[99]

An article of faith in the asylum movement was, in the words of the pioneering French psychiatrist Etienne Esquirol, that "insanity is a disease of civilization, and the number of the insane is in direct proportion to its progress."[100] Edward Jarvis, who after his interventions on Emerson's behalf at McLean would go on to become a central exponent and theorist of the moral treatment movement, elaborated on Esquirol's thoughts as follows: "With the increase of wealth and fashion there comes also, more artificial life, more neglect of the natural laws, of self-government, more unseasonable hours for food and for sleep, more dissipation of the open, allowable, and genteel kind, and also more of the baser, disreputable, and concealed sorts."[101] (Here he sounds much like Emerson: "Society acquires new arts, and loses old instincts," he wrote in "Self-Reliance." "What a contrast between the well-clad, reading, writing, thinking American, with a watch, a pencil, and a bill of exchange in his pocket, and the naked New Zealander, whose property is a club, a spear, a mat, and an undivided twentieth of a shed to sleep under! But compare the health of the two men, and you shall see that the white man has lost his aboriginal strength."[102]) Accordingly, asylums were carefully set in bucolic landscapes, away from the artificiality, stress, and social instability of cities; similar logic sent Thoreau to Walden Pond, where Emerson underwrote his experiment in self-reliance.[103] Asylum superintendents sought to reharmonize the lives of patients not only with nature but also within a stable social environment. The capitalist marketplace in particular was a source of unhealthy ambition and material striving that caused vulnerable minds to crack; the asylum was there to repair the damage. For early psychiatry, overspecialization was a constant source of mental illness. Excessive study or devotion to a single idea or pursuit caused physical deformation of the brain, literalizing Emerson's complaint that even intellectuals were pathologically specialized. "The multitude of scholars and authors," he wrote, have a talent that grows out of "some exaggerated faculty, some overgrown member, so that their strength is a disease."[104]

Emerson jokingly referred to Jones Very's illness as either "monomania or mono Sania," which is the closest we have to a contemporaneous diagnosis.[105] The ubiquitous mental illness called monomania, in which the patient becomes fixated on one particular idea to the point of delusion, is the medical correlative of what Emerson described as the soul-sickness stemming from the *"divided* or social state" of modern life.[106] The holism of the asylum movement was a corrective for this overspecialization and social division; when Emerson wrote in "The Young American" of "the tranquil-izing, sanative influences" of the land which "brings us into just relations with men and things,"[107] he could have been speaking of his brother's res-toration in the sanative landscape at McLean after his nervous collapse, owing to fixation on his studies at the expense of the rest of his life. Viewed one way, Emerson extended the logic of the asylum beyond its walls; in another, the asylum superintendents enclosed and formalized the romantic therapeutic landscape, removing contingency and chaos from a sanitizing "nature" by applying to it a tight regimen of medical and administrative control. A similar overlap occurs between the asylum movement's harmoni-zation of labor and creativity and transcendentalist invectives against social fragmentation. McLean, like the state asylums modeled after it, stressed the importance of "diversion" and labor in their therapeutic regime; mean-while, at Brook Farm, the experimental transcendentalist commune, every member was to be a laborer as well as an artist.

These similarities should not obscure the profound differences between transcendentalism and the asylum movement. Transcendentalists were in most respects followers of Immanuel Kant, who held that the soul con-tains its own moral laws, whereas the asylum keepers believed, with Locke, that all knowledge was derived from sensation (the collecting of sensory data) and association (the ordering of that data). Because these early psy-chiatrists believed that external influences defined an individual's psycho-logical makeup, they believed that cures rested on tightly controlling such influences.[108] In this way, asylums were really much closer in spirit to the older generation of Unitarians, whose Lockean theology similarly stressed the linkage of character formation and social order, than to the transcen-dentalists, who were railing against these ideas.[109] The transcendentalists' accommodation to institutional psychiatry, however, represents one area where Emerson and the rest of the *enfants terribles* did not entirely throw off the world view of the organized religionists whose precepts they flouted so openly.

Emerson wrote little on Very's collapse that gives modern readers a di-rect indication of how he squared medical understandings of insanity or the social authority of asylum medicine with his own philosophical system. But several other members of the transcendentalist group did write about it in ways that showed their discomfort in broadening the attack they had leveled on the Unitarian establishment by turning fire on an allied institution. Elizabeth Palmer Peabody's first impulse was to guard against counterattack. In the series of letters she wrote to Emerson shortly after Very was released from McLean, she repeatedly warned the master of the popular linkage of Very's madness and Emerson's influence:

> The thought which has pressed itself on my mind most is — how some people have taken it all — as nothing but *transcendentalism*—which shows how very entirely they do *not* apprehend *the ground* of a *real belief* in *Inspiration*. What a frightful shallowness of thought in the community—that sees no difference between the evidence of the most manifest insanity & the Ideas of Reason![110]

By denying Very access to the "Ideas of Reason," Peabody is referring to a crucial concept in transcendentalists' self-definition;[111] Reason, to them, was the highest form of knowledge, an immediate, intuitive, nonrational form of insight. In Emerson's usage, Reason was contrasted with "Understanding," a more prosaic type of knowledge that is necessary to live in the world: the organization and analysis of our sense perception, or that type of knowledge that "adds, divides, combines, measures, and finds nutriment and room for activity." Despite Reason's primacy, it depended on the lower forms of knowledge, for "Reason transfers all these lessons into its own world of thought, by perceiving the analogy that marries Matter and mind."[112] Borrowed from Kant and his romantic followers, "Reason" functioned as a code word for transcendentalists, signaling their rejection of the rationalistic, empiricist world of Locke and the Unitarians. The universal mind, they argued, was something more exalted than the merely physical thing-ness of the brain.

As Barbara Packer has shown, the distinction between Reason and Understanding ultimately became a catchall for "every knotty problem" that perplexed the transcendentalists; Emerson himself described the distinction as "a philosophy in itself. . . . The manifold applications of the distinction to Literature to the Church to Life will show how good a key it is."[113] The uninitiated, Peabody argued, saw transcendentalist Reason as insanity and vice versa, which revealed only the philistines' prosaic minds. But by taking this ostensible swipe at the critics of her group, she also drummed Jones Very out of the community.[114] His ideas could have nothing to do with "the Ideas of Reason"; the two must be cleanly separated for Emerson and the others to avoid the spreading stain of his insanity.

Peabody accepted that Very was insane, but she offered no transcendentalist reading of Very's insanity other than a negative one: his crazy vision had nothing to do with the movement or its ideals. Bronson Alcott likewise did not dispute the term "insanity," but in a journal entry for December 1838, he gave Very's vision a spin more consonant with transcendentalist ideals:

> Is he insane? If so, there yet linger glimpses of wisdom in his memory. He is insane with God—diswitted in the contemplation of the holiness of Divinity. He distrusts intellect. He would have living in the concrete without the interposition of the meddling, analytic head. Curiosity he deems impious. He would have no one stop to account to himself for what he has done, deeming this hiatus of doing a suicidal act of the profane mind. Intellect, as intellect, he deems the author of all error. Living, not thinking, he regards as the worship meet for the soul. This is mysticism in its highest form.[115]

In contrast to Peabody's account, here Very's insanity enables a rapturous form of immediate spiritual perception that is not unlike Emerson's Reason—a kind of apprehension that jumps all rational and intellectual circuits. (Emerson himself would later write in "The Over-Soul" that "a certain tendency to insanity has always attended the opening of the religious sense in men, as if they had been 'blasted with excess of light.'"[116]) But perhaps Very's experience of holiness was too immediate. No transcendentalist ever rejected intellectual work as "impious" in the way that Alcott sees Very doing. In Emerson's *Nature*, after all, Reason is not in simple opposition to Understanding—in fact, Reason can only be attained by "transfer[ring] all these lessons [of Understanding] into its own world of thought." If Peabody saw Very as devoid of Reason, Alcott saw him getting there too soon, at the expense of his ability to function in the real world. Indeed, he wrote of Very a month later, "I think he will decease soon. He dies slowly by slowly retreating from the senses, yet existing in them by memory, when men or things are obtruded upon his thought."[117] Perhaps to Alcott's chagrin, Very would live another forty-one years.

For Peabody, Very's insanity had nothing to do with the transcendentalist movement or its ideals; for Alcott, it was a diseased mutation of them. In either case—and despite Alcott's more sympathetic reading—Very was implicitly made a transcendental outcast. For Alcott, insanity even implied death. Less willing to sacrifice Very was James Freeman Clarke, the man usually credited with spreading the transcendentalist message westward through his Kentucky-based journal, *The Western Messenger*. (In 1886, six years after Very's death, Clarke would also publish the fullest edition of Very's work until Helen R. Deese's 1993 collection *Jones Very: The Complete Poems.*) In an introduction to a series of Very's sonnets that he printed in his journal, Clarke referred to the popular notion of the poet's insanity as the sort of charge that "is almost always brought against any man who endeavours to introduce to the common mind any very original ideas." Calling Very insane was a way for people to avoid being moved from "the sphere of thought which is habitual to us, into a higher and purer one," because "nobody is obliged to attend to the 'insane ravings' of a maniac." Even granting—which Clarke says he is not willing to do—some "limited" form of insanity in Very, it would seem to be only a loss of "the use of his practical intellect . . . a partial derangement of the lower intellectual organs, or perhaps an extravagant pushing of some views to their last results." In other words, Very suffered from a mere defect of Understanding, which left his transcendent mind free to roam "in the loftiest contemplations, and which utterly disregarded all which did not come into that high sphere of thought."[118]

Clarke momentarily hedged in his defense of Very's mental health: he was sane, but if he wasn't, only his "lower intellectual organs" were affected. What is interesting here is not only the transcendentalist reading of what early psychiatrists were calling religious monomania, but that there is practically no difference between the psychiatric and transcendentalist readings at all. (In this light, it seems fitting that Clarke was publishing Edward Jarvis in his newspaper and convincing him to move out to Kentucky at about the same time he was publishing his defense of Jones Very.[119]) The reigning medical explanation of mental functioning at the time of the moral treatment was that of "faculty psychology," which divides the human brain into compartments or faculties, each one associated with some kind of thinking or acting; mental illness occurs when one of these faculties becomes overdeveloped.[120] In this model, the spiritual faculties could be affected; but this was different from saying that the spirit itself—or the mind—could become insane. The theoreticians of the moral treatment movement, no less than the transcendentalists, were thoroughgoing dualists who believed that the "mind" was immaterial and immortal, and could not be touched by disease; the brain was simply a physical instrument by which the mind carried out its will.[121] This was a view that saved the asylum's founders from charges of irreligion, and a view that allowed ministers such as Upham and Brazer to accept psychiatry's claim that insanity was a medical problem, rather than a spiritual one.

This shared dualism was the unspoken frame for the whole circuit of interchanges surrounding Jones Very's supposed insanity and the justification of his incarceration at McLean. For virtually all commentators, interpreting Very's ordeal revolved solely around the question of the location of his spiritual ideas: did they emanate from the infallible, eternal, immaterial mind (or, Reason), which was untouchable by disease or strain? Or were they misfirings of a leaden, corruptible, unbalanced brain—a defect in Understanding? By agreeing to this frame, the transcendentalists missed a key opportunity to widen the discussion by asking whether the forcible detention in an asylum of an excited young man who—while making a serious nuisance of himself—was doing no one any particular harm was an injustice, whatever his mental condition. And despite its prominence in Emerson's life during his formative years as a public intellectual, McLean—and the asylum movement which it helped to generate—was for him not so much an institution to be justified or challenged, as it was a social fact that escaped his critical notice.

Nonetheless, the shadow of McLean did linger in his writing and public career. Emerson's first published mention of asylums came in the last paragraph of *Nature* (1836), where they are cast as one of the "disagreeable" things of the world that will be swept away by the "revolution" caused by "the influx of the spirit": "So fast will disagreeable appearances, swine, spiders, snakes, pests, madhouses, prisons, enemies, vanish; they are temporary and shall be no more seen."[122] The prophetic cast of this statement perhaps implies that in the here and now, when spirit has not yet pervaded the world, madhouses are inevitable. The grounds for his real-world accommodation to asylums are hinted at in a journal entry during his warm-up for the "Divinity School Address," in which he warned himself to "beware of Antinomianism" because "the loss of the old checks will sometimes be a temptation which the unripeness of the new will not countervail."[123] One wonders what are the "old checks" that are lost when one overthrows all of social authority. As Caleb Smith has argued, prisons were one. Emerson's reluctance to slide into an antinomianism that overthrows all authority led him tacitly to accept the premises of prison reform, even turning "prison architecture into an imagery of the mind." Emerson's conception of freedom, according to Smith, does not depend on smashing all systems of confinement, but in fact is an abstracted and internalized version of the solitary self-correction that was the hallmark of early nineteenth-century prison reform. While man in society is "clapped into jail by his own consciousness," Emerson wrote in "Self-Reliance" (1841), the self-reliant man will "receive the benefits of attendance on Divine service . . . without stirring from their [solitary] cells." [124]

A close reading of this landmark essay suggests that insane asylums have perhaps an even more complex relationship to his notion of liberation than do prisons. Strikingly, at several points in the essay, he casts the battle between conformism and self-reliance as one between oppressive traditions or institutions and an individual struggling to maintain sanity: "As men's prayers are a disease of the will, so are their creeds a disease of the intellect," and "the centuries are conspirators against the sanity and authority of the soul." [125] In this last quote, he appears to refer back to the controversy surrounding the "Address," in which "worship of the past" ("the centuries") is an obstacle to the reception of "divine wisdom" ("the sanity and authority of the soul"). Implying sympathy with the soul wounded by a tradition-based authority, Emerson positions himself on the side of the target of social control. But, as in the essay "Friendship," where he more explicitly refers to Jones Very, he does not question the grounds on which that control is effected: the centuries (*i.e.,* those on the side of tradition and social order) may do the conspiring, but the soul's sanity and authority really *are* vulnerable. And so they needed to be repaired.

And how should a society respond to those it has damaged? One main thrust of Emerson's essay suggests that organized attempts at relief of social problems only create new constraints on individuals, most prominent of which is the social expectation that one will donate to an abstract cause in order to expiate oneself:

> Do not tell me, as a good man did to-day, of my obligation to put all poor men in good situations. Are they *my* poor? I tell thee, foolish philanthropist, that I grudge the dollar, the dime, the cent, I give to such men as do not belong to me and to whom I do not belong. There is a class of persons to whom by all spiritual affinity I am bought and sold; for them I will go to prison, if need be; but your miscellaneous popular charities; the education at college of fools; the building of meeting-houses to the vain end to which many now stand; alms to sots; and the thousandfold Relief Societies;—though I confess with shame I sometimes succumb and give the dollar, it is a wicked dollar which by and by I shall have the manhood to withhold.[126]

This famously troubling passage hints at Emerson's contempt for the dependent and weak willed ("Are they *my* poor?"), but in the main, it expresses disdain for institutional reform and charity efforts: relief societies, scholarship funds, and what might now be called faith-based organizations. He favors instead one-on-one exchanges, where the donor is linked to the recipient through a "spiritual affinity." For these persons, he would "go to prison," implying that his own personal liberty is less important to him than is standing up for his ties to fellow men.

In the next paragraph, the figure of the institutionalized insane obtrudes, imperfectly assimilated into Emerson's train of thought:

> Men do what is called a good action, as some piece of courage or charity, much as they would pay a fine in expiation of daily non-appearance on parade. Their works are done as an apology or extenuation of their living in the world,—as invalids and the insane pay a high board. Their virtues are penances. I do not wish to expiate, but to live. My life is for itself and not for a spectacle.[127]

What are we to make of the "invalids and the insane" who are analogized to the hypocritical donors of charity, whose "works are done as an apology or extenuation of their living in the world"? The simile resists simple unfolding, as does so much of Emerson's prose. On the surface, it seems to suggest that for the social conformist—the guiltily non-self-reliant—"giving" is experienced as a sort of penance, a price paid for the privilege of "living." But how do "invalids and the insane" pay such a price? The simple answer is that they are punished by being locked up, which for Emerson might be analogous to conforming to society's expectations. But on closer inspection, what he mentions is not the fact of incarceration, but the "high board" that the invalids and insane must pay (presumably at private institutions).

Of course, invalids and the insane did not usually pay this "high board" themselves, as Emerson knew so well, having helped pay for the care of two brothers at McLean. Is his conflation of patient and payer an unconscious effort to repress his real role in managing those who suffered from his family's "constitutional calamity"? Or is it the expression of an equally unconscious wish that the loved ones whom he either ushered into McLean himself or whom he impotently watched being carried off went there of their own accord, even paying their way? Either way, the actual "board" charged to insanity that this passage most plausibly records was paid by the outsider: it was the financial and emotional cost to family members of supporting their afflicted loved ones, perhaps even the stigma of being associated with the insane. What happens, or should happen, to the "invalids and the insane" who flit through "Self-Reliance" is never made clear: Emerson's is a philosophy for those on the outside.

No matter how we read this slippery passage, mention of the "invalids and the insane" conspicuously does not trigger an assault on the asylum movement as a species of "foolish philanthropy," even in a piece of writing whose ostensible force is to condemn the "wicked dollar" that supports institutions of humanitarian reform. The contradiction is not as severe as it might seem, however. As disability studies scholars Sharon Snyder and David Mitchell have argued, Emerson implicitly supported his culture's distinction between the deserving and undeserving poor.[128] In connection with this "wicked dollar," we might presume that Emerson would have been opposed to state financing of insane asylums, as this would create an "obligation to put all poor men in good situations," regardless of the merits of the individual case. Paying for a brother or supporting a friend's treatment in a private institution, on the other hand, might be an acceptable arrangement (although Emerson inverts the usual structure of such relationships by suggesting that he might "go to prison" for such a soul). At any rate, the logic of institutional confinement—or care—is more affirmed by this famously anti-institutional essay than it is attacked.

If Emerson did not attempt to question the social and medical revolution in the treatment of the mad, one could argue that his various engagements with McLean did, by the end of the Jones Very affair, change him. In his arm's-length embrace of Jones Very after his release from McLean and in his own career over the next decade, Emerson experienced the specter of the asylum as a check against his own wildest antinomian impulses: a sort of safety net for the self-reliant, nonconformist soul that has strayed too far, too fast from tradition, authority, and propriety. He published Very's work but robbed it of much of its visionary or pathological character; he called Very his eternal friend but referred to his most cherished beliefs as "a fit of insanity." In his writings immediately following the "Divinity School Address," he continued to fire away at organized religion, but on safer ground—in a series of lectures that he himself had organized, where he preached largely to a paying audience of the converted. His words became both more measured and more vague; instead of throwing verbal spears at the Unitarian establishment seated in front of him, he broadly lamented that "the formal church has overlaid the real." [129] And at points he warned about the consequences of too shrill or prolonged an opposition. Maturity, he intoned, consists of moving beyond the protests of youth to an affirmative stance toward life: "He has done protesting: now he begins to affirm: all art affirms: and with every new stroke with greater serenity and joy." [130]

Lawrence Buell refers to the "Divinity School Address" as Emerson's "most contrarian act of intellectual radicalism." [131] Never again would he take such an intellectual and professional risk as he had in the summer of 1838, when he spoke what he perceived to be hard truths directly to an entrenched and powerful institution from which he himself had accrued benefits. His affirmative and apolitical stances allowed him, in his later career, to be taken up increasingly by the intellectual mainstream rather than by vanguard political and intellectual movements.[132] By the 1840s, he had systematically renounced almost all of the more radical experiments undertaken by his transcendentalist compatriots; by the end of the decade, he was increasingly at ease playing the role of public lecturer and moral pedagogue, whom Thomas Augst describes as guiding Americans "in the democratic art of living under capitalism."[133] A fighting Emerson would reemerge with his participation in the abolitionist crusade of the 1850s; but in contrast to his earlier battles, he was reluctant to join; even several family members became activists in the cause before he did.[134] Emerson's participation in the movement was a crucial event in marshalling intellectual opposition in the North against slavery. But as he himself noted, he waited until the fight found him, complaining in one speech on the 1850 Fugitive Slave Law that speaking on politics is "odious and hurtful and it seems like meddling or leaving your work," and in another resigning himself to the fact that "the last year has forced us all into politics."[135] "Forced us all": he was riding the tide, confirming its power, rather than swimming against it. Accordingly, he emerged from the Civil War as New England's "great man" rather than its scourge, the "mad dog" of his early career. If, in 1838, Emerson did not take on the authority of the insane asylum, the asylum, one could argue, played a role in taming Emerson, taking a bite out of his impassioned, visionary, and—some said—mad critique of modern life.

CODA: "I WAS SICK AND IN PRISON"

And what did Jones Very make of his experience at McLean? The record is frustratingly thin, but one can make several surmises. First, despite his brief stay there and the apparently gentle treatment by Dr. Bell, he likely encountered certain indignities, if not outright humiliations. One former patient, Robert Fuller, recounted in 1833 the admissions routine for unwilling patients. A married man with four children who had been under enormous stress because of failed business ventures and a dispute with the Cambridge school board, of which he was a member, he had begun to exhibit erratic behavior and volubility. One morning, while speaking with his wife and mother in front of his house, he was confronted by a group of neighbors who demanded that he speak with a doctor. When he refused, the neighbors grabbed him and held him inside his house until the doctor arrived in a carriage. At this point, Fuller realized he would be taken by force, and indeed he was bound and driven to McLean, where he was put into a cell with iron grates. The attending physician gave him two pills, which he pretended to swallow but managed to spit out (Elizabeth Peabody's advice to Very to "take your medicine" suggests that Very may also have resisted McLean's drug therapy), and he asked to see his wife. The doctors seemed at first to assent, but when Fuller saw that he was fooled, he began to scream and shake the bars. He was taken to

> a dark room or inner prison, where they laid me on a bed and literally robbed me. . . . I could not bear the indignities that had been heaped upon me, and in my wrath, I cried to God for vengeance on my enemies. In this situation, my imagination became disordered, and my miserable condition became still more pitiable by the horrible visions, that flitted across my mind. For eight or ten days, I walked around my straightened abode, crying and praying to God for deliverance. In Him I trusted, and through his goodness, I have been relieved.[136]

Despite his religious faith, Fuller saw the existence of McLean and other insane asylums as an affront primarily to a secular authority, the state. After all, he wrote:

> the best index of the freedom of a government is the protection it affords to personal liberty. . . . So careful is our law of the freedom of the citizens, that every man charged with a criminal offence is entitled to a hearing before a jury of his country. Yet there is this seeming anomaly—a man charged with insanity can be taken away without trial, and shut up within the walls of a prison. . . . On the charge of insanity, many a rich father can shut up his disorderly or idiot child; he pays liberally for his imprisonment, and the public are none the wiser for it. It is time for the Legislature to remedy the evil.[137]

In a concluding patriotic flourish, he wrote: "The liberty which we have enjoyed, and which the half finished monument on Bunker Hill was intended to commemorate, has vanished.—Let that monument be torn from its base,—we are no longer worthy of it."[138] Fuller's response to his two-and-a-half month stay may be more bitter than that of many or even most former patients, but it articulates the rage and sense of injustice felt by many former patients in both state and corporate institutions whose complaints found their way into print. Not even McLean's exceptional commitment to the tenets of the moral treatment—the granting of physical mobility, the plentiful diversions and beautiful grounds, the better class of patients—could exempt it from the most basic complaints that it was an artfully constructed prison.

Very stayed only a month at McLean, as we know, and he appears to have avoided the worst treatment that former patients alleged in their memoirs. One comes away from reading these other accounts feeling that Very was lucky. Perhaps the notoriety of his case convinced the authorities not to take harsh measures with him. In the fall and winter of 1838, a continuous stream of religious poetry and essays flowed out of him—or through him, according to his belief in their divine composition. Although scholars have been unable to date most of these precisely, a good deal of this writing must have been done in the asylum. Given the intense spirituality of his output and the fact that Bell released him so quickly, one senses a reluctance to treat the symptoms of his supposed insanity with any force. Writing in the asylum, as we have seen, was always conducted under heavy surveillance, and Very's writings, judged apostate by the Unitarian clergy, would hardly have seemed less so to the secular guardians of rationality in the asylum. But rather than try to break the flow and perhaps make Very a martyr to the transcendentalist cause, they let the author free. Or maybe Lydia Very finally made herself obnoxious enough to win the release of her son, who was transferred back to her care.

Other religious visionaries locked up at McLean were not so fortunate. Elizabeth Stone, who published her memoir in 1841, was a former Lowell mill worker, born into a strict Congregationalist family, who left work to study religion. Initially she became disillusioned because she felt that sectarian bickering betrayed "the simple religion of Jesus Christ." [139] Overcome with a sense of guilt, she vowed to give up food, drink, and sleep until she found God—who ultimately came to her in the middle of the night and asked her to open her heart. The voice then led her to a revival meeting, where she experienced rapture.

> As we rose I opened my mouth and words flowed faster than I could speak, I blessed and praised God and asked them all to forgive me for the opposition that I had manifested towards them for their entreating me to be reconciled to God. There was great rejoicing over me. Some wept, some prayed, and some sang.

She decided then to become a missionary, but unfortunately for her, the Spirit directed her to make her parents her first converts: "I told them that I had met with a change, but said but little, as I did not wish to argue the point, for they were both against me and said they thought I had got my brain *turned* by studying too much." [140] After she tried to convert other members of her family, her brother took her riding, insisted that she visit a doctor, and—when she protested—carted her off to an asylum. "Is this done in a free and happy land?" she wrote. "Because I differed from some of my family in my religious opinion must I be taken and imprisoned?"[141]

At McLean, Dr. Bell quizzed her intently on her religious visions. "I did not know why I must relate my Christian experience to a Doctor and an unconverted man at such a time, for it seemed to me like mockery. I refused again and again, but, *no*, I must relate it."[142] She spent a sleepless night in bewilderment, fancying herself in a prison for prostitutes, and was told the next morning by a doctor "that I must not think I was so filled with the spirit; any minister would laugh at me." She tried to quote scripture at him, but he threw it back in her face and forced her to take some medicine. This, she found, "effected [*sic*] my brain, the back part of my head, hardened or petrified it, and the brain is the seat of the nerves, and any one can conceive of the distress that I must be thrown into all over in my body, every nerve in me drawing and straining convulsively."[143] She managed to speak with a sympathetic and religious attendant, who expressed some concern that "poor Christians [were] troubled about their religion in that house." This good woman then gave Stone a warning, and some advice:

> She desired me to control my feelings as much as possible. If I did not, I should be showered. I then enquired what that meant; she then described it to me, that I should be stripped of all my clothes, and cold water poured upon me, and I should be carried on to another gallery, where the society would not be so pleasant, neither the accommodations so good.[144]

Stone apparently avoided the dreaded shower, but—in her telling—the assault on her beliefs, consisting of harangues and drugs, continued. As she felt herself losing God, she tried to hang herself, but the sheet she used for the purpose tore. She concluded by addressing her readers: "I wish you to understand it is that praying spirit that can be taken from you by medicine."[145]

Very's stay at McLean appears to have overlapped with Stone's; if her account is to be believed, it is with amazement that one reads Very's sole poem about his career as a madman, which was written seventeen years after his confinement. In a poem called "McLean Asylum, Somerville," (1855), he appears to look nostalgically back on his stay there:

> Oh! House of refuge; for those weary souls,
>   Trembling on dizzy heights, mid gloom and shade,
> While Reason from their path her light withholds,
>   Oh! House of Refuge! Thou for them wast made.

Oh! House of Refuge! Ever stand thou there—
　　A refuge thou from fiery Passion's sway—
A shelter from the scorching heat of care—
　　A holy Refuge, in grief's wintry day.

The hand of kindness reared thy stately pile,
　　A goodness kinder keeps thee fair within;
Thy gates are open, and a welcome smile
　　Here greets the weary wanderer—enter in.

Oh! House of Refuge; thou receivest all,
　　The young, the old, the innocent, the gay;
The sighs, the groans, the burning tears that fall,
　　Oh! Holy Refuge! thou wilt chase away.

Oh! House of blissful Hope! The orb of day
　　First robes thy lofty domes with morning light
So the first dawn of orient Reason's ray
　　Beneath thy walls lights up the soul's dark night.

A House of Refuge, and a home of love.
　　A blest retreat, to me, thou wast for years,
When discord, doubt, and fear for mastery strove—
　　There, first, His bow of peace shone amid falling tears.[146]

At the time of this gauzy remembrance, Very's literary reputation had almost been forgotten, but his social rehabilitation was nearly complete. For one thing, he had returned to the Unitarian fold and was working as a supply minister for various congregations. He was still writing the occasional poem—occasional both in the sense of intermittent and in the sense of public, to be read mainly aloud in social settings. And as such this poem was likely a vehicle for testifying to his renewed institutional faith: his faith in the asylum is faith in progress, rationality, and humanitarianism; his release from "fiery passion's sway" is a renunciation of the enthusiastic excesses against which the Unitarians warned. In the poem, he treats the asylum much as his Unitarian persecutors had in the 1830s. Dorothea Dix herself might well have used such language to lobby the state of Massachusetts to build another asylum.

The language of "McLean Asylum, Somerville" however, belies the continuing messianic fervor he had still shown upon his release; and it belies the turmoil that had attended his readmission into the transcendentalist community. McLean may well have been a "House of Refuge" in certain respects, but it certainly did not shed the light of Reason on him, release him from "fiery Passion," or light up his "soul's dark night." In the context of Very's late-in-life rehabilitation within the Unitarian community, the poem reads as an attempt to renounce the ecstatic and decidedly un-Unitarian experience that had made him notorious as a young man.

Another poem ("On Finding the Truth"), written two years earlier, sounds a more plausible and bittersweet note in looking back on the period of his rapture (or madness). Although it does not mention his confinement at McLean, it rhapsodizes on his earlier religious convictions with a sense of regret at their passing:

> With sweet surprise, as when one finds a flower,
> Which in some lonely spot, unheeded, grows;
> Such were my feelings, in the favored hour,
> When Truth to me her beauty did disclose.
> Quickened I gazed anew on heaven and earth,
> For a new glory beamed from earth and sky;
> All things around me shared the second birth,
> Restored with me, and nevermore to die.
> The happy habitants of other spheres,
> As in times past, from heaven to earth came down;
> Swift fled in converse sweet the unnumbered years,
> And angel-help did human weakness crown!
> The former things, with Time, had passed away,
> And Man, and Nature lived again for aye.[147]

Rather than reading his ecstatic period as brought about by a deprivation of Reason, which McLean would restore to him, here he regards the state that others defined as madness as his "favored hour." The only signal of his renunciation of those ideas is the past tense of the poem itself. Neither the exertions of the doctors, the importuning of the Unitarians, the fickle embrace of the transcendentalists, nor even his own will convinced Jones Very to cast off his vision. The only apparent agent in his release is "Time."

All through the period of Very's involvement with the transcendentalists—whether the "favored hour" or the hour of "fiery Passion's sway"—God spoke through him. A letter he wrote to the Unitarian minister Henry Whitney Bellows in December 1838, two months after his release from McLean, informs his friend that he was placed "contrary to my will in the Asylum." In contrast to his account in his 1855 "McLean Asylum" poem, he implied to Bellows that he, like Elizabeth Stone, learned to modify his behavior enough to satisfy the authorities, while never renouncing his vision: "There I remained a month in which under the influences of the spirit my usual manner returned in all things save that I now obey it as my natural impulse." Most of the letter details his unchanged religious outlook: his double consciousness, his renunciation of his own will, his obedience to the voice of God within him, his sense that his sufferings confirm his status as the Second Coming. At the bottom of the letter, written in someone else's hand—probably Bellows'—are the words, "During his aberration of mind." [148]

Very also informed Bellows that the sonnets he was then writing were a direct transcription of what "I hear of the word." Indeed, the emotional world of this poetry—much of it achingly beautiful—ostensibly follows the passion of Christ. The most famous of them, "The New Birth," "The Slave," and "He Was Acquainted With Grief"—still anthologized today—sound a triumphal messianic note: "And I a child of God by Christ made free / Start from death's slumbers to eternity"; "No more without the flaming gate to stray, / No more for sin's dark stain the debt of death to pay"; "Thou too must suffer as it [the spirit] suffers here, / The death in Christ to know the Father's love; / Then in the strains that angels love to hear, / Thou too shalt hear the spirit's song above." [149] But through these sonnets also course darker, more personal themes: confinement, bondage, betrayal, mockery. These are all quickly—within the space of fourteen lines—transmuted into Christian trials and redemptions. But even the titles of some of the poems (many left uncollected in the Emerson edition of 1839) give a sense of the human ordeal that Very was trying so desperately to convert into signs of his religious calling: "The Slave," "Help," "The Prisoner," and—most poignantly, "I Was Sick And In Prison." This last poem envisions a moment when the poetic persona will be able to answer God's call, at which point a period of "brotherhood of peace" will begin, and his "song" (perhaps the poem itself) will redeem prisoners and send them all to heaven. From a poet who himself had recently been "sick and in prison," this is a triumphal repositioning of himself from captive to liberator.

Images of involuntary confinement flicker through these poems. In one, a call to the sinner to renounce his traitorous will—which is like an inner Judas—there is this warning: "The foe is on you! Haste, he's at the door! / Soon, soon thy limbs will be securely bound, / And you in chains your former sloth deplore." [150] In this image, Brazer and Upham, knocking on the door, become the sounds of his own devilish will trying to gain control of his spirit; his captivity is punishment not for his religious vision, but for his failure to live up to it. In another poem, "Behold He Is At Hand That Doth

Betray Me," he seems to comment on the stigma of his confinement: the mocking, the insults, the persecution.

> Why come you out to me with clubs and staves,
> That you on every side have fenced me so?
> In every act you dig for me deep graves;
> In which my feet must walk where'er I go.[151]

Although Very does not specify the "you" whom he is addressing, the last lines of the poem must have made Emerson uncomfortable: "And you in turn must bear the stripes I bear, / And in his sufferings learn alike to share."[152] One can imagine Emerson reading this, feeling accused of sharing the younger man's vision, but letting Very alone suffer the consequences of living up to it. He was cast, in short, as Judas betraying Very with a kiss. Emerson did not see fit to publish it.

——— ✳ ———

CHAPTER FIVE

What's the Point of a Revolution?

Edgar Allan Poe and the Origins of the Asylum

IN HIS POLEMICAL classic, *Reflections on the Revolution in France* (1790), Edmund Burke compared the forces unleashed by the revolution in the name of the rights of man to a lunatic escaping from his cell. "Is it because liberty in the abstract may be classed among the blessings of mankind," Burke asked rhetorically, "that I am seriously to felicitate a madman, who has escaped from the protecting restraint and wholesome darkness of his cell, on his restoration to the enjoyment of light and liberty?"[1] In this analogy, civilization—especially all the restraints, laws, and traditions that uphold it—is akin to a well-regulated asylum; revolution is a shattering not only of the old order but of civility itself. When these restraints give way, they can produce, in Burke's view, only more disorder and madness: "If that which is only submission to necessity should be made the object of choice, the law is broken, nature is disobeyed, and the rebellious are outlawed, cast forth, and exiled, from this world of reason, and order and peace, and virtue, and fruitful penitence, into the antagonist world of madness, discord, vice, confusion, and unavailing sorrow."[2] For Burke, the madman was a figure for all those irrational latent forces in society that need constantly to be held in check by authority; revolution both emanates from those forces and causes them to proliferate.

Burke's linkage of insanity and revolution was hardly anomalous in French Revolution-era discussions of politics and the social order. In eighteenth-century France, the label of insanity was one of the tools at the disposal of the monarchy and the politically connected to remove obstacles to their authority. Schemers with any connection to royalty could obtain a royal *lettre de cachet* to incarcerate an enemy (or a misbehaving child, or a relative who blocked a potential inheritance) on the grounds of insanity.[3] This royal prerogative seemed to many revolutionaries to epitomize the wanton abuse of power in the *ancien regime*. Some revolutionaries even believed that the new order would sweep away not only asylums but the social misery that they enclosed. In the midst of the Revolution, the Jacobin utopian revolutionary Bertrand Barère offered a proleptic caption for the imminent liberation: "Put above the door of these asylums inscriptions that announce their imminent demise. For if, once the Revolution is over, unfortunate creatures still exist among us, our Revolutionary labours will have been in vain."[4] Interestingly, both the revolutionary Barère and the conservative Burke imagined asylums in a purely negative relation to the Revolution: for both men, they were impressive symbols—and indeed agents—of the old order's power to restrain, to suppress, and to maintain order and control.

The Revolution, however, did not bring about the release from bondage of all those labeled mad, nor did it bring down the asylum walls. In fact, the golden age of the asylum was coincident with the revolutionary age—and in nineteenth-century psychiatric lore, the advent of the asylum was the fulfillment of the Revolution, rather than its antithesis. Nowhere was this more forcefully conveyed than in an apocryphal story that gained increasing traction, eventually reaching mythic status during the 1830s and 1840s as insane asylums were built across Europe and America at a dizzying rate. As the legend goes, upon becoming the superintendent of Asylum de Bicêtre, located just outside of Paris, in 1792, Philippe Pinel famously unchained fifty-three maniacs and went on to rule them with compassion, reason, and humanity rather than force. (He was said to have unchained the patients at Salpêtrière asylum for women when he moved there two years later.) The result was, according to Amariah Brigham, "a revolution in the treatment of this unfortunate but hitherto neglected portion of our fellow creatures."[5] The relation between Pinel's "revolution" and the revolutions that spread across the Atlantic from the end of the eighteenth century through the middle of the nineteenth prompted endless commentary by psychiatrists, and, to some extent, the lay public. What did "freeing" the insane mean, and what role did the new psychiatric profession have in it? Did the political revolutions that were necessary to depoliticize the care of the mentally ill produce their own mental health risks? Could a liberal society—with asylums at their helm—convert brute unreason into civility and rationality, or were restraints and punishments still necessary?

All of this may sound like background for Peter Weiss's well-known 1964 play *The Persecution and Assassination of Jean-Paul Marat as Performed by the Inmates of the Asylum of Charenton Under the Direction of the Marquis de Sade* (better known as *Marat/Sade*). Using Sade's actual confinement at the Charenton asylum after the Revolution as a jumping-off point, Weiss imagines Sade authoring a play in which patients reenact and comment upon the assassination of Marat, offering an over-the-top commentary on the incompleteness of the Revolution in the context of the bourgeois consolidation of power.[6]

But an earlier literary text uncannily anticipates Weiss by restaging the upheavals of the age of Revolution in a private asylum. This is Edgar Allan Poe's 1844 story "The System of Doctor Tarr and Professor Fether." The story is set in a "Maison de Santé, or private Mad House" run along moral treatment principles (called here "the soothing system") in an abandoned chateau in the south of France. Beyond its French setting, the story's revolutionary context is alluded to in the title (tarring and feathering was a punishment reserved for Tory sympathizers during the American Revolution, as well as for runaway slaves who might incite insurrections of their own); in the name of Poe's asylum superintendent, Monsieur Maillard (Stanislaus-Marie Maillard was a hero of the storming of the Bastille); and in the narrative's revelation of a previous uprising of patients against their keepers and graphic picturing of a counterrevolution, which is played out as the asylum band plays a frenzied version of "Yankee Doodle" in discordant tones. However, few critics have discussed this story's treatment of insanity in a revolutionary age, because another layer of symbolism points in a different direction: its captives-turned-rebels theme and terrifying racial imagery at the ending certainly suggest Poe's less-than-sanguine view of the state of American race relations.[7] The story's climax, in which a group of angry, dark, apelike figures crashes into the mansion and violently subdues their "Southern" keepers, unavoidably calls up associations with slave uprisings, as do such other Poe tales as "Hop-Frog" and *The Adventures of Arthur Gordon Pym*.[8]

Chapter 2 has shown how discussions of race and slavery were entangled with discussions of insanity and asylum care in politics, law, medicine, and popular culture. Poe's tale can certainly add to that story, and in this chapter I will draw out some of the implications of Poe's treatment of black (or blackened) inmates taking over the asylum in a "Southern" setting. But the story's context must be widened beyond the national preoccupation with slavery to the transatlantic aftershocks of the Revolution, rumblings caused not just by the ongoing upheavals conducted in the name of Reason, but by the persistence of uncontainable, inextinguishable, possibly even spreading elements of irrationality and madness that Enlightenment-inspired revolutions could not stamp out. In this story, Poe implicitly accepts the claim of early psychiatry that the asylum was a key legacy of the revolution and a hallmark of liberal society, but for him these are not to the asylum's credit.

Recent theorists of disability have argued that the problem of incapacitated minds has always been a blind spot in theories of liberalism, which depend on rational actors to make decisions freely. The needs of the mentally ill or cognitively impaired are therefore determined by others, who presumably can act in their interest better than they can act for themselves. The result is that in liberal societies, those deemed mentally deficient are cast as outsiders, with no real capacity to determine the structure of the society that labels them, confines them, and supposedly rehabilitates them. Martha Nussbaum has argued that the solution to this problem is a sort of ethical extension: mental and other kinds of disability should be viewed as states of dependency into which all of us fall at some point during our lives ("We are needy temporal animal beings who begin as babies and end, often, in other forms of dependency"[9]). If we view disability in this way, then caring for the mentally and physically disabled will not create a dependent class and a class of caregivers, but a society in which everyone's eventual vulnerability (or "animality") will be addressed.

Poe would have found this to be alarmingly naive. While the inversions of his story—and the arc of his literary career—suggest that he would agree that madness is a state into which we all might fall (it is not the patients but the *keepers* who go on a rampage at the end), he would disagree sharply that a liberal society can simply extend its purview to solve the problem. While in Poe's world madness lurks in everyone, it is activated or aggravated by social conflict and therefore cannot be solved by the social system that brings those conflicts into being. The asylum, as child of the revolution and solution to the revolution's problems, creates new conflicts which it also proposes to resolve. Founded by violence but appealing to reason, a postrevolutionary society (and the asylums that are such an important part of them) can never achieve stability. The best they can attain is the temporary mastery of one class—who hide their desire for power behind a cloak of reason—over that of another, whose humiliations bleed over into resentment, madness, and violence.

As in Weiss's play, the themes Poe engages are broad: revolutions abroad and possible revolutions at home; the dream of a society based on reason rather than acquired privilege or brute force; the tensions between humanitarianism and the need for security; the place of unreason in a liberal society; the incompatibility of slavery and democracy; the surging of the bourgeoisie and the allure of the old aristocratic order; the dependence of the master class on the myth of their own superior breeding and rationality; the humiliations and rage of the serving class that is forced to indulge them. Unlike Weiss, who saw himself as a Marxist furthering the dialectic of revolution,[10] Poe — being Poe — does not offer definitive positions on any of these matters; rather, his story amounts to an absurdist, almost nihilistic counterweight to the humanitarian gloss on the revolution. His position is not unlike that of Sade in the play, who muses on the righteous revolutionary certitude of Marat:

> Marat
> these cells of the inner self
> are worse than the deepest stone dungeon and
>   as long as they are locked
> all your revolution remains
> only a prison mutiny
> to be put down
> by corrupted fellow-prisoners [11]

For Sade, unlocking the doors within is the final step in the revolution; for Poe, too, all revolutions will end with an unshackling of the "inner self" — but for him, that is the way to the abyss.

FOR ALL its absurdity, grotesque humor, and conspicuous winking, "The System of Doctor Tarr and Professor Fether" is in certain respects a faithful treatment of a private asylum catering to the nouveaux riches in a postrevolutionary society. The narrator of Poe's story is a tourist in southern France who, traveling with a friend, decides to visit a *"Maison de Santé, or private Mad House,"* which on the surface seems a more or less accurate representation of the moral treatment movement. Here he has heard that "all punishments were avoided — that even confinement was seldom resorted to — that the patients, while secretly watched, were left much apparent liberty, and that most of them were permitted to roam about the house and grounds."[12] The narrator's first glimpse of the interior of the asylum confirms that it is — or has been — run along the lines of the moral treatment, a system in which, the superintendent Monsieur Maillard tells him, "we put much faith in amusements of a simple kind, such as music, dancing, gymnastic exercises generally, cards, certain classes of books, and so forth."[13] Indeed, Maillard greets him in an elaborately refined parlor "containing among other indications of refined taste, many books, drawings, pots of flowers, and musical instruments." A young woman, whom the narrator takes to be a patient, sings arias from Bellini, and the narrator warms to a feeling of the nobility of the scene, only slightly exaggerating the piousness felt—or claimed to be felt—by many nineteenth-century tourists of humanitarian carceral institutions: "She excited in my bosom a feeling of mingled respect, interest, and admiration."[14] Of course, this is a Poe story, and so that feeling disintegrates throughout the narrative into ever-deepening levels of perplexity, chaos, and eventually horror—a horror that implicates not only the moral treatment movement, but the social order from which it emanates.

The first twist comes when Maillard explains that the era of the "soothing system" is actually over, the patients having been too often "aroused to a dangerous frenzy by injudicious persons who called to inspect the house," and that a "rigid system of exclusion" has now been put in place.[15] Over the course of an evening of surpassing strangeness, the narrator dines with Maillard and a cast of eccentrics whom the doctor insists are his "friends and keepers" but whom the narrator suspects are actually patients. They purport to tell the narrator tales of the patients' strange behavior, but in so telling, they duplicate it: one clucks like a chicken, another is convinced he has two heads, another that he is a tea kettle, and a fourth that it is more proper to get "outside, instead of inside of her clothes."[16] Maillard assures him, however, that these ludicrous behaviors are due simply to the provincial habits of the asylum keepers: "Odd!—queer! Why, do you *really* think so? We are not very prudish, to be sure, here in the South—do pretty much as we please—enjoy life, and all that sort of thing."[17] The keepers have, however, been through a recent trauma. As Maillard explains it, one of the patients, "who, by some means, had taken it into his head that he had invented a better system of government than any ever heard of before—of lunatic government, I mean . . . persuaded the rest of the patients to join him in a conspiracy for the overthrow of the reigning powers."[18] Under this new regime, "the keepers and kept were soon made to change places," with the former "shut up in cells forthwith, and treated, I am sorry to say, in a very cavalier manner."[19]

Before Maillard can explain how a "counter revolution" was effected, he and the narrator are interrupted by "loud shouts and imprecations" coming from beneath the windows. Again, in an eerie foreshadowing of the ending of Weiss's play, where the patients form a military column and "suddenly the whole stage is fighting," even spilling out toward the audience in an orgy of violence and sexual energy, Poe's story ends with a rapid shattering of the facade of civility promoted by the moral treatment movement: "Gracious Heavens!" says the narrator, "the lunatics have most undoubtedly broken loose!"[20] Howling incoherently, the intruders smash windows, beat the door with "what appeared to be a sledge-hammer," and terrify the revelers within. Several members of the dinner party have been playing musical instruments, and they strike up a version of "'Yankee Doodle,' which they performed, if not exactly in tune, at least with an energy superhuman" as their tarred and feathered captives rush in, like so many "Ourang-Outangs, or big black baboons of the Cape of Good Hope."[21] (In *Marat/Sade*, too, the patients sing a revolutionary song as they lash out in fury at the end.) After receiving a beating at the hands of the asylum attendants–turned-captives–turned-rebels, the narrator rolls under a sofa, where he realizes the truth about his host, Maillard.

> In giving me the account of the lunatic who had excited his fellows to rebellion [he] had been merely relating his own exploits. This gentleman had, indeed, some two or three years before, been the superintendent of the establishment; but grew crazy himself, and so became a patient. The keepers, ten in number, having been suddenly overpowered, were first well tarred, then carefully feathered, and then shut up in underground cells. They had been so imprisoned for more than a month, during which period Monsieur Maillard had generously allowed them not only the tar and feathers (which constituted his "system") but some bread and abundance of water. The latter was pumped on them daily. At length, one escaping through a sewer, gave freedom to all the rest.
>
> The "soothing system," with important modifications, has been resumed at the *chateau;* yet I cannot help agreeing with Monsieur Maillard, that his own "treatment" was a very capital one of its kind. As he justly observed, it was "simple—neat—and gave no trouble at all—not the least."[22]

Angry, dark, apelike figures crashing into the mansion, upsetting a genteel dinner party and violently subduing their bon vivant Southern keepers: unsurprisingly, this ending has generated numerous critical readings that turn the story into a parable for a slave uprising. (Simian characters in Poe's stories "Murders of the Rue Morgue" and "Hop-Frog" are often read as the author's stand-ins for racist images of blacks: subrational human simulacra whose resemblance to humans masks a barbarous tendency for violence.[23]) The most subtle of these readers is J. Gerald Kennedy, who suggests that Poe was "attempting to register his apprehensions about abolitionism and immediate emancipation without dismissing the cruelty of bondage," by constructing "a problematic analogy between madness and blackness that the tale itself ultimately deconstructs." The twists and turns of the story, according to Kennedy, ultimately yield two incompatible but necessary implications: "1) all abolitionists are insane, or 2) anyone who assumes the position of a slave feels a justifiable longing for freedom."[24] The revolt is frightening, nearly apocalyptic, and it calls up images of an intractable race war that Thomas Jefferson had predicted as the eventual outcome of abolition in his *Notes on the State of Virginia:* "Deep-rooted prejudices entertained by the whites; ten thousand recollections, by the blacks, of the injuries they have sustained; new provocations; the real distinctions which nature has made; and many other circumstances, will divide us into parties, and produce convulsions, which will probably never end but in the extermination of the one or the other race."[25] As in Jefferson's vision, "Tarr and Fether" provides ample justification for the captives to turn on their masters in the "injuries they have sustained," and yet—again following Jefferson—immediate emancipation would seem only to unleash retribution more barbarous than the "provocations" that justified it.

This racial allegory does not fully explain the situation of the "big black baboons," who are—after all—former keepers and difficult to parallel cleanly to slaves. And yet the racial symbolism is indisputably *there* in their blackened features and simian howling: Poe taps into the imagery of animalism that had coursed through Western representations of racial difference and insanity for centuries. Poe himself participated directly in this strand of natural history, helping to translate Baron Cuvier's famous work on the resemblances and distinctions between apes and humans. Other works of popular natural history, some of which Poe no doubt read, emphasized apes' natural ferocity and propensity to attack humans.[26] This linkage finds its way into his story "The Murders in the Rue Morgue," where a detective—citing Cuvier as an authority—establishes that an escaped orangutan has run amok in the streets of Paris, killing two white women.

For a moment, as the former keepers burst forth from the cellar, they appear to embody what Sander Gilman has called "the nexus of blackness and madness," which structured perceptions of each group through the lens of the other.[27] Just as blacks were frequently understood as a sub- or semihuman race, the notion of animal madness has a long provenance in the history of perceptions of insanity, which Gilman traces back at least as far as the biblical description of Nebuchadnezzar, who "was driven from men and did eat grass as oxen."[28] The late sixteenth- and early seventeenth-century

French doctor André du Laurens, who wrote one of the first popular treatises on madness, viewed madness as a form of bestiality:

> Consider the action of a frenetic or a maniac, you'll find nothing human there; he bites, he screams, he bellows with a savage voice, rolls burning eyes, his hair stands on end, he throws himself about and often kills himself so. Look at a melancholic and how he lowers himself so that he becomes a companion of beasts and only likes solitary places.[29]

If madness was a reversion of humanity to bestiality, it was akin to racial otherness. Gilman even shows that as far back as the medieval period, madmen were represented as having darkened skin, which was taken as evidence of their excess of "black bile."[30] Accordingly, as with the study of racial differences, the empirical search for evidence of madness often had recourse to the surfaces of the body. This tactic recurred through the Enlightenment, where it provided impetus for physiognomists like Johann Caspar Lavater to scrutinize the bodily (especially facial) markings of the insane, on the theory that "everything in the world has an internal as well as external aspect, which stand in direct relationship to each other."[31] And in the nineteenth century, phrenologists also attempted to generalize about the skull formation of the insane, with frequent comparisons to black subjects: "It is striking," wrote one phrenologist, "how similar the pronounced jaw line [of an "idiotic" woman] is to the skull of a Black. For it is evident that decadent structures among civilized peoples are often similar to the typologies of uncivilized peoples."[32] Such attempts to make mental or psychological deviance visible on the skin, to stabilize its disorder as an essentially somatic or quasiracial state, persisted well into the late nineteenth and early twentieth centuries, when theories of racial degeneration prompted the mass sterilization of "mental defectives."[33]

The leaders of the moral treatment in asylum medicine, however, thought of themselves as challenging earlier dehumanizing scientific understandings of insanity. They regularly deplored earlier treatments of the insane as fit only for beasts; in the words of Edward Jarvis, Pinel "had the unprecedented courage in 1792, to unchain [the asylum's] miserable occupants, and to treat them as human beings."[34] In the legal arena, they fought to include the category of "partial insanity" (meaning either a temporary bout or an affliction of only part of the brain) as exculpatory, replacing earlier definitions of insanity that demanded a continuous and visible state of "furious mania" and a reversion to near-bestiality[35] (fig. 10). The notion that insanity was a regression from civility to barbarity (if not outright an-

FIGURE 10. "Madness," in *Essays on the Anatomy of Expression in Painting* by Charles Bell (London: Longman, Hurst, Rees, and Orme, 1806).

imalism) persisted, but this was largely a matter of environmental, rather than purely hereditary or racial susceptibility. Poe's friend Pliny Earle, superintendent of the Bloomingdale asylum in New York, attempted to reverse the age-old stigmatization of the insane as "a race of beings entirely distinct."[36] In his essay "The Poetry of Insanity," which drew attention to the creative powers of asylum patients, he castigated a low curiosity in the antics of the insane and the popular view that they were animalistic monsters. Instead, the insane still cherish "the germs of moral beauty," and can be "bowed even unto childish tenderness by the power of filial affection." In fact, "the little child is in no place more secure from harm, and no where more caressed than in the halls of a Lunatic asylum."[37]

The apparent "big black baboons" that break out of Poe's *maison de santé* seem to reactivate all the associations of animality, monstrosity, violence, and otherness that Earle's sentimental rhetoric tries to combat. Poe's asylum is most decidedly not a place in which one might entrust a "little child" to the tender caresses of a lunatic. In fact, it is really something like a zoo with no bars or glass panes separating the observer from the beasts within. The clucking, braying, and lewd behavior of the patients is both ironized and real: the narrator would have been well advised to heed the warning from the friend with whom he has set out on his adventure. The friend, declining to enter the asylum, cites "his very usual horror at the sight of a lunatic"—a horror that eventually infects the narrator when he sees the "fighting, stamping, scratching, and howling . . . army"[38] breaking through the windows. Such imagery recalls not only traditional views of bestial lunatics, but fearful whites' renditions of the Haitian uprising (1791–1804), in which slaves were aroused to a pitch of animalistic fury. One observer wrote of frantic whites choosing suicide over falling prey to the voracity of black violence: "Their hideous howlings and shouts of exultation rose far above the noise of the cannon and musquetry, and raised forebodings of horror which made every [white] heart tremble."[39] Poe's reactivation of this horror seems to argue that reintegrating the insane (or the blacks) into the civilized human family is folly, a perversion that will only boomerang on the liberal humanitarians who oversee the project and lead to a spasm of orgiastic violence. He fears what Sade celebrates in Weiss's play: "What's the point of a revolution / without general copulation?"[40]

BUT WHO are these "big black baboons," and why do they burst forth with such fury? When one unravels the story, the neat symmetry between lunatics and slaves descended from Africa evaporates, for the fact is that the blackened, simian figures who smash through the dinner party are not staging a revolt but a counterrevolution. Instead of representing the pent-up, animalistic fury of slaves or the bestial, regressive tendency of lunatics, their fury is that of the rightful enforcers of the social order who have been turned into its victims. If one traces their fury back to its roots, one might be tempted to read the story as a shrewd anatomy of simmering class resentments in a postrevolutionary bourgeois society rather than as a warning of an apocalyptic race war or as a commentary on the bestiality of the insane.

The first detail that bears remarking is that the narrative takes place in a "private Mad House" rather than a "public hospital."[41] Private asylums by their nature held patients from elite backgrounds; the social standing of the attendants and perhaps even the doctors would therefore be below that of most of the patients (fig. 11). Those whom we see first as eccentric keepers but then realize are patients are "apparently, people of rank—certainly of high breeding."[42] The medical historian Roy Porter has argued that the earliest private asylums were created in the context of a shift to a service economy, in which patients (and families) of means paid for services that once were performed within the community. They demanded a certain level of service from those below them, and Porter makes it clear that the cure was generally secondary to the function of service.[43] Poe emphasizes that "the regulations of these private mad-houses were more rigid than the public hospital laws," but the regulations seem to apply more to the asylum's attendants than to the patients. Under the "soothing system," the attendants were enjoined, Maillard tells the narrator, never to use the word "lunacy" and to "repose confidence in the understanding or discretion of [the] madman."[44] But if the pride of the patients was protected, what about the dignity of the keepers? At a "private Mad House," one can easily imagine the pressures on such a group to know their place and to remain tactful, discreet, and subservient, even while holding the keys to the patients' barred rooms. Who, after all, would calmly persuade Eugénie Salsafette to get back inside her clothes when she had chosen to dress herself by getting outside of them? Who would gently coax Bouffon Le Grand down from the dinner table where he declaimed in the voice of Cicero from one of his heads and the voice of Demosthenes from another? Behind the scenes and between the lines, one might wonder who would clean the feces from the wall, all the while indulging the patients' high regard for themselves and their breeding? Here Poe hints at a class disturbance that is actually more far-reaching than Weiss's: the avowedly Marxist playwright analogizes the patients to the oppressed proletariat but never sees that the asylum workforce might have its own grudges against their social superiors.

Adding to the routine challenges and even the humiliations of their trade, Poe's asylum attendants had to face an acute spike in job insecurity. Because the patients were given so much freedom and authority ("a great point was to set each lunatic to guard the actions of all the others"), asylum management was "enabled to dispense with an expensive body of keepers."[45] Surpassing the routine silent humiliations of their professional existence in the asylum is the outrage that occurs when their own supervisor,

FIGURE 11. Illustration from Edgar Allan Poe's "The System of Doctor Tarr and Professor Fether," in *Nouvelles Histoires Extraordinaires* (Paris: A. Quantin, 1884).

Monsieur Maillard, turns on them capriciously and joins the patients whom they have overseen, giving patients run of the asylum and confining the keepers to the dungeon—tarring and feathering them, for good measure, and putting them on a bread-and-water diet while the rightful inmates frolic in the old chateau above. All this is certainly a recipe for a murderous, even revolutionary (or counterrevolutionary) outburst.

But why does Maillard switch sides? In the story's rapid unraveling, the narrator informs us that some years earlier, Maillard "grew crazy himself, and so became a patient,"[46] and then led the patients in an uprising against their former captors. But rather than release all of the liberated inmates, he chooses to keep them on as "friends and keepers . . . my very good friends and assistants." They all seem perfectly content to stay in the former chateau, ransacking the wine cellar and appropriating the fantastical clothing of the (perhaps guillotined) family that had once lived there. The narrator, in one of his early intimations that something might be wrong, notices that the keepers' "habiliments, I thought, were extravagantly rich, partaking somewhat too much of the ostentatious finery of the *vielle cour* [*sic*]," though most of the clothes are ill-fitting and "by no means . . . what a Parisian would consider good taste at the present day."[47] Their strange tics and delusions betray that they are not well, but Maillard himself seems quite in control, quite rational throughout the story. So why does he choose to stay among them? For what reason does he continue to put on the show of running the asylum, when his new "keepers" are deranged and the former ones are howling below? The story presents a simple answer, one as plain to see as the famous envelope in "The Purloined Letter." Maillard is "a portly, fine-looking gentleman of the old school, with a polished manner."[48] He likes tea parties. He likes opera. He likes banquets with witty (if deranged) repartee. Like other asylum superintendents of his day, he is a social climber, desiring professional authority but perhaps also a life of grace and elegance.[49] One can imagine that in postrevolutionary France, such a figure would have experienced the Revolution as a glorious opening onto a future in which men of his class and training can take over the elevated roles in society once held by the aristocracy—especially given the hagiography surrounding Pinel. And yet here he is, a solitary figure of authority in an asylum (a converted chateau, no less), with the presumably proletarian attendants below him and "Monsieur Kock" and "Mlle. Laplace" held in silken fetters. Who would be the better dinner companions? Who the more sensitive artistic souls? Which side would he choose to be on?

Maillard, in a sense, appears to have chosen class solidarity over institutional order, a dissipated life at the top rather than an orderly life enforced by those from below. When the patients lock up their keepers, it is in one sense a simple reversal: those in shackles lock up those in control. But in another sense, it is simply a clarification of who is really on top in a private asylum–an institution committed to the indulgence rather than the restraint of privileged mental patients.

To widen the analysis back out to the Revolutionary context, Poe's story appears to hint at what Marx—according to Hannah Arendt—found to be the reason for the Revolution's failure to bring about freedom: "that it had failed to solve the social problem" of structural economic inequality.[50] Evidence of this failure was proliferating throughout Europe, especially in the workers' unrest that would lead to the Revolution of 1848. In this sense, Poe casts Maillard's "storming of the Bastille" not as a real liberation from tyranny but simply as an unchaining of bourgeois lunatics and imprisoning of the asylum work force. (As Weiss's Marat says: "Fellow citizens / did we fight for the freedom of those/who now exploit us again."[51]) The rightful patients are members of the bourgeoisie who strive to imitate the old aristocracy, wearing their clothes, drinking their wine, and lording it over their social inferiors. The freedom from restraint that the patients enjoyed under the "soothing system" (echoes of Pinel liberating the insane, of the historical Maillard storming the Bastille) gives them a sense of entitlement that knows no bounds and leads to the chaining of those who would place any limits on their behavior. Not that Poe offers a Marxian lament about the limits of revolution and its institutional aftereffects. Poe is far more pessimistic, even apocalyptic, than that. The story's resolution is hardly an advertisement for a final revolution that will settle "the social problem" once and for all. We are not offered the perspective of the keepers-turned-captives in this story; they are presented to us only as a mob of angry, bestial, even simian (counter) revolutionaries howling and scratching at the windows.

LIKE MARX, nineteenth-century asylum boosters believed that the Revolution and the democratic systems it spawned did not adequately address "the social problem"; unlike Marx, however, they located the source of this lingering conflict in the psychic stress of receiving too much liberty too fast, rather than in the lack of social equality in the new order. Despite Burke's vision of the asylum as a space of restraint rather than humanitarianism, their critique of revolution is in some sense more like Burke's than like Marx's or Weiss's. It is not far from Burke's fear that revolutions would exile the newly liberated "from this world of reason, and order and peace, and virtue, and fruitful penitence, into the antagonist world of madness, discord, vice, confusion, and unavailing sorrow" to Amariah Brigham's comment (quot-

FIGURE 12. Engraving from Tony Robert-Fleury's painting, "Pinel Freeing the Insane" (1876). (Yale University, Harvey Cushing/John Hay Whitney Medical Library)

ing the French physician Pariset) that "the more there is of liberty . . . the more numerous are the chances of mental derangement." The solution for Brigham and his generation of asylum superintendents, however, was not to favor despotism or a return to the stability of an established order, but to follow liberty and democracy's path toward humanitarianism, for "liberty is favorable also to the expansion of human reason."[52] The humanitarianism of asylums was, in their view, a direct manifestation of revolutionary liberty, but it also served to check the spread of destabilizing revolutionary impulses. Modern-day asylums were, in short, the outcome of the Revolution and a stay against social breakdown. Poe's story seems designed to dismantle this kind of thinking, which found its articulation most forcefully in the fashioning of a cult of Pinel rather than in fully fleshed-out argument.

Pinel's (supposed) great act of liberation—ultimately memorialized in Tony Robert-Fleury's great 1876 painting, *Pinel Freeing the Insane* (fig. 12)—

was, for the boosters of the moral treatment movement in asylum medicine, the symbol of a more just, rationally ordered society administered by
trained professionals. Pinel himself had gained his education in Enlightenment circles in both Toulouse and Paris; after encountering Benjamin
Franklin in the famous salon of Madame Helvetius, he was so impressed
that he considered moving to the United States.[53] Instead, in 1784 he became
the house doctor in a private mental hospital for wealthy patients. Increasingly, however, his interest focused on the fate of the insane poor, whose
treatment he urged both on humanitarian and scientific grounds. This was
often considered proof of his egalitarian sensibility, but according to Klaus
Doerner, Pinel believed that only by treating indigent patients could physicians make a proper scientific study of insanity, because the poor had fewer
means to resist the experimental treatments of their socially superior keepers than did the rich.[54]

Pinel was originally a strong supporter of the Revolution, and his ideas
about the proper treatment of the insane were given reinforcement by the
Declaration of Human and Civil Rights of August 25, 1789, which viewed
the insane as "free" and "equal" and stated that no person could be arbi-
trarily incarcerated. This led to an investigation of the *hopitaux généraux,*
where paupers, political dissidents, and those labeled insane were all held,
sometimes by *lettres de cachet.*[55] Directors of these institutions were rep-
resentatives of the monarch, and they enjoyed absolute control over the
populations they housed.[56] In December of the same year, the Revolutionary Constituent Assembly declared that all *hopitaux* were to be abolished
or at least brought into accordance with the new laws of the republic. In
March 1790, the Constituent Assembly ordered the release of all those held
through *lettres de cachet,* "except for sentenced or accused criminals and the
insane"; the latter group was to be either released or cared for in special
hospitals for the insane. But the problem was that there *were* no special
hospitals for the insane. Since many religious churches' shelters for the insane had been closed in the wake of the Revolution, the only solution was
to concentrate the mentally ill paupers at Bicêtre and Salpêtrière. Adding to
this, public fear of the insane mandated new laws that held communal ad-
ministrations responsible for the harmful actions of released lunatics. And
so—in an ironic reversal of Barrère's prediction—the number of mental
patients increased after the Revolution.[57]

Amariah Brigham would later define Pinel's appointment as medical director of Bicêtre in 1792 as a watershed moment in the treatment of the insane. It was due to this event, in the eyes of Brigham and other nineteenth-

century American asylum superintendents, "that Correct views respecting the treatment of the insane began to prevail."[58] Brigham, Jarvis, and other psychiatrists considered Pinel's heroic unchaining of the fifty-three maniacs an emblem of mental medicine's liberation of the treatment of the mentally ill from the tyrannous exploitations of the old regime. Recent historians have presented two problems with this interpretation. First, Pinel did not unchain the patients at all: Dora Weiner has shown that only 10 of the 270 patients at Bicêtre were chained when Pinel took charge and that Pinel himself "accepted the traditional use of chains to restrain the violent insane as a matter of course."[59] Second, the humanitarianism of Pinel's administration (he did renounce punishments and attempted to engage each of his patients in serious conversation about their problems) borrowed heavily from eighteenth-century nonmedical practices, particularly those developed by lay superintendents of asylums in England and France, and so his mode of treatment was not simply an extension of his republican faith.[60] These borrowings from earlier practices and continued reliance on constraint do not invalidate Pinel's republican credentials, but they do make Edward Jarvis's claim that Pinel single-handedly "opened men's eyes and the prison doors of the insane" hyperbolic.[61]

Pinel's intellectual affinities with Enlightenment and political sympathies for republicanism mark him as a creature of the revolutionary age, as do his complaints that the French aristocracy had a stranglehold on the medical establishment: "I very much wish that in medicine a sound judgment, a natural wisdom, and inventive mind, *devoid of all other privilege*, counted for something."[62] Good supporter of the bourgeois revolution that he was, he delighted in his triumph over the aristocrats and their tightly controlled medical circles, and he advocated opening science to the free marketplace of ideas. However, that same bourgeois mentality led him to a rather more conservative position once the Revolution had been completed: his class was among the victors and wanted to protect its position. Pinel, unlike Poe's Maillard, never took his revolutionary commitments to the extremes of a Burkean nightmare. "Tarr and Fether" presents a scene of retribution against the asylum keepers—feeding them only bread and water, chaining them "hand and foot" and treating them "in a very cavalier manner"[63]—that was in some ways akin to the Reign of Terror that Burke predicted in his *Reflections*. Pinel, on the other hand, recoiled from the excesses of the Jacobins. Upon the execution of the king and the advent of the Reign of Terror, Pinel withdrew from political life and focused on medical reform, which would provide guidelines for the rational organization of the new society rather than a continuing attack against vestiges of the old regime.[64] And in marked contrast to the utopian optimism of Barrère, he believed that the Revolution actually produced new types of insanity. In his *A Treatise On Insanity* (1801), he argued that revolution unleashed dangerous passions and that education and order were necessary to control those passions.[65] His reign at Bicêtre and later at Salpêtrière was authoritarian (even as he devoted himself to the principle of *douceur*, or gentleness): the superintendent, he believed, should have ultimate control over every aspect of administration and the daily lives of patients. In this, he set the tone for the following generation of asylum authorities.

Enlightenment-era faith in reason and nature and an attempt to moderate the effects of revolution course through Pinel's case studies, several of which read like background papers for Poe's story. There is the case of the tailor who was convinced that his disagreement with the Jacobin punishment of Louis XVI would cause him to be guillotined. Pinel treated him, like so many others, with his theater of reason (see chapter 2): he staged a mock-tribunal, which pronounced him not guilty, whereupon the patient was cured of his delusion.[66] Or there is the case of the man who fancied that he had a snake inside of him. Pinel gave the man an emetic, causing him to vomit, and then arranged to have a live snake placed in the vomit. The man believed that he was divested of his parasite, and the delusional behavior ceased. In much the same way, Poe's inmates are *"menagés,* humored." As Maillard explains it:

> We contradicted *no* fancies which entered the brains of the mad. On the contrary, we not only indulged but encouraged them; and many of our most permanent cures have been thus effected. There is no argument which so touches the feeble reason of the madman as the *reductio ad absurdum*. We have had men, for example, who fancied themselves chickens. The cure was, to insist upon the thing as a fact—to accuse the patient of stupidity in not sufficiently perceiving it to be a fact—and thus to refuse him any other diet for a week than that which properly appertains to a chicken. In this manner a little corn and gravel were made to perform wonders.[67]

Pinel's system marked his faith in the powers of reason to triumph over delusion, in rational structures to contain disorder, in a trained professional class to manage the excesses of the Revolution. Delusion takes itself to its own extreme, confronts itself with its own inner absurdity, and will fall apart in the face of reason, personified by the doctor himself. Poe's Maillard repeats this logic, and yet the story itself denies it. In telling of how the asylum keepers constructed dramatic scenes in which patients play out their fantasies, he is actually constructing a new drama for the narrator, in which delusions are presented merely as harmless eccentricities, in which madness is cloaked as reason, and in which his own role as doctor/authority and patient/rebel are thoroughly intertwined. Rather than being struck by the light of reason, the narrator is instead struck by the ape-men themselves, who inflict on him "a terrible beating—after which I rolled under a sofa and lay still." [68] What collapses here is not unreason but reason itself, and the result is not a revolution conducted in the name of enlightenment (either a medical revolution or a political one), but a continuing spiral of violence and unchecked lunacy. Poe seems to agree with Pinel's followers that revolution produces madness; but he disagrees that bourgeois liberalism is the solution. For Poe, postrevolutionary society is a struggle between the genteel lunatics on top and the brute force of the mob below.

Notwithstanding Poe's biting irony, Pinel's theories were taken up enthusiastically within American culture, where faith that liberty and order could coexist impelled faith in correctional institutions that were both humane and protective. David Rothman writes that the image of Pinel unchaining the inmates at Bicêtre "had an immediate and obvious appeal to men in the new [American] republic. They too had just emerged from bondage and intended to bring freedom to others." [69] But while the medical authorities who claimed his mantle cited Pinel's "liberation" of the maniacs—casting themselves in the role of Stanislaus Maillard storming the Bastille—their position was really closer to the conservative posture of postrevolutionary Pinel. The self-consciously moderate American psychiatric interpretation of revolution begins with Benjamin Rush, signatory of the Declaration of Independence and the foremost medical authority of the early republic. In his *Medical Inquiries and Observations, Upon the Diseases of the Mind* (1812), Rush wrote that "certain forms of government predispose to madness," by which he meant the arbitrary rule of monarchs, which frustrates the people's "just and exquisite sense of liberty." So far, a good revolutionary position. But where "the conflicting tides of the public passions" surge, outbreaks of violence—assassinations and even revolutions—occur, causing epidemics of "derangement." And so while tyranny may cause madness, revolutions enacted to undo that tyranny only make matters worse, from a standpoint of mental health. Likewise, democracy was necessary to promote a free exercise of mind (repressed political urges could cause mental strain); however, too much political freedom promoted mental as well as social instability.[70] Accordingly, France's continued unrest meant that "there were three times as many cases of madness in Paris in the year 1795 as there were before the commencement of the French Revolution"; in contrast, in the relatively stable United States, where property-owning white men still held all the political power and Jacobin sympathizers like Thomas Paine were politically marginalized, madness has occurred "rarely from a political cause."[71] Rush's conservative embrace of the Revolution can be divined from some of the political/psychological disorders he diagnosed: on the one hand, opposition to the Revolution might lead to a disease called "revolutiona," and women could be cured of hysteria by supporting the Revolution; on the other, an excessive passion for liberty might lead to a disorder known as "anarchia."[72]

Rush ran the nation's first mental ward, in the Pennsylvania Hospital of Philadelphia. Although he accepted Pinel's theory of psychological treatment for some cases (including an emphasis on amusements, directed reading, musical instruments, and carriage rides), his methods of confronting delusion tended more toward humiliation and ridicule than humoring and reasoning.[73] He cited approvingly the case of a man who thought he was a plant and was cured of his delusion when "one of his companions, who favoured his delusion, persuaded him he could not thrive without being watered, and while he made the patient believe, for some time, he was pouring water from the spout of a tea-pot, discharged his urine upon his head. The remedy in this case was resentment and mortification."[74] And in general, much of Rush's treatment regime was an elaboration of the "heroic" school of medicine. He purged; he bled; he even invented a "gyrator," which spun patients around on a board to increase the pulse, and a tranquilizer chair, which bound lunatics at the head and hands to reduce the flow of blood to the brain.[75] The remedy for chronic lying was to be beaten by a rod, shut up in solitary confinement, or starved; problems of faith—either a failure to recognize "the truths of the Christian religion" or those who "deny their belief in the utility of medicine" could be addressed by subjecting the patient to "great physical pain."[76] In the view of Nancy Tomes, his overall stance toward patients was that of the animal trainer; he even allowed visitors to pay a small fee to visit, creating a "zoo-like atmosphere" in the hospital.[77]

The subsequent generation of American mental health practitioners—the first to form a professional network, the Association of Medical Superintendents of American Asylums for the Insane (AMSAII)—often cited Rush, like Pinel, as a precursor, but they backed away from Rush's "heroic" methods in favor of the gentler psychological therapeutics of moral treatment, always presenting themselves as benevolent despots who would return those damaged by modernity and liberty to a position in which they could rule themselves. As the director of the Charenton asylum in *Marat/Sade* puts it:

> We're modern enlightened and we don't agree
> With locking up patients We prefer therapy
> Through education and especially art
> Faithfully following according to our lights
> The Declaration of Human Rights[78]

And yet, like the director, their authority was absolute. According to Robert Castel:

> The liberal society and the totalitarian institution functioned like a dialectical pair. . . . To the very extent that the contractual society became generalized, it required the rejection of those who could not play its game. . . . In a laissez-faire context dominated by a market economy, the criminal and the insane could most assuredly not be left to their own devices.[79]

To Castel, liberal democracies used asylums to disqualify the illegitimate players in a contractual society; the "kindness" and "humanity" of the medical regime only masked the fact of their totalitarian power.[80]

Castel's thesis overreaches, because it does not take into account the enormous pressure on asylum superintendents—at least in the American context—to release patients from their care within a short period of time. The extraordinarily high cure rates cited in asylum reports year after year put self-generating pressure on superintendents to make their authoritarian reign over the lives of the mad a temporary one, in service to a larger liberty that was psychologically precarious to navigate. The doctors took pains to impress upon the public, as well as their patients, that despite their absolute sovereignty, they were guarantors of the patients' liberties, rather than captors. One issue of the *American Journal of Insanity* included an article entitled "Celebration of the Birth-Day of Pinel at the State Lunatic Asylum, Utica, N.Y. April 11, 1846." It included the information that the event was "got up" at the suggestion of the patients, "with the approbation of Dr. Brigham, to manifest their deep sense of reverence for the character and memory of that great friend of humanity, and their gratitude for the benefit which they, with thousands of others in like circumstances, had received from the results of his labors of love in that great cause." Taking place in the asylum chapel, which was decorated with French and American flags and engraved with portraits of Pinel and his successor Esquirol, it featured performances by patients, letters from important asylum superintendents who could not attend in person, and visits from local authorities. The asylum choir sang a hymn in Pinel's name ("From fettered limbs, imprisoned hearts/He struck the galling chain;/And in the image of his God/The maniac rose again"); the asylum chaplain gave a prayer, and then a patient gave an oration on the life of Pinel and his importance in the treatment of the insane. Finally, patients read odes, including one written especially for the occasion by Lydia Sigourney—a friend of Dr. Brigham's and one of the best-loved poets in the country:

> Whereso'er, to reason blind,
> Moans the sick, imprison'd mind,
> Whereso'er, from misery's rein
> Springs to health and peace again,
> Set by hallow'd science free,
> There, Pinel, thy praise shall be.
>
> So thy name shall never die,
> And beneath this western sky,
> In the country of the free,
> Grateful hearts remember thee,
> And on this, thy natal day,
> Wake for thee, the votive lay,
> Who in mercy's cause so brave
> Didst the lost and hopeless save.[81]

The massive ideological coercion of the event contrasted almost laughably with the emphasis on patients' consent and freedom. (The patients were said to have "got up" the exhibit; they spoke and sang in their own voices; they were figured as the descendants of the unchained prisoners at Bicêtre, and so forth.) As with their efforts to promote the *Opal*, authorities were invested in making the patients speak—as if freely—the institutional line.

Such heavy-handed pageantry—or perhaps puppetry—notwithstanding, the authorities' preoccupation with the inherent contradictions of their role in a democratic culture bespeaks sensitivity to the relations between social organization and mental health that have been lost in our contemporary society. Even Poe's story, which is a fierce corrective to the superintendents' posturing, is a sign of another time, a literary trace of a lost world in which what happened to the insane might reflect on an entire society, especially one that prided itself on reason, liberty, and justice. That Poe's narrator would stop to visit the asylum at all on his travels through France reflects a culture-wide curiosity about the social situation of the mad that has been all but lost.

AT THE END, however, we are still left with the troubling image of the apelike men running amok through the asylum. F.O. Matthiessen famously excluded Poe from his pantheon of the American Renaissance because he was "bitterly hostile to democracy"[82]; if we accept the PR of the asylum movement that it was an institutional guarantor of democracy, then Poe's ape-men certainly smash through this democratic institution in a bitterly hostile way. The racial imagery can qualify this: Poe might be suggesting, as some of his more recent critics have argued, that the animalistic qualities of those of African descent will make abolition a catastrophic mistake. The complaint, then, would not be so much against liberty and democracy, but against their extension to black persons. Or it could be, as Kennedy suggests above, that slavery itself is the problem—that slaves will eventually call on the same revolutionary principles to attack their keepers as their keepers called on to liberate themselves. (The "Yankee Doodle" theme playing at the end certainly brings this to mind.) Finally, the strong hints of labor unrest in the story imply yet another reading: the bourgeoisie, having deluded themselves that they are the new elite, the new kings of the castle, will create another powder keg by finding new ways to exploit—and misrecognize—the labor on which they depend.

That readings of the story as a racial allegory have to some degree supplanted critical interest in Poe's treatment of insanity *as* insanity and asylums *as* asylums (instead of as metaphorical plantations) is symptomatic of the relative invisibility of mental illness as an area of concern in humanities scholarship.[83] I am not suggesting that the story is about insanity any more than it is about race (or revolution, or class and labor); Poe's artistry is such that an easy solution to the story's riddles is impossible. What the narrator flees at the end may be the necessity of untangling the story, of tracing out the implications of foreboding that are so clear in the unfolding tableau at the *maison de santé*. What links the issues together, is that they all point to the problem of the nonrational actor's place within a liberal, postrevolutionary society. In this way, Poe thematically anticipates certain strands of disability studies, which show how categories of race and physical and/or mental disability have been mutually constitutive in American history, defining each other by shuttling tropes and images across zones of discourse, and defining liberal individualism by presenting images of its negation.[84]

This linkage was not theoretical or abstract for Poe. As a Southerner (he was born in Boston but raised on his uncle's Virginia plantation) writing to a national audience in the face of growing sectarian tensions over slavery, Poe was acutely aware of the volatility of American race relations.[85] But as a man whose erratic behavior and literary celebrity made his psychological state a frequent matter of public speculation, his concern with the national discourse surrounding insanity was no less pressing. Gleefully chronicling Poe's alcoholism and strange—sometimes one-sided—battles within the literary world, several newspapers printed rumors that Poe was on his way to an asylum.[86] A year after he wrote "Tarr and Fether," one of his antagonists, fellow writer Thomas Dunn English (whom Poe had recently sued for slanderously suggesting that Poe had committed forgery), published a novel in which a character clearly modeled on Poe is locked up at Utica in a murderous, drunken rage.[87] Although Poe never did become a mental patient, his extremes of frenetic activity and despondency along with his copious drinking made him the subject of a case study by the British alienist Henry Maudsley, which was reprinted in 1860 in the *American Journal of Insanity*.[88] Through the nineteenth century and well into the twentieth, a significant strand of Poe criticism involved diagnosing his mental illness and finding its effects in his writings.[89] And so while the "big black baboons" of the story may, in a sense, stand for racial otherness, if madness was a kind of psychological blackness, then the ape-men were also something that he may have feared within himself.[90]

Much of Poe's literary career suggests a kind of overcompensation for his fears of the baboon within: he wrote tales of ratiocination that featured a detective capable of deciphering any irrational disturbances in the social order with an almost superhuman logic; he delighted in solving coded messages his readers sent to his newspapers; he crafted essays in aesthetic theory that stressed the poet's need for rational control over every element of his literary universe. In this stance, he posed as the hyperrational asylum superintendent who could decipher any apparently random, disordered, crazy, or violent behavior and bring it back into the light. But "The System of Doctor Tarr and Professor Fether" suggests that if he thought of himself as a superintendent, he was more like Maillard than like his famous detective Dupin or the supremely confident followers of Pinel. He could easily go over to the other side, because the irrational world was lodged inside him, ready to come "fighting, stamping, scratching, and howling" at the window like so many orangutans.

If *Marat/Sade* questions whether the bourgeois revolution has really advanced the cause of freedom, Poe's story questions whether freedom is ever compatible with security: social, political, or psychological. Although his portrait of the asylum leaves little hope for resolving the contradictions inherent in managing disorder in a liberal society, it does at least face the hard questions so painfully evaded in Emerson's work. In challenging the authority of depersonalizing, normalizing institutions in the democratic culture he so hoped to foster, Emerson blinked when it came to asylums. The moral treatment movement, however, also had its blindness. In depending so heavily on the universal convertibility of unreason to civility, it examined neither its own presuppositions nor the resistance it might encounter. For all Poe's nihilism, he had the virtue of never flinching, in part because he had made a career of staring down the animal within.

CHAPTER SIX

———— ✳ ————

Out of the Attic

Gender, Captivity, and Asylum Exposés

VIRTUALLY COINCIDENT with the rise of the asylum movement in the nineteenth century was the rise of a new genre of captivity narrative: that of the patient wrongfully deemed insane who, upon release from an asylum, bravely exposes the institution that deprived him or her of the rights of an American citizen. After narrating his harrowing stay at McLean in the early 1830s, Robert Fuller moralized that "the liberty which we have enjoyed, and which the half finished monument on Bunker Hill was intended to commemorate, has vanished.—Let that monument be torn from its base,— we are no longer worthy of it."[1] In this literature of countersubversion, the back asylum wards—where the unruly patients were kept, out of sight of visitors—are filthy, violent, raucous places where the mania of the patients is matched by the wanton sadism of the attendants. In one account, a man is killed for kicking over a water pail.[2] In another particularly gruesome tale—one pilloried by asylum authorities as evidence of continued mental illness—attendants kill several patients on a whim, even roasting one alive.[3] Nearly every former patient who published a memoir protested that his or her incarceration in an asylum was a matter of disciplining deviant political and/or religious views. Far from representing American ideals of life, liberty, and the pursuit of happiness, they were bastilles, slave pens, or institutions more worthy of the Inquisition than of the American republic.

Some of these narratives sold well, although not always on terms that the authors intended. Phebe Davis's exposé of the Utica asylum, which the author of another exposé faulted as being detrimental to the cause, nevertheless went through four print editions; but in its sequel, she noted painfully that her local paper had mentioned that "the extensive sale of her work proves that there are more lunatics out of the Asylum than inside of it."[4] Internal evidence in many of these texts suggests that authors read each other's work. Moses Swan, for instance, wrote that "since I left the asylum I have availed myself of books written by different authors who have been shut up in lunatic asylums, whose disclosures correspond with the facts herein set forth in regard to the treatment of patients."[5] This self-conscious participation in a literary community indicates not just a narrative genre in the making, but the developing seeds of a protest tradition, one that would extend through the nineteenth century with the reportage of Nelly Bly (published in book form in 1887 as *Ten Days in a Madhouse*) and into the twentieth with such insiders' narratives of institutional life as Clarissa Lathrop's *A Secret Institution* (1890), Clifford Beers's *A Mind that Found Itself* (1908), Mary Jane Ward's *The Snake Pit* (1946), Ken Kesey's *One Flew Over the Cuckoo's Nest* (1962), Sylvia Plath's *The Bell Jar* (1963), and Kate Millett's *The Loony-Bin Trip* (1990). Most but not all of these were driven by a desire either to reform or to dismantle the power of psychiatric hospitals.

Radical as some of this later writing is, the first wave of American protest writing against institutional psychiatry generally shied away from the absolutist position that asylums should be abolished. Most writers in this burgeoning tradition accepted the central tenets of the moral treatment movement: that mental illness was a disease that should be cured by doctors; that treating patients in an enclosed environment would both protect them from perverting influences and keep society safe from the threat they posed; and that most of the patients inside were indeed insane.[6] Time and again, after detailing horrific abuses, the writers stop to praise this or that superintendent and to acknowledge the necessity and even essential humaneness of such institutions. Elizabeth T. Stone, whose 1842 memoir of her incarceration at McLean detailed her persecution for her religious views, conceded that "there is no dispute but what there should be such an institution as an Insane Assylum [sic]." Her protest was specifically against private asylums and seemed to endorse the logic of state-run institutions: "But let it come under the jurisdiction of the Legislature and not have all the power consigned into the hands of a few individuals, over a distressed class of beings, a money-making system, at the expense of happiness, in a great measure."[7] Protests against public asylums also by and large accepted their necessity, albeit in some reformed state. "Although I have received maltreatment, in asylums in New York and Vermont States," wrote Moses Swan, "I am not altogether opposed to these institutions, for there are insane persons who have no homes, yet I protest against maltreatment."[8] Such acceptance could be motivated by humanitarianism, as in Swan's case, or by a desire for law and order. In the midst of detailing the monumental idiocy of her captors, Mrs. George Lunt assures her readers that she does not contravene "the rational opinion of every social, intelligent being" that insane asylums are necessary. She is careful not to have imputed to herself a dangerous position: "As though some one would abolish them, or would, through falsely enthusiastic philanthropy, free all the inmates at once, thus launching upon society a fresh race of helpless beings incapable of self-protection"—or, she seems to imply, peaceable behavior.[9]

Typically, therefore, these protesters champion some sort of reformist agenda rather than a revolutionary liberation of all the inmates. Former patient Hiram Chase, a Methodist minister from Troy, New York, wanted to require a board of at least five asylum overseers chosen by the people to make a determination of each prospective patient's sanity, to be followed by a jury trial. Those five board members were to be doctors familiar with state asylums. This would ensure that the asylum superintendent did not have total control of "the destinies of so many hundreds of souls." Additionally, he advocated regulations governing doctors' use of medicine beyond a certain period of confinement and treatment.[10] Phebe Davis wanted the physicians to be older, for "we need fathers here, but we have only boys."[11] She was also opposed to the admission of "foreigners" in "any of the public institutions in the United States." (She found that Catholics in particular "took delight in annoying the American ladies."[12]) Finally, she felt that "insane institutions are built much too large and too far apart. There should be about four in the State of New York, where there is now only one, for I noticed that the nearer a patient's friends were to the institution, the better they were treated."[13] Most of the others simply wanted asylum superintendents to live up to the ideals of the asylum movement instead of abandoning them.

The reasons for this moderation on the part of the protesters are several. First, unlike advocates of the abolition of slavery, who formed the greatest protest movement of the nineteenth century, these men and women primarily argued not on behalf of an entire class of people, but on behalf of themselves. They were motivated at least as much by efforts to reclaim their social standing and reputations as by any sympathy for their brothers and sisters in bondage. They did not want to eradicate the social distinction between sanity and insanity—as most black (and some white) abolitionists wanted to eradicate the social distinctions between the races—but simply wanted to prove to the world that they were sane. That distinction, of course, depended on the notion that others truly *were* insane; and so the pages of these memoirs are filled with descriptions of the delusional, bizarre, and sometimes frightening behavior of fellow patients. Writing of the patients he encountered on the notorious eleventh hall of the Utica asylum, Hiram Chase declared: "Many of them are so crazy they are obliged to be kept bound, some in cribs, some hand-cuffed, some tied down in seats, some with muffs, and many of them in strait jackets. I am not censuring anybody for this, unless it be the patients themselves, who have brought themselves to this state by imprudence and debauchery." [14] Moses Swan described patients who "are more fit for penitentiaries than places like these." [15]

Despite the protesters' desire for more humane treatment, the effect of these narratives, then, was often to legitimize the custodial aspects of the asylum and to call into question the more ennobling goals of the moral treatment movement. If the patients who could benefit from medical treatment, elaborate cultural programming, and finely kept grounds were in fact threatened by being thrown in with violent maniacs, then perhaps the best response was to retain only the hardest cases and to release the "curables"— those in whose name the asylums had been established in the first place. The narratives alone, of course, did not cause the downfall of the moral treatment movement in asylum medicine. The hopelessly inflated cure rates offered by asylum superintendents were in time exposed; this gave cost-cutting legislatures strong arguments to reduce funding for state institutions. The Civil War added new financial burdens on the states and diverted the nation's attention from the problems of mental illness and the promise of new treatments; additionally, it introduced a new generation of shell-shocked veterans whose disturbances presented challenges that the often complacent and programmatic asylum superintendents were ill equipped to handle. Even more threatening to the old asylum regime was the emergence of a new generation of neurologists who prided themselves on empirical research and derided the older asylum keepers (not entirely unfairly) as bourgeois gentlemen who had no scientific basis for their claims. And new theories of degeneracy being developed by European alienists classed insanity as a dangerous, hereditary condition that posed a threat to the strength of nations. The enterprise of returning the insane to civilized society was not only misguided; it was dangerous to the species.[16] Charles Darwin himself wrote, in *The Descent of Man* (1871) that "civilized men" built "asylums for the imbecile, the maimed, and the sick" while "our medical men exert their utmost skill to save the life of every one to the last moment. . . . Thus the weak members of civilized societies propagate their kind." [17] In the age of social Darwinism, neurologists and many others came to view the civilizing mission of the mid-nineteenth-century asylum as at best an anachronism and at worst a positive threat to humanity.

Amplifying these economic, political, and intellectual forces were the words of former patients critical of the asylum regime. One woman's work in particular helped to bring some of the reformists' agenda to pass by weakening the authority of the superintendents, an important factor in the downfall of the utopian asylum movement. This was Elizabeth Parsons Ware Packard, whose memoir of her confinement in the state insane asylum in Jacksonville, Illinois, sold well enough to support her in the years after her release and helped usher in a wave of legislation—known as the Packard laws—limiting superintendents' powers to admit and detain patients (especially female ones) in numerous states.[18] Her allegations were spectacular: that her husband, a Calvinist minister, had confined her in order to keep her from spreading her own more feminized version of Protestantism (she believed that the Holy Ghost was "the Mother of the heavenly Christ"[19]) and also to keep his children from her influence; that the asylum superintendent, Dr. Andrew McFarland, admitted her only on the word of her husband and two physicians who were in her husband's Bible group; that McFarland essentially held her as a prisoner in order to satisfy her husband, while knowing full well that she was sane; and that McFarland's motives for holding her included a sexual attraction for her, which—despite her early affection for him—she rebuffed. She recounted horrifying stories of the abuse of patients, and—particularly poignant in this postbellum narrative—frequently compared the plight of patients to slaves. Like most of the other asylum protests, however, Packard's did not call for the abandonment of the asylum system. She simply wanted greater oversight: "legislation—such as will hold the Husband and Superintendent both amenable to the laws of this Republic in the exercise of their legal power over the wife and the insane patient"[20] (fig. 13).

By aligning "the Husband" with "the Superintendent," Packard marked the asylum as a bulwark of American patriarchy that was aligned with the institution of marriage; she is remembered today as much as a protofeminist as an advocate of patient rights.[21] Indeed, upon her release from the asylum, she found herself imprisoned in her husband's home, subject to the whims of a tyrant far more abusive than the one who ran the institution which she charged with mounting "inquisitions, which [Americans] are blindly sustaining, under the popular name of charitable, humanitarian institutions."[22] In addition to reforming the admissions procedures for

No. 1.   No. 2.

Kidnapping Mrs. Packard.

"Is there no man in this crowd to protect this woman!"   See page 59.

No. 1.—"And this is the protection you promised my Mother! What is your gas worth to me!"   See page 61.

No. 2.—"I will get my dear Mamma out of prison! My Mamma shan't be locked up in a prison!"   See page 62.

FIGURE 13. Illustration in Modern Persecution, or, Insane Asylums Unveiled by Elizabeth Parsons Ware Packard (Hartford, CT: Case, Brainard, and Lockwood, 1873).

insane asylums, then, her political agenda included reforming marriage laws to ensure women's property rights after marriage, a goal that—in the immediate aftermath of the Civil War—she referred to as "Married Woman's Emancipation." [23] Again and again, she compared her condition as an asylum inmate to that of a slave: "Like the fugitive, I claim protection under the higher law, regardless of the claims of the lower." [24]

The ideological conflation of women's rights and abolition is a story well told in American history; it usually begins with the Seneca Falls convention in 1848, organized in part by Lucretia Mott, an abolitionist who was outraged at being denied a seat at an international antislavery meeting in London. Increasingly, female abolitionists came to question their own disenfranchisement and second-class citizenship, a condition whose similarity to slavery was acknowledged by figures such as Frederick Douglass, who attended the convention, and by the most famous white abolitionist, William Lloyd Garrison, who addressed the Fourth National Women's Rights Convention in 1853. For all the moderation of her legislative goals, it was Elizabeth Packard's significant achievement to include designations of insanity along with those of race and gender in the national discussion about freedom that abolitionists and feminists had regenerated. (Garrison, however, inadvertently anticipated her on this score in his remarks at the convention: "The Common Law, by giving to the husband the custody of his wife's person, does virtually place her on a level with criminals, lunatics and fools, since these are the only classes of adult persons over whom the law-makers have thought it necessary to place keepers." [25])

But why was the most successful of former patients' attacks on institutional psychiatry during the moral treatment regime conducted by a woman, in the name of women's rights? And if reforming the asylum meant reforming other powerful American institutions, why was it marriage that came in the line of fire? It is true, as Packard protested, that many state laws allowed husbands to commit their wives to insane asylums "without the evidence of insanity required in other cases." [26] But male patients occupied asylum wards in roughly the same numbers as females, and as numerous narratives by male former patients make clear, the susceptibility of women to the authority of their male superintendents and husbands in no way implies that men were exempt from arbitrary detention and the specter of the stigma of insanity. In fact, one could argue that institutionalization was more of a threat to nineteenth-century masculinity than to femininity, since many of the chief liberties that were rescinded by the asylum authorities were male prerogatives: the rights to vote, draw up wills, and, in some instances, hold property (women ceded these latter rights to their husbands under the law of coverture.) Recent scholarship has shown that men's illnesses were more likely than women's to be ascribed to immoral behavior like alcohol abuse or sexual promiscuity; that women—unlike men—were more likely to be sedated rather than physically restrained for violent behavior; and that women were more likely to be discharged cured than were men.[27]

The convergence of asylum reform and women's rights is particularly striking when we consider that the abolition of slavery often highlighted the struggles of black men, and for over a century afterward the figure of the "freedman" rather than the "freedwoman" was considered the standard bearer of abolition. In iconography, the end of slavery is represented most memorably by Thomas Ball's Emancipation Memorial in Washington, DC, with its image of a standing Lincoln reading the Emancipation Proclamation while a kneeling male slave breaks the chains of slavery. The nearest analogue in asylum reform is Tony Robert-Fleury's 1876 painting *Pinel Freeing the Insane*, which represents male wardens liberating a disheveled young woman while Pinel stands erect, gazing on the spectacle of chained madwomen in various states of undress (see fig. 12 in chapter 5). Elaine Showalter reads the spectacle of female depravity on display in this painting as an indication of the association of madness with femininity, and yet, one might view it as anticipating the convergence of feminism and the critique of institutional authority that came in the twentieth century by suggesting that institutional confinement was mainly a method of controlling—or abusing—women.[28] Although the painting does not so much propagandize for the liberation of women as it does for their transfer from an abusive authority to a properly paternalistic one, it indicates visually the narrow rhetorical opening that institutional confinement could offer for women, rather than for men. For Elizabeth Packard, freeing herself from the institutional matrix of authoritarian marriage laws and a patriarchal asylum regime allowed her to fulfill her role as a wife and a mother. It is hard, conversely, to imagine a former male patient adapting Frederick Douglass's famously macho line about the emasculation of slavery and the potency of freedom: "You have seen how a man was made a lunatic (slave); you shall see how a lunatic (slave) was made a man"[29] (a fight with his overseer ensues, in which the overseer is given a sound thrashing).

A generation of feminist critics and historians in the United States has essentially elaborated on the conflation of the women's rights movement with the asylum protest tradition that Packard's appeals brought to prominence. In her influential *Women and Madness*, Phyllis Chesler argued in 1971 that "madness and asylums generally function as mirror images of the female experience, and as penalties for *being* 'female,' as well as for desiring or daring not to be."[30] Chesler viewed Packard as a trailblazer who revealed that psychiatric institutions "tend to mirror or support the institution of marriage," a situation Chesler found held as true at the end of the twentieth century as it had during Packard's lifetime.[31] Sandra Gilbert and Susan Gilbar's *The Madwoman in the Attic* (1979), a pioneering work of feminist literary analysis, does not explicitly address the historical conflation of feminism and asylum reform; but, like Chesler, the authors found that women (especially women writers) in the nineteenth century were doubly oppressed by restrictive social conditions and by an association with madness. The recurrent image of the confined madwoman in nineteenth-century women's fiction, they argued, was a figure for women's frustrated creative energies in a patriarchal society that denied them avenues of expression; the madwoman was a "double" for the writer's own secret self who allowed the writer to express "her own raging desires to escape male houses and male texts."[32] Elaine Showalter, in *The Female Malady* (1985), argued against the dangerous romanticism of madness indicated in Gilbert and Gubar; instead, she viewed feminine madness as "the desperate communication of the powerless." Showalter acknowledged that women were not always more susceptible to confinement in institutions than men were; nonetheless, she accepted Chesler's notion that the conjunction of madness and femininity was pervasive both in cultural and medical realms in the last two centuries of social and literary history. "Madness," she wrote, "even when experienced by men, is metaphorically and symbolically represented as feminine: a female malady."[33] Finally, in her feminist analysis of asylum memoirs, *The Writing on the Wall* (1994), Mary Helene Wood returned to Packard herself, reading her narrative as a forceful protest against a patriarchal culture that defined in an extraordinarily confining way "to what extent women could be considered rational beings."[34]

Each of these works builds powerfully, directly or indirectly, on Packard's protofeminist attack on the authority of the asylum by highlighting the ways in which psychiatric institutions could be used to do a patriarchal society's bidding. But they do not explain where Packard's attack came from, what conditions in the nineteenth century enabled her to come out of the attic—that is, what enabled her to represent her situation as a lunatic in a way that emphasized gender politics, and what allowed her message to be heard when the cries of many other former patients—and virtually all male patients—went unheard. The history of the asylum, in this light, is remarkable as much for the unusual role it opened up for women to speak out against a powerful institution as it was for levying what Chesler called the "penalties" for being female.

One reason Packard found an opening for protest where so many men did not is that Packard frequently cast her appeals as defending traditional gender roles, rather than attacking them. Her husband, she argues, had abandoned his proper role as her "protector" by persecuting her: "It was the *protection* of my identity or individuality which I was thus claiming from my husband, instead of its subjection, as *he* claimed." [35] Critics of Packard's reformist agenda sometimes pointed out that Packard admitted in her memoirs that she fell in love with Dr. McFarland and hinted that spurned affection may have prompted her vendetta against him and the institution he represented. But Packard addresses this issue in the memoir itself, citing her earlier love for McFarland as the natural feelings of a woman who has been thrown from one protector to another: "In choosing him as my only earthly protector, I merely accepted of the destiny my friends and the State had assigned me, and in return for this boon thus forced upon me, I willingly offered him a woman's *heart* of grateful love in return, as the only prize left me to bestow." [36] In the words of Packard's biographer, "She wanted to be married and protected by a husband. In the absence of protection by him, she wanted protection from him." [37]

A broader factor licensing Packard's protest is that despite the paternalism of insane asylums and hospitals, care for the indigent and sick was still traditionally considered to be women's work. One of the few nineteenth-century institutions other than schools over which women exerted authority was orphan asylums, where female leadership was consistent with the exalted roles for women in the domestic sphere. [38] Insane asylums, too, were domestic spaces writ large; the asylum's model of a well-regulated family was of a piece with the proliferating child-rearing literature of the nineteenth century, much of it written by women such as Catherine Beecher and Lydia Maria Child, who—according to David Rothman—"wished to bring the rules of the asylum into the home." [39] And so a political program that attacked a prominent antebellum institution in the name of women's rights could avoid being cast as unfeminine because it spoke from a position of domestic, rather than overtly political, authority. [40] After all, the greatest champion of the asylum movement was a woman, Dorothea Dix, who saw herself as doing a woman's traditional work of caring for the needy while she plunged into the masculine realm of politics. Even as she took on state legislatures and formed political alliances at the national level, Dix opposed the reforms of the Seneca Falls convention and declined to give speeches in public out of a sense of feminine decorum.[41] And so a political role had been created for a woman like Packard before she came along to inhabit it: that of the critic of the asylum's institutional authority as an abuse, rather than a defense, of domestic order.

Finally, asylum care was in some ways less stigmatizing for women than it was for men. The leading causes of insanity for women were disturbances in their domestic roles, such as the physical stress of childbirth and nursing, intense emotions, uncontrolled passion, or tight lacing of corsets. For men, insanity was thought to be brought on by intemperance, prolonged study, intense application to business, or sexual indulgence (especially masturbation), all of which were either dangers brought on by the competitive world of nineteenth-century capitalism or were thought of as threats to success in a marketplace that demanded regulated behaviors.[42] Female patients could be cured by accepting the authority of the male physicians and transferring that acceptance back into their submissive roles as wives and daughters. In contrast, men were in something of a double bind: they had to passively accept authority within the asylum, but that acceptance was to be transmuted, somehow, into self-mastery and self-control on the outside. Carroll Smith-Rosenberg has argued that "the sick role" paradoxically empowered some women, who were temporarily released from the pressures of housework and relished a dynamic in which they could expect to be tended to rather than having constantly to care for others. Through bouts of hysteria or other women's illnesses, they "could express — in most cases unconsciously — dissatisfaction with one or several aspects of their lives."[43] Asylum care was an ordeal that most women would not wish for, but others wrote letters to their doctors thanking them for their care and remembering the asylum as a respite from their domestic duties. As one former patient of the Bloomingdale asylum wrote to Pliny Earle, "I think so much of you all that I shall continually recommend your establishment to all my acquaintances and friends and tell my husband to take me to no other place should Providence afflict me again as heretofore."[44] Men could be appreciative, too, but friendly letters from former male patients to Earle tend to be nervous in their acknowledgment: one man, who donated fifty dollars to the State Hospital for the Insane in Northampton, Massachusetts (where Earle had been chief physician since 1864) years after his release, wrote that "I am glad you did not mention my name in your report and would like it kept private all though I forgot to say so at the time."[45] Whereas men could lose their standing by entering an asylum, women could, in a sense, have theirs enhanced. Smith-Rosenberg writes that in such scenarios, it was not uncommon for women to manipulate their doctors by willfully refusing to be cured.[46]

And so when Elizabeth Packard spoke of her asylum tribulations, she still had a certain amount of gendered social capital to draw upon, in that her asylum stay did not rob her of her feminine authority in the way that a confined male might lose his masculine prerogative. As a writer, she drew strength from certain developments in literary culture as well. The grounds for Packard's campaign of asylum reform had been elaborately laid, in heavily gendered terms, in popular literature—especially in the very forms of writing that asylum superintendents warned the public against reading. In this explosive literature—whether coded as sensational or sentimental—the narrative of wrongful confinement almost invariably conformed to nineteenth-century literary conventions that feminized victims of social injustice. Packard's literary role was one that, paradoxically, treated women (including "madwomen") as passive victims of nefarious male power, but in so doing, it created an opening for a gender-based challenge to institutional authority.

IN THE WORLD of nineteenth-century popular fiction, it is only a small exaggeration to say that the moral treatment movement in asylum medicine never happened—or that if it did, it was an elaborate ruse for the confinement of women, the punishment of deviants, the gratification of unscrupulous relatives (usually husbands), and the sadistic pleasures of doctors and their attendants. Rothman identifies popular women's literature as a natural ally of the asylum movement in its frequently didactic appeal to regulating the emotions and sanctifying the values of the middle-class home; curiously, however, when this literature explicitly pictured the asylum, it frequently presented it as a site of abuse of women.[47] In the so-called sentimental novels so popular among middle-class women, the entrance of the asylum into the plot line almost inevitably signaled the oppression of a strong-willed woman by a scheming husband or another male villain. In Fanny Fern's enormously successful *Ruth Hall* (1855), the protagonist and her daughter visit a friend, Mary, who is a patient at an asylum architecturally modeled on the leading designs of the day: "Fair rose the building in its architectural proportions; the well-kept lawn was beautiful to the eye." They gaze at first on its "terraced banks, smoothly-rolled gravel walks, plats of flowers, and grape-trellised arbors," and then inquire of the gate-keeper about Mary, a beautiful, "queenly" woman confined at the will of her husband, who has

evidently grown tired of her frequent headaches and her reluctance to engage in "common female employments and recreations."[48] The gate-keeper
informs them that "her husband left her here for her health, while he went
to Europe" but that Mary had died.[49] Inside, the superintendent reveals
that he is "an intimate friend" of Mary's husband, a "fine man" who "left
her under my care." Ruth persuades him to let her see the corpse; and as
the matron leads her toward the body, she hears a woman screaming. The
chief female attendant explains that it is "only a crazy woman in that room
yonder, screaming for her child. Her husband ran away from her and carried off her child with him, to spite her, and now she fancies every footstep
she hears is his."[50] She goes on to explain that the woman had complained
to a judge about the loss of her children, but learns that "the law . . . as it
generally is, was on the man's side. She's a sight of trouble to manage. If she
was to catch sight of your little girl out there in the garden, she'd spring at
her through them bars like a panther; but we don't have to whip her *very*
often."[51]

A similar sequence occurs at the denouement of E.D.E.N. Southworth's
best-selling *The Hidden Hand* (1859). The novel recounts the story of a plucky
young orphan girl, Capitola Black, who is rescued from the streets of New
York where she has been passing as a boy in order to find work. Eventually,
Capitola discovers that she is the rightful heiress of a large Southern plantation, and the novel's swirling adventures all coalesce around the mystery
of Capitola's missing mother. It turns out that she had been the victim of
her nefarious brother-in-law, who, upon the death of his brother, schemed
to steal Capitola and lock up her mother in order to claim his brother's inheritance. First, in true gothic fashion, he locks her in an attic; then, as the
plot thickens, she is drugged with a delirium-inducing sedative and dragged
to a private mad house outside of New Orleans. She tells the superintendent her story, but he dismisses it as a hallucination; and so whenever he
presses her she lapses into a haughty silence: "Why should I speak when
every word I utter you believe, or affect to believe, to be the ravings of a
maniac?" Toward the end, she is found languishing at the asylum, "a large,
low, white building, surrounded with piazzas and shaded by fragrant and
flowering southern trees, [which] looked like the luxurious country seat of
some wealthy merchant or planter, rather than a prison for the insane."[52]
But a prison it is indeed, used "by some unscrupulous men, who wished to
get certain women out of their way, yet who shrank from bloodshed."[53]

In these sequences, virtually all of the themes that Elizabeth Packard
would stress thirteen years later are already present in fictional form: the

asylum as a space of male authority in which "difficult" women are put away at the convenience of men; the contrast between the outward serenity and inward chaos of the institution, as well as between its reputation as a space of healing and comfort and its actual practice of brutality; the connections between women's lack of legal standing and their subjugation both in marriage and in medicine; the use of the asylum as a tool to challenge women's natural role as primary caregivers for their children; the women's pleas of wrongful incarceration taken as further evidence of their insanity. Each of these novels used the plot of institutional confinement to make a challenging point about women's subordinate position in society (and especially in marriage); one critic notes that Southworth's male characters tend toward "tyranny . . . brutality, and stupidity" and that the novel undercuts the period's elevation of marriage to a sacred ideal.[54] One could easily say the same of Fern's novel, where the fiercely independent protagonist's liberation comes when she recognizes that in order to find her true calling (as a writer) she must do so outside of the confines of marriage; otherwise, she may find herself screaming in the back wards of an asylum.

Interestingly, the image of the asylum as a site for incarcerating troublesome women took on such a life of its own that in other forms of popular fiction, it came to symbolize other types of oppression and did political work quite apart from (and sometimes at odds with) the liberation of women or the reform of marriage laws. In the racy and violent urban gothic fiction favored by readers of the "mechanic" classes and indulged as a guilty pleasure by many young clerks, the wrongfully incarcerated woman was both a semipornographic image of captive femininity and a figure for the economic exploitation of workers by capitalists and moral reformers. Toward the end of *The Quaker City* (1844), George Lippard's rich fantasia of city crimes set in Philadelphia, readers are given an exterior view of an apparently genteel private hospital for the insane run by Signor Ravoni: "Twelve massive pillars of dark-hued marble rose from the variegated floor, to the dome above, and around each pillar, were clustered vases of solid stone, filled with rare and beautiful flowers, mingling their hues and perfume, while they rustled gently in the light. . . . Beyond these pillars, was a cloistered space, but dimly penetrated by the light, yet full of music and beauty."[55] The scene is complete with images of exotic plants, twelve shimmering fountains and a courtyard with chirping birds, an almost over-the-top version of the self-image of the insane asylum during the heyday of the moral treatment movement. But even the casual reader of Lippard and other urban gothic writers will know that the facade of Ravoni's institution is sure to conceal a chamber of horrors, since institutions of humanitarian reform are invariably figured in their work as sites in which the social elite abuse, enslave, and rape those who come under their control. In this case, the asylum turns out to confine beautiful brainwashed women who become the mad doctor's slaves; and the asylum subplot culminates in a postmortem operating theater, in which the dissecting table becomes the altar for Signor Ravoni's ascent to a demonic priesthood. In an orgiastic revelation of Ravoni's prophesy of a state of existence in which death is conquered, he raises his scalpel above the body of a decapitated ex-patient: "And then the bosom, ha, ha! The Scalpel makes love to it now!"[56]

Lippard's asylum/dissecting table scene was imitated and perhaps topped by his colleague and competitor George Thompson, whose 1855 novel *Dashington; Or, the Mysteries and Iniquities of a Private Madhouse* tells of a beautiful young somnambulist who is framed for a murder and "treated" in an asylum by a doctor who rapes female patients and threatens to kill troublemakers and sell their bodies to scientists for dissection.[57] Lippard's and Thompson's work, printed in the cheap yellow-covered format (identified by superintendents such as Isaac Ray as signals of disease-generating literature), has generally been understood as appealing to a working-class readership hungry for scenes that turned the tables on their social superiors, both by casting the urban elite as sadistic hypocrites and by openly indulging in a taste for sex and violence that bourgeois reformers were trying to stamp out.[58] At first blush, it is difficult to read these scenes in *The Quaker City* and *Dashington* as simple class-based criticisms of the asylum. Neither the workers who constitute the core implied readership for these novels, nor the noble working-class male characters who form their (weak) moral core are in danger of being confined in the institutions that are pictured; for the asylum scenes of the novels are set in expensive private mad houses rather than state-run lunatic asylums. But in each of them, the mental patient—and particularly the beautiful young female patient—becomes a surrogate for the suffering of the downtrodden. Significantly, in Thompson's novel, she is rescued by an asylum worker, a good-hearted attendant whom Thompson characterizes as *"nature's gentleman."*[59] What attracts Lippard and Thompson to these private mad houses is the ways in which defenseless human beings are turned into money for others; unscrupulous relatives try to fix wills in their favor by disposing of inconvenient family members; doctors are only too happy to lock up these unfortunates indefinitely as long as the family members continue to pay. The mental patient is in this way a figure for the economically abused; and philanthropy toward the insane is exposed as a cover for the economic exploitation of the vulnerable.

These novels vacillated between images of victimization (rape, dissection, and bondage) and revenge (violent retribution, exposure of hypocrisy, and attainment of wealth). In keeping with the intensely masculine perspective of the narratives, revenge was a male prerogative, and victim status was feminized. But the "madwoman in the attic" meets her grisly fate in the asylum in a wide range of fictional texts, from the gritty urban underworld of Lippard and Thompson to Fern's and Southworth's world of a female middle class striving for autonomy and respectability. Why would writers from such disparate social positions who were writing toward such different ends settle on the same figure? Part of the answer is that the feminization of victims was a long-standing literary strategy, one that could yield payoffs in a number of contexts. The ubiquitous captivity narratives that detailed the threats posed to European settlers living among "savages" classically featured white female captives held in bondage to red men.[60] By the mid-nineteenth century, picturing the confinement of defenseless women was a nearly universal strategy in writing about inequality. According to Amy Schrager Lang, reformers routinely feminized the objects of their philanthropic schemes in an effort to mask or minimize the threat that releasing them would pose to the bourgeois social order. In classic reformist texts such as Harriet Beecher Stowe's *Uncle Tom's Cabin* and Rebecca Harding Davis's *Life in the Iron Mills*, gender is at once "the lens through which substantial inequality becomes visible" and an obstacle to viewing the origins of social inequality in class.[61] To treat women as victims—or, in the case of Uncle Tom, to feminize victims—is to appeal to a male code of honor; if the victims were imagined as masculine, championing their cause might seem to threaten the prevailing order rather affirm its inherent justice. Even in the works of Lippard and Thompson, the fallen woman—either incarcerated in an asylum or forced into prostitution—might serve as a safety valve for readers' more radical urges; while the authors raise their readers' hackles at the injustice of the economic order, they also reaffirm the hierarchies of gender by saving the women from their sadistically imagined doom.

Elizabeth Packard, then, made her appeals on behalf of women's rights in a form that was familiar to readers as a method of restoring—rather than challenging—patriarchy.[62] Women novelists such as Fern and Southworth had subtly reworked the old image of the entrapped woman in order to question the patriarchal institutions (marriage and psychiatry) that held her, and Packard's critique of the social order that allowed her husband and her doctor to hold her in bondage reflected that movement. At her most radical moments, she compared the married woman's lot with that of the slave before the Emancipation Proclamation: "It is our legal position of *nonentity*, which renders us so liable and exposed to suffering and persecution." Women's special vulnerability to incarceration in the asylum makes their slave-like status clear: "If it were not for this *slave* labor, the State would be compelled to have double the number of attendants to do all this work, which it now gets as a gratuity out of its prisoners." But in the end, she simply wanted a reformed patriarchy, just as she wanted a reformed asylum regime. Despite her calls to allow married women to retain property rights and to equalize other aspects of the marriage bond, she affirmed that "Woman's love for man is based on the principle of reverence. We can never truly love a man who has never inspired in us the feeling of fear, or reverence. . . . Fear, respect, and reverence, are emotions which superiority alone can inspire." [63] To remove herself from one type of subordination, she pictured another, more perfect one.

BUT WHAT of male asylum protesters? What recourse did they have to redress their wrongs? And what language did the culture offer for them to shape their experiences? At first blush, it appears, practically none. In a culture that stressed male self-making, workplace productivity, and business competitiveness, an appeal to victim status could only reinforce one's alienation from the mainstream. Just as the broader culture lionized up-from-the-bootstraps masculinity, asylum physicians pathologized male laziness, failure, and nonproductive behaviors outside of the asylum, which they purported to cure by disciplining and reenergizing the male body.

Taming the male body but also reenergizing it: this was the special task of asylum physicians in regard to male patients. Elizabeth Packard learned how to speak within the domestic circuit that linked asylums to nineteenth-century notions of the home: in both spheres, she was a woman in search of protection, but she found it in neither. Men, however, could not hope so easily for a rescue, for a knight in shining armor to afford them protection: this was not a voice that they could find in the broader culture. Instead, the voice had to assert its own manliness, something that the asylum itself stripped away time and again. Male critics of the asylum resort to ever more fantastic images of conspiracy and violation in order to detail how their own self-control could be robbed from them, how they could find themselves wrongfully locked in the asylum to begin with. For instance, Hiram Chase wrote that he was removed from his position as minister by scheming congregants who objected to his being retained beyond the traditional two-year period. Once he was committed, he did begin to suffer religious hallucinations, but this was an *effect* rather than a cause of his confinement, in which he was forced by attendants to eat table scraps, in which his every action was under surveillance, and in which he feared to complain because he knew that these complaints would be interpreted as signs of his continuing illness.[64] The superintendent, he writes, is a tyrant who brooks no opposition to the smallest demand, and Chase's memoir is a narrative of being broken, being forced into a total submission to the asylum regime.

It is not surprising that when he published his memoir upon his release, the superintendent at Utica saw fit to contradict his charges, as well as to question his manhood. In the 1868 annual report of the institution, superintendent John P. Gray rebutted Chase's charges by reprinting notes on Chase's case from the patient casebooks. Though Gray does not name Chase's ailment (or its cause), here we find a portrait of a classic masturbator: "He is feeble in health, thin to emaciation, has no appetite, even loathes food; is sleepless, depressed under the delusion that he is utterly lost; that he has committed the unpardonable sin, mourns constantly over his state; declares that his family is coming to starvation, and that some have already perished." [65] And upon his release, he writes a book that is evidence only of his return to his former state:

> The next thing we hear of our clerical friend is through a sensational book, a loose, disjointed production, full of evidence of a threatened return of his former condition. This book of the unfortunate man, written under the shadow of disease, or rather, under the illumination of a disordered fancy, he calls his experience; and it may be received by many as such, although it is but the reminiscence and reflected flashes of his insane delusions during his stay in the asylum, and is just as true and real as those, and just as worthy of confidence.[66]

Chase was trapped by his own speaking position, that of the man too feeble to resist his tormentors or his own delusions, whether inside the asylum or out of it. Any attempt to stand up for himself and speak back to the doctors is a delusion brought on by his "disordered fancy," a mere simulacrum of male self-mastery. The figure of the "passive man"—thin, feeble, devoid of energy, unable to shift for himself—was the ruinous masculine correlative to the perfect female speaking position. The "sensational book" that Chase produced was in some sense like those other books that asylum physicians railed against: the ones that led boys and men to libraries and bookshops in search of the ubiquitous volume that "has something, prose, poetry, or picture, which can be perverted" to the service of male self-amatory practices.[67]

Luther Bell's anti-masturbation tract, *An Hour's Conference with Fathers and Sons, in Relation to a Common and Fatal Indulgence* (1840), reported that in both public and private asylums, masturbation was a leading—if not the leading—cause of insanity among men;[68] Nathan Benedict of the state asylum at Utica confirmed in 1851 that it was the leading cause there, too, mainly among men;[69] and Samuel Woodward of Worcester State Hospital for Lunatics wrote that "no cause is more influential in producing Insanity" than masturbation.[70] Bell found that especially prevalent among "the pale student of the school, the college, or the seminary," the foul practice turned once vigorous youth into profoundly passive sloths, minds and bodies wasted not from want of muscular capacity or nourishment, but instead from an "unnatural draught upon the nervous influence."[71] At least since Samuel Woodward's graphic reports of male patients masturbating openly in the Massachusetts asylum at Worcester, male patients were thought to be prolific onanists—masturbation being at once a leading cause and an indication of insanity. (There were scattered cases of erotomania and onanism in female wards of the asylum, but superintendents devoted scant attention to female self-pleasure; and in the popular imagination, female masturbators tended to become prostitutes rather than mental patients.)[72] Youths drawn toward the vice will forego sports and other "exciting plays of boys" for "some trashy novel, or sedentary amusement, because that energy and excitability of the system, which nature instinctively requires to be worked off in muscular exercise, has been expended, exhausted, wasted, in this unnaturally debilitating process."[73] Once gratified, the predilection fed upon itself:

> This same nervous exhaustion displays itself in a constant disposition to assume a recumbent position; to loll about on chairs, or the sofa; to lay on the bed in the day time, not for the purpose of sleeping, but to gratify this feeling of weakness; to read in bed at night, and to continue in bed in the morning, after being awaked. The mind becomes fascinated with the morbid gratification of exciting and libidinous reading and imaginings; the power of fixing the attention steadily and deeply is lost; and of grappling with any thing that is abstruse in studies. The imagination runs riot; day dreams, fanciful castle-building in the air, involving especially the sensual, usurp the place of the practical, and common sense views of things.[74]

The reading scene pictured is a kind of harem of one: it is both what the masturbator seeks and what beckons to him, luring him away from productive behaviors. It was crucial in the asylum not only to correct such nasty habits (through use of restraining straps, constant surveillance, blistering the genitals, and occasionally even surgical procedures), but also to provide rational and healthful amusements that would discourage such dissipation. Andrew McFarland (Elizabeth Packard's tormentor in the Illinois State Hospital for the Insane) wrote that asylum amusements were necessary distractions to keep patients from giving in to the "secret vices that gnaw . . . in the hidden recesses of the soul." [75]

Ellen Dwyer reports that many women in the nineteenth century turned themselves in to asylums in order to protect themselves from abusive and/ or alcoholic husbands,[76] but if male patients had been abused, it was most likely self-abuse that was at issue. As Russ Castronovo has argued, masturbation was frequently understood as a sort of auto-enslavement practiced by white males. An article in the *Library of Health* made the analogy clear:

> The public mind is, at the present time, all excitement about slavery—the slavery of two or three millions of our fellow men, by a nation professing to love and regard personal liberty beyond any nation on the globe. And why should it not be so? . . . Yet admitting it to be much more dreadful than it is, what is this sort of slavery compared with the slavery of man to himself, or rather, to his own appetites and lusts? And what is freedom, dear as in itself it truly is, to those who are carried captives by Satan at his will; who bow down their necks to the yoke of passion, fashion, appetite; and even rejoice in their own bondage?[77]

Even abolitionists sometimes accepted the comparison between masturbation and slavery; Garrison's antislavery newspaper, the *Liberator,* for instance, railed almost as forcefully against self-abuse as it did against Southern bondage. One reformer even saw the emancipation from self-abuse as the first stage in the assault on bondage of all forms: "We are not fit to plead the cause of Freedom until we get free from the tyranny of our own passions." [78] If men like Chase were charging that the asylum was a space of tyranny, the asylum authorities could turn the charge right back on the patients, submitting wild fantasies as evidence of a greater tyranny: the tyranny of their own passions.

In a culture that lionized male self-possession, then, to speak out as a victim was to court ruinous associations. Whether one had been sent to an asylum for masturbation or not, the male former patient was effectively neutered as an agent of protest by the very system that had entrapped him. Compared to the outpouring of sympathy that met Elizabeth Packard's crusade against the wrongful confinement of women, protests by wrongfully confined men met a deafening silence, proceeding from a culture reluctant to hear (or fearful of hearing) the voices of failed men. This is a dynamic that is explored with extraordinary artistry by Herman Melville in his short story "Bartleby the Scrivener." Melville himself seems to call up his culture's association of lassitude with masturbation when his narrator obliquely speculates that Bartleby might be a closet masturbator. One Sunday morning, as the narrator makes a visit to his office while killing time before hearing a "celebrated preacher," he is perturbed to find the door locked from the inside. When the key turns from within, he is greeted with the vision of Bartleby in his shirt sleeves, and otherwise "in a strangely tattered dishabille, saying quietly that he was sorry, but he was deeply engaged just then, and—preferred not admitting me at present." As the narrator slinks away from the office, he works himself up into a state of moral outrage. He wonders if "anything amiss" is going but ultimately convinces himself that Bartleby, whatever his eccentricities, would never "violate the proprieties of the day," nor the purity of the office space.[79]

By the end of Melville's story, Bartleby has been removed not to an insane asylum, but to the Tombs, where he is held as a vagrant. But in asylums, pale young clerks, nervously exhausted preachers, and other men who found themselves unable to master their passions and conform to the demands of the workplace haunted the halls. (Indeed, Samuel Woodward's portrait of one male masturbator sounds curiously like that of the most famous of nineteenth-century nonproductive men: "He was pale, feeble, nervous—lost his resolution—had no appetite—took to his bed much of the time, and became dull, almost speechless, and wholly abstracted in melancholy."[80]) And yet the sequestered masturbator remained largely a figure of fear, an externalization of an ambient dread of male incapacity, sterility, and failure. If female patients could be pictured—or occasionally could picture themselves—as slaves to the male-controlled institutions of marriage and asylum medicine, male patients' cries of victimhood were too easily read as an entrapment by oneself, a failure to transcend the body, a submission to pernicious fantasies and the poisoning elements of nineteenth-century culture.

EMERSON WROTE, in "The American Scholar," that one of the "auspicious signs of the coming days" which will see the emergence of a new, postrevolutionary cultural disposition, is that

> instead of the sublime and beautiful, the near, the low, the common was explored and poetized. That which had been negligently trodden under foot by

those who were harnessing and provisioning themselves for long journeys into far countries, is suddenly found to be richer than all foreign parts. The literature of the poor, the feelings of the child, the philosophy of the street, the meaning of household life, are the topics of the time. It is a great stride. It is a sign—is it not? of new vigor, when the extremities are made active, when currents of warm life run in to the hands and the feet.[81]

Emerson's comment could refer to the extraordinary interest shown to patients' writing in the *Opal*, or, for that matter, to former patients detailing their sufferings to the reading public. But what did the extremities have to say to those in the mainstream, and what could be heard? Melville's story anatomizes the impossible demands of a culture that presses, even forces, its Others to speak, but structures the language in such a way that no real communication is possible. Nineteenth-century asylums were full of chatter: doctors and attendants lecturing patients on morals and correct behavior; patient/pupils reciting lessons and compositions, debating each other to show their reasoning skills, and masquerading as minstrels or other ludicrous characters to show their mastery of folly; chaplains and their wards uttering the vows of a rationalized religion; visitors and legislators conversing with doctors and patients to satisfy themselves about the benefits of the institutions. The extremities may have been activated, but in each of these scenarios, patients were asked to play proper roles, to speak as if of their own free will but to tell their superiors what they wanted to hear. The superiors then would be confirmed in their benevolence, their humanitarian concern: they wanted to think of themselves as listening to society's victims rather than simply shutting them away. Elizabeth Packard found a way to carry on a dialogue under these terms while still retaining her sense of self and even criticizing the institution that structured her role. Melville's story recounts a perhaps more common response, from one who found himself unable to say anything meaningful at all. As the narrator presses Bartleby to speak, to tell him something, anything about himself that might explain his strange behavior, the clerk answers simply, and maddeningly, "I would prefer not to."

Echoes

HISTORIES OF psychiatry tell us that the moral treatment movement in America ended in the decades after the Civil War. And yet it is not entirely over, even today. In a strange coincidence that has prompted me to think about its legacy, my parents are—as I write this—en route to western Massachusetts, where my father, a psychiatrist, will be Erikson Scholar–in–residence at the Austen Riggs Center, a progressive psychiatric hospital that has carried on and developed some key features of the movement. I have written about the moral treatment in a historical light; he will have a chance to observe some of its traces in a living milieu.

As it happens, my father is not the first person in my life to make a connection with Riggs. In researching this book, I have thought frequently of Ike Schambelan, a friend who spent seven years as Riggs's theater director in the 1980s. On its Web site, Riggs explains that its focus on "therapeutic community" fosters patients' sense of citizenship through focus groups and "patient-government structures" as well as work programs and "an innovative program of arts and crafts." The latter was introduced by Joan Erikson, wife of the influential ego psychologist (and Riggs staff member) Erik Erikson. She described it this way:

> Art, crafts, drama, intellectual pursuits, involvement in the nursery school or greenhouse program are productive for personal growth and development in any individual. These activities . . . promote change in a positive direction, support competence, and enhance the dignity and identity of the person involved.

Today, the Web site tells us, "artisans and teachers—specialists in their fields, and not trained as clinicians—work with individuals and groups, opening possibilities for creative expression and the use of new skills." Patients perform serious full-length works in their own seventy-five-seat theater; they learn woodworking, ceramics, and other visual arts in studio space owned by the center; they maintain an on-campus greenhouse; and they serve as interns and aides in a Montessori preschool for local children, also on campus.[1]

Schambelan describes the theater program warmly, emphasizing the sense of autonomy and socialization it has engendered in patients, as well as its ability to train their attention in the way that only art can do. Key here was something that went well beyond the conception of the moral treatment's proponents: Schambelan's job was conceived as separate from the therapeutic dimensions of the hospital. He was not given information about patients' diagnoses, nor did he work directly with other staff to integrate the theatrical performances with other dimensions of patient care. He was expected to report back to his employer about patients' progress, but this was only in the context of their involvement in the artwork. In contrast to the steady surveillance of the nineteenth-century asylum, where art and writing were an integral part of the "total institution," at Riggs, art has, as Schambelan suggests, its own intrinsic therapeutic properties, which worked by the rules of art, not the rules of medicine or administration. And those artistic rules were stern: the patients, working often with local actors from the "outside," put on plays by Shakespeare, Brecht, Miller, and other demanding playwrights. Reviewers from local papers were not afraid to criticize actors, sometimes not knowing which of them were patients. The previous director even staged a patient performance of *Marat/Sade* (which Schambelan, understandably, felt hard-pressed to top).

The Austen Riggs Center was founded in 1907, a full generation after the demise of the moral treatment movement, but much of its philosophy would have met with the approval of Amariah Brigham, Pliny Earle, and their cohorts. (What Schambelan describes as its "loose and free" code of patient conduct, however, would not.) Interestingly—and sadly—it is a philosophy that has migrated back to the milieu in which it originated: elite, modest-sized private institutions that are well beyond the means of most of the nation's mentally ill. Several of the private asylums I have studied continue to function as elite psychiatric hospitals. McLean Hospital (since 1895 situated in Belmont, Massachusetts) is one of the most recognizable such institutions, offering "milieu therapy" to typically upscale patients.[2] It boasts on its Web site of having "the largest research program of any private psychiatric hospital worldwide" and ties to Harvard University's psychiatric neuroscience program.[3] Additionally, its well-known cast of former patients (including Ray Charles, James Taylor, Sylvia Plath, and Susanna Kaysen) testifies to its allure for established creative spirits who have lost their way. Still, perhaps the greatest appeal to potential patients and their families is suggested by its regular advertisements in such tony publications as the *New Yorker* and the Harvard and Yale alumni magazines, where the hospital's "unsurpassed discretion and services" are emphasized over medical and scientific advances. Unintentionally emphasizing the way in which such "discretion and services" are available only to a very small segment of the mentally ill population, both McLean and Riggs feature on their Web sites a seal indicating their stature among *U.S. News and World Report*'s "Best Hospitals of 2006." They are to psychiatric hospitals what Harvard and Williams are to institutions of higher learning—with the difference being that outstanding higher education is also available at public institutions in many states, while public mental health care for the disadvantaged is in crisis.

Riggs and McLean, among others, represent the endurance and maturation of some of the moral treatment movement's loftiest goals, albeit those available to only a narrow segment of society. Lovingly set in bucolic landscapes that are close to cultural centers, they attempt to promote dignity and to create a holistic—if regimented—social life for patients, often featuring artistic and creative endeavors, along with medical treatment and research. Another strand of the moral treatment movement persists in the art (or science, depending on one's perspective) of psychoanalysis. The concern with patients' expressivity exhibited in the nineteenth-century asylum movement's promotion of theater, writing, oratory, and debate has been inverted since Freud. Whereas for the moral treatment movement, cultural activity was offered as a way to control or tame madness, psychoanalysis sees artistic expression as an outlet for madness, a way to let it out in the open, where it will escape the filters of repression (often masquerading as civility) and come into a dialogue with reason. Indeed, the psychoanalytic therapy session is in some ways an artistic endeavor, where the analyst and analysand try to talk through the patient's inner disturbance, rather than to talk over it—as was the case in nineteenth-century asylums.

Both settings, however—the private "retreat" and the psychoanalyst's couch—are increasingly off-limits to non-wealthy patients and their families. And neither is in favor with insurance companies, drug companies, managed care corporations, and other private interests that shape an often ad-hoc policy toward the mentally ill.[4] Those whose madness cannot be held at bay by the new drugs and who cannot afford private institutions or expensive and time-consuming therapy sessions find themselves at extraordinary personal risk. Their options are often homelessness and intermittent stays in public (or publicly funded) psychiatric wards, hospitals, or halfway houses that are—as several recent series of exposés attest—underfunded, underscrutinized, overcrowded, and incompetently staffed. A 2002 *New York Times* exposé detailed the "stunning array of disorder and abuse" at privately run group homes that have received state contracts to care for the mentally ill since the closing of state psychiatric wards in the 1980s.[5] A recent investigative series in my hometown newspaper found 115 unexplained deaths in Georgia's public hospitals and concluded that "dangerous conditions in the hospitals arise from decades of disregard by public officials, chronic overcrowding and understaffing, and public indifference."[6] A federal investigation of the state system is underway.[7]

In literature and popular culture, a vogue for mental illness persists and in some ways has crested, as in the "outsider art" that exoticizes the creativity of the usually untutored mentally ill and sells it for high prices. Every year, it seems, a new Hollywood film or bestselling novel or memoir explores its protagonist's descent into madness. But we seem to want to hear stories of those who fall and bounce back, without thinking about why it is that only some can bounce. Few of these popular works portray the truly desperate situations of those lacking sufficient connections or funds to escape falling through the many holes in our social safety net. Susanna Kaysen's memoir *Girl, Interrupted* (1993)—one of the most sensitive (and commercially successful) recent portrayals of the life of the institutionalized insane, is set in McLean in the 1960s. Kaysen occasionally draws connections between the mentally ill and oppressed racial minorities, but she does not let us forget her privilege. After watching "Bobby Seale bound and gagged in a Chicago courtroom" on her television, one patient cries "They do that to me!" To her credit, Kaysen won't allow this kind of easy identification to stand without irony: "We were safe in our expensive, well-appointed hospital, locked up with our rages and rebellions. Easy for us to say 'Right on!'"[8] And yet she does not think past her own gilded cage, imagining the lives of those for whom the parallel might be more apt.

The problem does not end there, however, for in the 1960s and 70s, when the social situation of madness at the margins of society *was* represented powerfully to large audiences, the unintentional results may have been to weaken the protections given to the most vulnerable. Frederick Wiseman's searing documentary *Titicut Follies* (1967) and Ken Kesey's novel *One Flew Over the Cuckoo's Nest* (1962) presented damning visions of public institutions, perhaps helping to pave the way for small-government conservatives to reduce funding for state hospitals and leave the mentally ill to fend for themselves. At a time when Foucault, Szasz, and Goffman were leveling their critiques of institutional power, few voices were asking what would fill the void if such institutions were to vanish. *Titicut Follies*, which frames brutal scenes of patients being placed naked in solitary confinement and having feeding tubes forced up their noses with scenes from a patient-staff theatrical show, sends the message that patients' artistic pursuits are window dressing for an essentially barbarous institution. If vestiges of the moral treatment remain in view, they have been reduced to a depressing, half-hearted attempt to put a happy face on social death. And the film version of *One Flew Over the Cuckoo's Nest* (1975) ends with the protagonist—beaten down by the system—being euthanized by a fellow patient, suggesting that physical death is preferable to life in an institution.[9] The film thus presents an all-or-nothing choice that was in keeping with the more strident critiques of the period, but it does not suggest the possible difficulties if patients were cast out into the streets.

Powerful visual reminders of the collapse of the public investment in mental health dot our landscape. Many of the great public asylums constructed during the utopian moral treatment movement now lie in disuse, disrepair, or near-ruination. Typically built with thick stone walls separating small rooms with little functionality beyond their original design, and hugely expensive to maintain (and to cool and heat), they present major challenges to the small army of architects and historians who are interested in preserving them. Their crumbling edifices, smashed windows, overgrown landscaping, and locations at the periphery of urban centers are mute testimony to an almost-forgotten period in psychiatric care. What has been forgotten is not so much the goals or ambitions—McLean, Riggs, and their ilk have to some extent carried these on—but the sense of a shared civic obligation that these buildings once represented. Stand on the campus of one of these gigantic ruins and think that the public bore the expense for building and maintaining them; remember that their network spread through the Northeast and (by the middle of the nineteenth century) well into the South and Midwest; remember the audacity of Dorothea Dix's federal proposal and the narrowness of its defeat; and ask whether our society's collective response to the problem of mental illness measures up to that of an earlier age.

FIGURE 14. Pillar of Old Main building of the Mohawk Valley Psychiatric Center (formerly, the New York State Lunatic Asylum) in Utica, New York. (Photo by author)

I am not advocating a return to the moral treatment movement. Even given the most generous reading, the movement contained the seeds of its own undoing. To insist that controlling the environment could cure mental illness begged the question of who was doing the controlling, and on what terms. The claim of near-universal cure rates set up a calamitous fall from grace for the institution and hardened attitudes toward those who were manifestly not cured. Standardized methods of treatment for a dizzying array of psychobiological problems amounted to a denial of the particularity and diversity of human suffering, and superintendents' dogmatic insistence on their system without any kind of research program to question or refine it often amounted to a willful embrace of ignorance. Throwing drugs at patients haphazardly no doubt did at least as much harm as good, and uniformly separating patients entirely from their families and friends and other supposedly unhealthy influences was often cruel. Finally, the lack of sustained intellectual debate about the legitimacy, policies, and functions of these institutions allowed the superintendents to inhabit a dream world that was unchecked by critical thinking.

And yet, given all that, it is almost fantastical to imagine that the person in rags whom we may see today conducting conversations with imaginary entities in public spaces might, in a different era, have been attending tea parties, lecture series, daguerreotype workshops, theatrical performances, classes, editorial meetings, and fairs conducted inside the pillared grandeur of publicly funded asylums. But this fantastic dream is an aspect of our history. Though I have tried to show that this dream was shot through with delusions of its own, and that it was often experienced by patients as a nightmare, it is worth remembering that our society once was capable of thinking broadly and creatively—if not critically enough—about its responsibility toward those whom it deemed incapable of managing their independence (fig. 14).

Notes

INTRODUCTION

1. In his first month in office (July 1850), he signaled his alliance with the moderate Whigs, who favored the proposal to allow new states to hold referendums on whether to admit slavery by appointing Daniel Webster—the leader of the pro-Compromise faction—secretary of state. The following month, he sent a message to Congress recommending that Texas be paid to abandon claims to a portion of New Mexico, thereby convincing a number of Whigs to give up their insistence on the Wilmot Proviso, which had stipulated that all land acquired in the war be free of slavery. During this tumultuous time, he also backed legislation placing federal officers at the disposal of slaveholders seeking fugitives, which he attempted to balance by abolishing the slave trade in the District of Columbia.

2. In Charles M. Snyder, ed., *The Lady and the President: The Letters of Dorothea Dix and Millard Fillmore* (Lexington: University Press of Kentucky, 1975), 95.

3. An illuminating account of these proposals in the context of national politics is Thomas J. Brown, *Dorothea Dix: New England Reformer* (Cambridge, MA: Harvard University Press, 1998), 148–216. For documentation of these debates, see the sequence beginning with "Senate Debates On The Land-Grant Bill For Indigent Insane Persons," in the "Library" section of the Disability History Museum Web site, http://www.disabilitymuseum.org/lib/docs/1220.htm.

4. Herman Melville, *Moby-Dick* (New York: W. W. Norton, 2002), 419. On the centrality of architectural design to discussions of the proper treatment of madness, see Carla Yanni, *The Architecture of Madness: Insane Asylums in the United States* (Minneapolis: University of Minnesota Press, 2007); on the ventilation and heating of asylums, see pp. 12, 26, 31–34, 122–24.

5. Robert Castel, *The Regulation of Madness: The Origins of Incarceration in France*, trans. W.D. Halls (Berkeley: University of California Press, 1988), 97.

6. Ibid., 80.

7. The phrase comes from Erving Goffman, *Asylums: Essays on the Social Situation of Mental Patients and Other Inmates* (New York: Anchor Books, 1961), 13.

8. See Anne Digby, *Madness, Morality, and Medicine: A Study of the York Retreat, 1796–1914* (Cambridge: Cambridge University Press, 1985). The best study of the relation between the original "moral treatment" movement and the medical movement that co-opted it in the United States is Lawrence Goodheart, *Mad Yankees: The Hartford Retreat for the Insane and Nineteenth-Century Psychiatry* (Amherst: University of Massachusetts Press, 2003).

9. These last three causes are listed in Edward Jarvis, "On the Supposed Increase of Insanity," *American Journal of Insanity* 8, no. 4 (April 1852): 348-50. Others are frequently listed in asylum annual reports.

10. In Castel's fine phrasing, the asylum superintendent was a "modern figure of the philosopher-king," ruling over "a miniature Plato's republic" (*Regulating Madness*, 80).

11. On the faulty cure rates, see Norman Dain, *Concepts of Insanity in the United States, 1789-1865* (New Brunswick, NJ: Rutgers University Press, 1964), 120-21; David J. Rothman, *The Discovery of the Asylum: Social Order and Disorder in the New Republic* (Boston: Little, Brown, 1971), 130-32; Nancy Tomes, *A Generous Confidence: Thomas Story Kirkbride and the Art of Asylum-Keeping, 1840-1883* (Cambridge: Cambridge University Press, 1984), 292-93.

12. Nathaniel Hawthorne, *The House of the Seven Gables*, ed. Robert S. Levine (New York: W. W. Norton, 2006), 124, 174-75.

13. Ralph Waldo Emerson, "Experience," in *Essays & Poems* (New York: Library of America, 1996), 476.

14. Ibid., 478.

15. For a reading of Hawthorne's novel that emphasizes Hawthorne's incomplete acceptance of norms of sanity, sexuality, and middle-class propriety, see Christopher Castiglia, "The Marvelous Queer Interiors of *The House of the Seven Gables*," in *The House of the Seven Gables*, 472-93.

16. New York State, *Annual Report of the Managers of the State Lunatic Asylum*, vol. 1 (Albany: Carroll and Cook, Publishers, 1844), 51 (choir singing); ibid., vol. 2 (1845), 39 (countryside walks, lectures); John M. Galt, *Essays on Asylums for Persons of Unsound Mind: Second Series* (Richmond, VA: Ritchies and Dunnavant, 1853), 12 (debating societies, scripture reading); Commonwealth of Massachusetts, *Annual Report of the Trustees of the State Lunatic Hospital at Worcester*, vol. 9 (Boston: Dutton and Wentworth, 1842), 88 (elocution).

17. Commonwealth of Massachusetts, *Annual Report*, vol. 12 (1845), 91.

18. Rev. D.S. Welling, *Information for the People; or, the Asylums of Ohio* (Pittsburgh: Geo. Parkin & Co., 1851), 281-82.

19. Ibid., 280.

20. On the role of reformers in raising the cultural tone of the lower orders, see Thomas Augst, *The Clerk's Tale: Young Men and Moral Life in Nineteenth-Century America* (Chicago: University of Chicago Press, 2003), esp. 158-206. On parallels between nineteenth-century urban reform and the colonial enterprise, see Ann Laura Stoler, "Tense and Tender Ties: The Politics of Comparison in North American History and (Post) Colonial Studies," *Journal of American History* 88, no. 3 (2001): 829-65. On the relevance of postcolonial studies to disability studies, see Lennard J. Davis, "Crips Strike Back: The Rise of Disability Studies," *American Literary History* 11, no. 3 (Autumn 1998): 500-12; and Davis, *Enforcing Normalcy: Disability, Deafness and the Body* (London: Verso, 1995), esp. 90-92.

21. Michel Foucault, *Abnormal: Lectures at the College De France, 1974-1975*, ed. Arnold I. Davidson, trans. Graham Burchell (New York: Picador, 2003), 18.

22. Rothman, *The Discovery of the Asylum*, 109.

23. Ibid., 111-12.

24. Jarvis, "On the Supposed Increase of Insanity," 357.

25. Amariah Brigham, "Insanity and Insane Hospitals," *North American Review* 44 (January 1837): 91-120 (quote is on p. 91).

26. Isaac Ray, *Mental Hygiene* (Boston: Ticknor and Fields, 1863), 234-35.

27. Galt, *Essays on Asylums*, 14.

28. Ibid., 12. Most other superintendents disagreed with this position.

29. Michel Foucault, *Madness and Civilization: A History of Insanity in the Age of Reason*, trans. Richard Howard (New York: Random House, 1965), 259.

30. For this critique of Foucault and Rothman, see Michael Ignatieff, "State, Civil Society and Total Institutions: A Critique of Recent Social Histories of Punishment," in *Social Control and the State*, ed. Stanley Cohen and Andrew Scull (New York: St. Martin's Press, 1983), 75-105; and Gareth Stedman Jones, "Class Expression Versus Social Control? A Critique of Recent Trends in the Social History of 'Leisure,'" in ibid., 39-49.

31. On medical superintendents' struggles to achieve authority, see Tomes, *A Generous Confidence*; and Constance M. McGovern, *Masters of Madness: Social Origins of the American Psychiatric Profession* (Hanover, NH: University Press of New England, 1985). On power struggles within asylums, see Ellen Dwyer, *Homes for the Mad: Life inside Two Nineteenth-Century Asylums* (New Brunswick, NJ: Rutgers University Press, 1987), esp. 55-84.

32. Michel Foucault, *Psychiatric Power: Lectures at the Collège de France, 1973-1974*, ed. Jacques Lagrange, trans. Graham Burchell (Houndsmills, Basingstoke: Palgrave Macmillan, 2006), 47 ("procedure"), 7 ("battlefield"), 9 ("scene," "wearing down"), 16 ("microphysics"), 23 ("disciplinary"), 49 ("tissue," "bodies"), 55 ("pangraphic"). This lecture series, now in book form, connects Foucault's early work on asylums to his later work on prisons and sexology. See *Discipline and Punish: The Birth of the Prison*, trans. Alan Sheridan (New York: Vintage Books, 1977); *The History of Sexuality: An Introduction*, trans. Robert Hurley (New York: Vintage Books, 1978).

33. See James C. Scott, *Domination and the Arts of Resistance: Hidden Transcripts* (New Haven, CT: Yale University Press, 1990), 1-4.

34. The phrase "whole way of conflict" comes from E.P. Thompson, excerpt from "Review of Raymond Williams' *The Long Revolution*," in *A Cultural Studies Reader: History, Theory, Practice*, ed. Jessica Munns and Gita Rajan (London: Longman, 1995), 185.

35. Goffman, *Asylums*, 37.

36. William Hotchkiss, *Five Months in the New-York State Lunatic Asylum* (Buffalo: L. Danforth and Co., 1848), 36.

37. Ibid.

38. "Schools in Lunatic Asylums," *American Journal of Insanity* 1, no. 4 (April 1845): 326-40.

39. Rosemarie Garland Thomson, "Seeing the Disabled: Visual Rhetorics of Disability in Popular Photography," in *The New Disability History: American Perspectives*, ed. Paul K. Longmore and Lauri Umansky (New York: New York University Press, 2001), 348.

40. John F. Sears, *Sacred Places: American Tourist Attractions in the Nineteenth Century* (New York: Oxford University Press, 1989), 87-121.

41. Ibid., 89.

42. Rothman, *The Discovery of the Asylum*, 142.

43. Rachel Adams, in her book *Sideshow U.S.A.: Freaks and the American Cultural Imagination* (Chicago: University of Chicago Press, 2001), imagines the relationship between "the institutionalization of the mentally and physically disabled" and freak shows somewhat differently: "Whereas the freak show paraded the deviant body for all to see, the institution concealed abnormality from view." However, like me, she sees both developments as linked in a dialectical relationship: "Ironically, both [institutions and freak shows] performed the work of normalization by establishing standards for segregating the deviant from the normal" (15).

44. Pliny Earle, "The Poetry of Insanity," *American Journal of Insanity* 1, no. 3 (January 1845): 194.

45. Earle, "The Poetry of Insanity," 218.

46. See David A. Gerber, "The 'Careers' of People Exhibited in Freak Shows: The Problem of Volition and Valorization," in *Freakery: Cultural Spectacles of the Extraordinary Body*, ed. Rosemarie Garland Thomson (New York: New York University Press, 1996), 38-54.

47. "Editor's Table," *Opal* 2, no. 10 (September 1852): 318. An indication of this writer's sense of the importance of cultural activity in the asylum is his half-joking proposal that "the halls be turned into nine-pin alleys [and] the rooms into literary lounges."

48. See Ronald J. Zboray and Mary Saracino Zboray, *Literary Dollars and Social Sense: A People's History of the Mass Market Book* (New York: Routledge, 2005), esp. xvii-xix.

49. For a genealogy of this idea, see Georges Canguilhem, *The Normal and the Pathological*, in *A Vital Rationalist: Selected Writings from Georges Canguilhem*, ed. François Delaporte, trans. Arthur Goldhammer (New York: Zone Books, 2000), 363-69.

50. See Sander L. Gilman, *Difference and Pathology: Stereotypes of Sexuality, Race, and Madness* (Ithaca, NY: Cornell University Press, 1985), 131-49.

51. George Fitzhugh, "Sociology for the South," in *Defending Slavery: Proslavery Thought in the Old South: A Brief History with Documents*, ed. Paul Finkelman (New York: Bedford Books, 2003), 193.

52. "The Colored Insane," *Frederick Douglass' Paper* April 1, 1852. Somewhat differently, an article in the *Cincinnati Colored Citizen* protested the denial of "admission of a colored woman to the Long View Lunatic Asylum" on the grounds that there were no separate wards for her. The issue was discrimination within the asylums, rather than the asylums' affront to individual liberties. The article was reprinted in "General Intelligence," *Christian Recorder* June 9, 1866.

53. Elaine Showalter, *The Female Malady: Women, Madness, and English Culture, 1830-1980* (New York: Pantheon, 1985), 28, 50.

54. Quoted in Barbara Sapinsley, *The Private War of Mrs. Packard* (New York: Paragon House, 1991), 150.

55. Shoshana Felman makes a similar point about the pervasive discussion of insanity in the 1970s: "The fact that madness has currently become a *common* discursive *place* is not the least of its paradoxes. Madness usually occupies a position of *exclusion*; it is the *outside* of a culture. But madness that is a *common* place occupies a position of *inclusion* and becomes the *inside* of a culture." See Felman, *Writing and Madness: Literature/Philosohpy/Psychoanalysis*, trans. Martha Noel Evans and Shoshana Felman, with the assistance of Brian Massumi (Palo Alto, CA: Stanford University Press, 2003), 13 (original emphasis).

56. Gilman, "On the Nexus of Blackness and Madness," in *Difference and Pathology*, 131-49.

CHAPTER ONE

1. All information about this patient is taken from New York State, *Utica State Hospital Patient Case Files*, vol. 1 (New York State Archives). I have not been officially constrained from revealing the identity of the patients, but whenever patients did not explicitly reveal their names to the public, I have chosen to leave them anonymous or pseudonymous.

2. The best study of the New York State Lunatic Asylum is Ellen Dwyer, *Homes for the Mad: Life inside Two Nineteenth-Century Asylums* (New Brunswick, NJ: Rutgers University Press, 1987). The architecture and landscape of the Utica asylum are described in Carla Yanni, *The Architecture of Madness: Insane Asylums in the United States* (Minneapolis: University of Minnesota Press, 2007), 43-45.

3. Pliny Earle, "The Poetry of Insanity," *American Journal of Insanity* 1, no. 3 (January 1845): 185-210.

4. The particular details of doctors' treatments, patients' behaviors, and punishments emerged from a reading of the asylum's annual reports, patient case notes, and exposés written by former patients.

5. Erving Goffman, *Asylums: Essays on the Social Situation of Mental Patients and Other Inmates* (New York: Anchor Books, 1961), 96.

6. Jann Matlock, "Doubling out of the Crazy House: Gender, Autobiography, and the Insane Asylum System in Nineteenth-Century France," *Representations* 34 (Spring 1991): 166-95 (the quote is on pp.168-69).

7. Maryrose Eannace, "Lunatic Literature: New York State's *The Opal*, 1850–1860" (PhD diss., University at Albany, State University of New York, 2001), 203, 3.

8. James C. Scott, *Domination and the Arts of Resistance: Hidden Transcripts* (New Haven, CT: Yale University Press, 1990), xiii ("hidden transcript"), 138 ("ideological debate").

9. See Michael Warner, *The Letters of the Republic: Publication and the Public Sphere in Eighteenth-Century America* (Cambridge, MA: Harvard University Press, 1990); and Warner, "The Mass Public and the Mass Subject," in *Habermas and the Public Sphere*, ed. Craig Calhoun (Cambridge, MA: MIT Press, 1992), 377–401.

10. See Elizabeth McHenry, *Forgotten Readers: Recovering the Lost History of African American Literary Societies* (Durham, NC: Duke University Press, 2003), 62.

11. On the history of patient-edited journals, see Amariah Brigham, "Progress of the Periodical Literature of Lunatic Asylums," *American Journal of Insanity* 2, no. 1 (July 1845): 77–80. Copies of the *Asylum Journal* can be found at the American Antiquarian Society; copies of the *Retreat Gazette* can be found in the archives of the Institute for Living in Hartford. The *Morning-Side Mirror* is mentioned in "Journals by the Insane," *Asylum Journal* 4, no. 2 (February 1846): n.p.

12. New York State, *Annual Report of the Managers of the State Lunatic Asylum*, vol. 3 (Albany, NY: E. Mack, 1846), 36–39.

13. "On the Claims of the Insane to the Respect and Interest of Society," *Opal* 2, no. 8 (August 1852): 241–43.

14. The three models are convincingly demonstrated in Eannace, "Lunatic Literature," 98. I find most salient the connections to the *Knickerbocker*, for reasons stated later in this chapter.

15. New York State, *Annual Report*, vol. 8 (Albany, NY: n.p., 1851), 52; Eannace, "Lunatic Literature," 98, 263. The journal did not mention that some of this collection predated the printing of the journal; Brigham noted in his 1846 annual report that a "large library" for patients was already in existence. See New York State, *Annual Report*, vol. 3 (1846), 37; see also "Reports from Hospitals for the Insane," *American Journal of Insanity* 9, no. 2 (October 1852): 183. On asylum libraries in general, see Priscilla Older, "Patient Libraries in Hospitals for the Insane in the United States, 1810–1861," *Libraries and Culture* 26, no. 3 (Summer 1991): 511–31; L.M. Dunkel, "Moral and Humane: Patients' Libraries in Early Nineteenth-Century Mental Hospitals," *Bulletin of the Medical Library Association of America* 71, no. 3 (July 1983): 274–81; and Philip W. Weimerskirch, "Benjamin Rush and John Minson Galt, II: Pioneers of Bibliotherapy in America," *Bulletin of the Medical Library Association of America* 53 (1965): 510–26.

16. A number of asylum exposés written by former patients portray the asylum regime as tyrannical and antidemocratic. See for example Robert Fuller, *An Account of the Imprisonment and Sufferings of Robert Fuller, of Cambridge* (Boston: privately printed, 1833); Phebe Davis, *Two Years and Three Months in the New York Lunatic Asylum at Utica* (Syracuse, NY: privately printed, 1865); and, most famously, Elizabeth Parsons Ware Packard, *The Prisoners' Hidden Life, or Insane Asylums Unveiled* (Chicago: privately printed, 1868).

17. "An Ode, Written for the Celebration at the New York State Lunatic Asylum, July 4th, 1854," *Opal* 4, no. 8 (August 1854): 225.

18. "An Address to Our Readers," *Opal* 3, no. 1 (January 1853): 3.

19. Isaac Ray, *Mental Hygiene* (Boston: Ticknor and Fields, 1863), 57–58.

20. Ibid., 58 ("supply and demand"), 285 ("a degree of nervous irritability"). On the mental-health threats of popular reading, see Isabelle Lehuu, *Carnival on the Page: Popular Print Media in Antebellum America* (Chapel Hill: University of North Carolina Press, 2000), 132–40. On an earlier history of the perceived moral hazards posed by reading fiction, see Michael Davitt Bell, *The Development of American Romance: The Sacrifice of Relation* (Chicago: University of Chicago Press, 1980), 11–13.

21. Pliny Earle, for instance, cited three cases of insanity brought on by novel reading among patients at the Bloomingdale Lunatic Asylum, as well as many other causes of "moral" insanity,

such as "faulty education," "religious excitement," and "dealing in lottery tickets." See Earle, "On the Causes of Insanity," *American Journal of Insanity* 4, no. 3 (January 1848): 185–210.

22. Ronald J. Zboray and Mary Saracino Zboray, *Literary Dollars and Social Sense: A People's History of the Mass Market Book* (New York: Routledge, 2005), xx. For a compelling study of the function of cultural reformation in one nonelite community's literary societies, see McHenry, *Forgotten Readers*.

23. On labor in the asylums generally, see David J. Rothman, *The Discovery of the Asylum: Social Order and Disorder in the New Republic* (Boston: Little, Brown, 1971), 144–47; on Utica in particular, see Dwyer, *Homes for the Mad*, 15–16. On the supposed voluntarism at Utica, see New York State, *Annual Report*, vol. 4 (Albany, NY: C. Van Benthuysen, 1847), 46.

24. New York State, *Annual Report*, vol. 5 (Albany, NY: C. Van Benthuysen, 1848), 38.

25. "On the Claims of the Insane."

26. Lynn Gamwell and Nancy Tomes, *Madness in America: Cultural and Medical Perceptions of Mental Illness before 1914* (Ithaca, NY: Cornell University Press, 1995), 59.

27. On the social position of the contributors to the *Opal*, see Eannace, "Lunatic Literature," 76–77.

28. New York State, *Annual Report*, vol. 6 (1849), 56.

29. "A Letter from a Patient," *Opal* 2, no. 8 (August 1852): 344–45.

30. "Thoughts as They Rise," *Opal* 2, no. 4 (April 1852): 117–18.

31. Edward Stiff, "The Opal," *Stiff's Radical Reformer* (Gadsden, AL), June 25, 1852, n.p.

32. "Fair at the New York State Lunatic Asylum," *Utica Daily Gazette*, November 29, 1850.

33. "Editorial Statement," *Asylum Journal* 1, no. 51 (October 24, 1843): n.p.

34. "A Crazy Newspaper," *New York Post*, December 3, 1850.

35. "Editor's Table," *Opal* 5, no. 6 (June 1855): 188.

36. "Editor's Table," *Opal* 7, no. 1 (January 1857): 23.

37. Nathan Benedict, letter to Dorothea Dix, November 3, 1857, Dorothea Dix Papers, Houghton Library, Harvard University, Cambridge, MA.

38. "Illustrations of Insanity, Furnished by the Conversation and Letters of the Insane, *American Journal of Insanity* 3, no. 4 (January 1847): 346. The writer of this anonymous article (part of a series that ran across four issues from 1847–1848) was almost certainly Brigham, as most of its examples of patients' writings are taken from the Utica asylum.

39. Isaac Ray, "A Modern Lettre de Cachet Reviewed," *Atlantic Monthly* (August 1868): 227–43.

40. Roy Porter, *A Social History of Madness: The World through the Eyes of the Insane* (New York: Weidenfeld & Nicolson, 1987), 34. Porter's assessment is more nuanced than Michel Foucault's famous pronouncement that "the language of psychiatry . . . is a monologue of reason *about* madness," predicated on the enforced silence of the mad. See Foucault, *Madness and Civilization: A History of Insanity in the Age of Reason*, trans. Richard Howard (New York: Random House, 1965), x–xi.

41. Richard H. Brodhead, *Cultures of Letters: Scenes of Reading and Writing in America* (Chicago: University of Chicago Press, 1993), 21.

42. Paul E. Johnson, *A Shopkeeper's Millennium: Society and Revivals in Rochester, New York 1815–1837* (New York: Hill and Wang, 1978).

43. See Nathan O. Hatch, *The Democratization of American Christianity* (New Haven and London: Yale University Press, 1991), 9–14. Hatch complicates—but does not contradict—Johnson's "social control" thesis by arguing that the revival movements were a "democratization" of Christianity. The movements, by and large, broke down traditional hierarchies of religious practice but nonetheless paved the way for new structures of bourgeois social control over worship.

44. See the listing of "causes" or "exciting causes" of insanity in Utica's annual reports. (New York State, *Annual Reports*, vols. 1–17 (1844–1860). From the third annual report onward,

Brigham and his followers were always careful to state that the underlying cause of insanity was not empirically knowable. One of Brigham's successors at Utica, John P. Gray—who served as superintendent for the last seven years of the *Opal*'s existence—eventually became famous in psychiatric history as one of the earliest proponents of the idea that all insanity had a somatic causation; and yet, through the 1850s, he listed "religious anxiety" as a leading cause. It appears that by the 1860s, he simply adopted a somatic explanation for the threat posed by the religious movements. On the superintendents' notions of the causation of mental illness, see Norman Dain, *Concepts of Insanity in the United States, 1789–1865* (New Brunswick, NJ: Rutgers University Press, 1964), 84-113.

45. Dwyer, *Homes for the Mad*, 60-61.

46. New York State, *Annual Report*, vol. 1 (Albany, NY: Carroll and Cook, 1844), 50.

47. See Mary P. Ryan, *Cradle of the Middle Class: The Family in Oneida County, New York, 1790–1865* (Cambridge: Cambridge University Press, 1981).

48. See especially Phyllis Chesler, *Women and Madness* (1972; repr., San Diego: Harcourt Brace Jovanovich, 1989), who argued that the treatment of women's madness in the nineteenth century was a "female biological, sexual, and cultural castration" (31), and that asylums served as a "warning specter" to women who would step out of prescribed gender roles (34).

49. For an excellent overview on the topic, see Nancy Tomes, "Feminist Histories of Psychiatry," in *Discovering the History of Psychiatry*, ed. Mark Micale and Roy Porter (Oxford: Oxford University Press, 1994), 348-83. See also chapter 6.

50. These comments are found sprinkled liberally through New York State, *Utica State Hospital Patient Case Files*, vols. 1-11 (1843-1854).

51. For the "female" editorial style of the *Opal*, see, for example, "Editor's Table," *Opal* 4, no. 1 (January 1854): 25-32. This column was written by an "editress" who took over while A.S.M. was temporarily incapacitated (this will be discussed later in the chapter). For conventionally gendered women's fiction, see "Alpina," *Opal* 2, no. 1 (January 1852): 1-7; and "A Glance at Montmorency," *Opal* 2, no. 1 (January 1852): 8-11. The gendered conventionality of this literary style is analyzed in Nina Baym, *Woman's Fiction: A Guide to Novels by and about Women in America, 1820–1870* (Ithaca, NY: Cornell University Press, 1978), esp. 22-50.

52. "Life in the Asylum," *Opal* 5, no. 3 (March 1855): 75-76.

53. "Life at Asylumia," *Opal* 5, no. 11 (November 1855): 347.

54. In addition to Foucault's famous comments about the imposition of "bourgeois morality" upon the insane; see also Klaus Doerner, who locates the origins of the asylum in a desire for "maximum economic utilization of the lower orders" (*Madmen and the Bourgeoisie: A Social History of Insanity and Psychiatry*, trans. Joachim Neugroschel and Jean Steinberg [Oxford: Basil Blackwell, 1981], 130). For a more nuanced examination of the class dynamics of early psychiatry, see Andrew Scull, *The Most Solitary of Afflictions: Madness and Society in Britain, 1700–1900* (New Haven, CT: Yale University Press, 1993), 1-45.

55. "Pinel," *Opal* 2, no.1 (January 1852): 22.

56. "Editor's Table," *Opal* 2, no. 3 (March 1852): 124.

57. For a still-powerful analysis of the *Knickerbocker*, see Perry Miller, *The Raven and the Whale; The War of Words and Wits in the Age of Melville and Poe* (New York: Harcourt, Brace & World, 1956), esp. 36, where he discusses the social meanings of anonymity. My readings of the cultural styles associated with different formations of literary labor has also been shaped by Michael Newbury, *Figuring Authorship in Antebellum America* (Palo Alto, CA: Stanford University Press, 1997), and Michael Denning, *Mechanic Accents: Dime Novels and Working-Class Culture in America* (London: Verso, 1987).

58. Warner, "The Mass Public and the Mass Subject," 382.

59. Herman Melville, *Pierre; Or, the Ambiguities* (1971; repr., Evanston, IL.: Northwestern University Press, 1995), 254.

60. For two analyses of Melville's novel along these lines, see Susan M. Ryan, "Misgivings: Melville, Race, and the Ambiguities of Benevolence," *American Literary History* 12, no. 2 (Winter 2000): 685–712; and David T. Mitchell and Sharon L. Snyder, "Masquerades of Impairment: Charity as a Confidence Game," *Leviathan* 8, no. 1 (March 2006): 35–60.

61. See John Sekora, "Black Message/White Envelope: Genre, Authenticity, and Authority in the Antebellum Slave Narrative," *Callaloo* 10, no. 3 (Summer 1987): 482–513; and Henry Louis Gates, Jr., "Foreword: In Her Own Write," in *The Collected Works of Phillis Wheatley*, ed. John C. Shields (New York: Oxford University Press, 1988), vii–xxii.

62. See "Inquiries, Doubts, Etc. Or, Derby Dean's Letter to Her Aunt," *Opal* 3, no. 3 (March 1853): 68–70.

63. Eannace makes an intriguing suggestion that the inclusion of "crazy" writing was meant to make the "rationality" of the other pieces seem more striking in contrast. See "Lunatic Literature," 224.

64. Etta Floyd [pseud.], "Poetry and Poets," *Opal* 4, no. 7 (July 1854): 194 ("refines and elevates"), 193 ("a person can not be taught"), 195 ("the plaudits of all").

65. New York State, *Annual Report*, vol. 6 (Albany, NY: Weed, Parsons, & Co., 1849), 33.

66. See Mary Elene Wood, *The Writing on the Wall: Women's Autobiography and the Asylum* (Urbana, IL: University of Illinois Press, 1994), 10, 14, 31.

67. "Editor's Table," *Opal* 4, no. 8 (August 1854), 253–54.

68. Isaac Ray, "The Popular Feeling toward Insane Hospitals," *American Journal of Insanity* 9, no. 1 (July 1852): 36–65.

69. Mrs. George Lunt, *Behind the Bars* (Boston: Lee and Shepard, 1871), 5.

70. Phebe Davis, *Two Years and Three Months in the New York Lunatic Asylum at Utica* (Syracuse, NY: privately printed, 1865), 57, 50.

71. Rev. Hiram Chase, *Two Years in a Lunatic Asylum* (Saratoga Springs, NY: Van Benthuysen and Sons, 1868), 3.

72. See Constance M. McGovern, *Masters of Madness: Social Origins of the American Psychiatric Profession* (Hanover, NH: University Press of New England, 1985), 44–61; Dwyer, *Homes for the Mad*, 29–53; and Paul Starr, *The Social Transformation of American Medicine* (New York: Basic Books, 1982), 60–78.

73. Edward Jarvis, "On the Supposed Increase of Insanity," *American Journal of Insanity* 8, no. 4 (April 1852): 351.

74. Ray, "Popular Feeling," 39.

75. Zboray and Zboray, *Literary Dollars*, xxii.

76. For a selection of writings from the *Cherokee Phoenix* and a good introduction to its competing functions within Cherokee and white readership, see Theda Perdue, ed., *Cherokee Editor: The Writings of Elias Boudinot* (Athens, GA: University of Georgia Press, 1996); on the *American Annals of the Deaf and Dumb*, see Douglas C. Baynton, "'A Silent Exile on this Earth,': The Metaphorical Construction of Deafness in the Nineteenth Century," *American Quarterly* 44, no. 2 (June 1992): 216–43; on the *Freedman's Journal*, see McHenry, *Forgotten Readers*, 92–100; and for a selection from the *Lowell Offering*, see Benita Eisler, ed., *The Lowell Offering: Writings by New England Mill Women, 1840–1845* (Philadelphia: J. B. Lippincott, 1977).

77. See Newbury, *Figuring Authorship in Antebellum America*, 29.

78. See Thomas Dublin, *Women at Work: The Transformation of Work and Community in Lowell, Massachusetts, 1826–1860* (New York: Columbia University Press, 1979), 41–48.

79. Newbury, *Figuring Authorship*, 71.

80. Ralph Remmington [pseud.], "A Crazy Man's Common Sense," *Opal* 4, no. 9 (April 1854): 267.

81. Ibid., 268.

82. "Editor's Table," *Opal* 2, no. 1 (January 1852): 59.

83. "Editor's Table," *Opal* 2, no. 2 (February 1852): 59.

84. Goffman, *Asylums*, 63.

85. "Insanity—Its Causes and Cure," *Opal* 3, no. 3 (March 1853): 87.

86. Goffman, *Asylums*, 63.

87. "A Dialogue Between Two Southern Gentlemen and a Negro," *Opal* 2, no. 5 (May 1852): 145–53; continued in *Opal* 2, no. 6 (June 1852): 178–82. Specific quotes are on pp. 151 ("An asylum is a retreat") and 179 ("alleviate woe").

88. Shoshana Felman, *Writing and Madness (Literature/Philosophy/Psychoanalysis)*, trans. Martha Noel Evans and Shoshana Felman, with Brian Massumi (Palo Alto, CA: Stanford University Press, 1978; 2003), 5.

89. "Editor's Table," *Opal* 5, no. 6 (June 1855): 189.

90. "Editor's Table," *Opal* 2, no. 1 (January 1852): 28.

91. "Editor's Table," *Opal* 2, no. 3 (March 1852): 96.

CHAPTER TWO

1. For the history of blackface minstrelsy, see Robert Toll, *Blacking Up: The Minstrel Show in Nineteenth-Century America* (New York: Oxford University Press, 1974); Eric Lott, *Love and Theft: Blackface Minstrelsy and the American Working Class* (New York: Oxford University Press, 1995); W.T. Lhamon, *Raising Cain: Blackface Performance from Jim Crow to Hip Hop* (Cambridge, MA: Harvard University Press, 1998); Lhamon, *Jump Jim Crow: Lost Plays, Lyrics, and Street Prose of the First Atlantic Culture* (Cambridge, MA: Harvard University Press, 2003); and Dale Cockrell, *Demons of Disorder: Early Blackface Minstrels and Their World* (Cambridge: Cambridge University Press, 1997). *Raising Cain* and *Demons of Disorder* are two accounts that stress the changing circumstances and social meanings of blackface performance.

2. Cockrell, *Demons of Disorder*, 147–52.

3. Lhamon agrees with this trajectory in broad outlines, but insists that it retained a vernacular, antielitist, and often antiracist power in spite of official attempts to co-opt it. See Lhamon, *Raising Cain*, 65, 116–20.

4. See Susan Gubar, *Race Changes: White Skin, Black Face in American Culture* (New York: Oxford University Press, 1997); and Michael Paul Rogin, *Blackface, White Noise: Jewish Immigrants in the Hollywood Melting Pot* (Berkeley: University of California Press, 1996).

5. Erving Goffman, *Asylums: Essays on the Social Situation of Mental Patients and Other Inmates* (New York: Anchor Books, 1961), 13.

6. On self-possession as the key to understanding antebellum arguments about restricting racial minorities from property rights, see Priscilla Wald, "Terms of Assimilation: Legislating Subjectivity in the Emerging Nation," in *Cultures of United States Imperialism*, ed. Donald Pease and Amy Kaplan (Durham, NC: Duke University Press, 1993), 59–84.

7. New York State, *Annual Report of the Managers of the State Lunatic Asylum*, vol. 5 (Albany, NY: C. Van Benthuysen, 1848), 51–52.

8. "The Blackbird Entertainment, by Ella," *Opal* 4, no. 12 (December 1854): 373.

9. "Editor's Table: Asylumian Theatricals," *The Opal* 6, no. 1 (1856): 21–22.

10. D. Tilden Brown, MD, "Theatrical Performances at the New York State Lunatic Asylum," *Medical Examiner* 3 (April 1847): 261.

11. New York State, *Annual Report*, vol. 5 (1848), 41.

12. New York State, *Annual Report*, vol. 6 (Albany, NY: Weed, Parsons, & Co., 1849), 56. On the importance of "diversion" to European psychiatric thought, see Henri Falret, "On the Construction and Organization of Establishments for the Insane," *American Journal of Insanity* 10, no. 4 (April 1854): 416.

13. John M. Galt, *Essays on Asylums for Persons of Unsound Mind: Second Series* (Richmond,

VA: Ritchies and Dunnavant, 1853), 16; Isaac Ray, *Mental Hygiene* (Boston: Ticknor and Fields, 1863), 219, 237–38.

14. Michael B. Katz, *In the Shadow of the Poorhouse: A Social History of Poverty in America* (New York: Basic Books, 1986), 12. Katz is following the work of Herbert Guttman and E. P. Thompson on time, work discipline, and industrial culture.

15. Brown, "Theatrical Performances," 260 ("employment in industrial pursuits" and "the exercise of self-control"), 261 ("combining present gratification" and "that restraining surveillance"). After his tenure at Utica, Brown would go on to become superintendent of the Bloomingdale Lunatic Asylum in New York City.

16. Quoted in Lhamon, *Raising Cain*, 37.

17. Ray, *Mental Hygiene*, 237–38 ("a prolific source"), 219 ("the lower sentiments").

18. Lott, *Love and Theft*, 27.

19. See Helen Lefkowitz Horowitz, *Rereading Sex: Battles over Sexual Knowledge and Suppression in Nineteenth-Century America* (New York: Random House, 2002), 86–122. For examples of early psychiatric writing on masturbation, see Luther Bell, *An Hour's Conference with Fathers and Sons, in Relation to a Common and Fatal Indulgence* (Boston: Whipple and Damrell, 1840), and Samuel Woodward, *Hints for the Young, in Relation to the Health of Body and Mind* (Boston: George W. Light, 1840; repr. in *The Beginnings of Mental Hygiene in America: Three Selected Essays, 1833–1850* [New York: Arno Press, 1973], 1–65).

20. New York State, *Annual Report*, vol. 8 (Albany, NY: n.p., 1851), 38–39.

21. Etta Floyd [pseud.], "The Music Mania," *Opal* 5, no. 9 (September 1855): 273–74.

22. Brown, "Theatrical Performances," 260.

23. Ray, *Mental Hygiene*, 219.

24. See Lhamon, *Raising Cain*, 45–54.

25. New York State, *Annual Report*, vol. 5 (1848), 42.

26. Ellen Dwyer cites this general rule for asylum performances at Utica in *Homes for the Mad: Life Inside Two Nineteenth-Century Asylums* (New Brunswick, NJ: Rutgers University Press, 1987), 14.

27. New York State, *Annual Report*, vol. 5 (1848), 42.

28. "Negro Melodies," *Opal* 4, no. 12 (December 1854), 372.

29. On the importance of such elements in the "moral architecture" of the asylum, see Nancy Tomes, *A Generous Confidence: Thomas Story Kirkbride and the Art of Asylum-Keeping, 1840–1883* (Cambridge: Cambridge University Press, 1984), esp. 131–32.

30. Galt, *Essays on Asylums*, 6, 15–16.

31. Phebe B. Davis, *The Travels and Experience of Miss Phebe B. Davis* (Syracuse, NY: J.G.K. Truair & Co., 1860), 17.

32. On Reil, see Robert J. Richards, "Rhapsodies on a Cat-Piano, or Joahann Christian Reil and the Foundations of Romantic Psychiatry," *Critical Inquiry* 24 (Spring 1998), 700–36 (quoted material is on pp. 720–21). For a mostly negative discussion of Reil's work in the United States, see Henri Falret, "On the Construction and Organization of Establishments for the Insane," *American Journal of Insanity* 10, no. 4 (April 1854): 413–14.

33. See Jan Goldstein, *Console and Classify: The French Psychiatric Profession in the Nineteenth Century* (Cambridge: Cambridge University Press, 1987), 87.

34. See Klaus Doerner, *Madmen and the Bourgeoisie: A Social History of Insanity and Psychiatry*, trans. Joachim Neugroschel and Jean Steinberg (Oxford: Basil Blackwell, 1981), 136–37.

35. Michel Foucault, *Madness and Civilization: A History of Insanity in the Age of Reason*, trans. Richard Howard (New York: Random House, 1965), 189.

36. Ibid., 191–92.

37. Brown, "Theatrical Performances," 260.

38. Brown, "Theatrical Performances," 262.

39. "The Busybodies' Association," *Opal* 5, no. 1 (1855): 12–14

40. "The Blackbird Entertainment, by Ella," *Opal* 4, no. 12 (1854): 373–74; "Parlor Scene, by the Observer, C.," *Opal* 4, no. 12 (1854): 367.

41. Dwyer calculates that the black population at Utica constituted 0.8% of the total. See *Homes for the Mad*, 106–8.

42. "Music for the Insane," *North Star* (Rochester, NY), April 17, 1851.

43. See chapter 6.

44. Lhamon, *Raising Cain*, 63.

45. Cockrell, *Demons of Disorder*, 85–86.

46. Mrs. George Lunt, *Behind the Bars* (Boston: Lee and Shepard, 1871), 42.

47. "NOTES OF MY STUDY, vol. 2, by A.W.L.S.," *Opal* 1, no. 1 (January 1851): 4.

48. "Negro Melodies," *Opal* 4, no. 12 (December 1854): 372.

49. "Parlor Scene, by the Observer, C.," 367 (original emphasis).

50. Floyd, "The Music Mania," 273–74.

51. Etta Floyd [pseud.], "The Musqueto Serenade," *Opal* 4, no. 10 (October 1854): 294.

52. Lott, *Love and Theft*, 62.

53. This line of analysis was suggested to me in Carroll Smith-Rosenberg's wonderful analysis of a different act of masking in the early American republic. See Smith-Rosenberg, "Surrogate Americans: Masculinity, Masquerade, and the Formation of a National Identity," *PMLA* 119, no. 5 (October 2004): 1325–35.

54. On whiteness, industrial discipline, and work—especially in relation to minstrelsy and popular culture—see David R. Roediger, *The Wages of Whiteness: Race and the Making of the American Working Class* (London: Verso, 1991), especially 115–32.

55. "A Valentine to Missy Dinah Crow," *Opal* 4, no. 2 (February 1854): 42.

56. Sander L. Gilman, *Difference and Pathology: Stereotypes of Sexuality, Race, and Madness* (Ithaca, NY: Cornell University Press, 1985), 146.

57. Sander L. Gilman, *Seeing the Insane* (Lincoln: University of Nebraska Press, 1996), 2–6 (the quotation from Shakespeare is on p. 4).

58. Sir Richard Blackmore, *A Treatise of the Spleen or Vapours*, quoted in Andrew Scull, *The Most Solitary of Afflictions: Madness and Society in Britain, 1700–1900* (New Haven, CT: Yale University Press, 1993), 50.

59. Georges Canguilhem, "The Normal and the Pathological," in *A Vital Rationalist: Selected Writings from Georges Canguilhem*, ed. Francoix Delaporte; trans. Arthur Goldhammer (New York: Zone Books, 1994), 366.

60. Robert Castel cites this analogy as a central rationale for the detention of the insane in postrevolutionary France: "Either the individual is an autonomous entity, since he is capable as such of carrying out rational exchanges, or his inability to enter a system of reciprocity renders him not responsible, and he must be assisted. The contractual basis of liberalism necessitates the comparison of the insane person with the child." Castel, *The Regulation of Madness: The Origins of Incarceration in France*, trans. W.D. Halls (Berkeley: University of California Press, 1988), 38.

61. George Fitzhugh, "Sociology for the South," in *Defending Slavery: Proslavery Thought in the Old South: A Brief History with Documents*, ed. Paul Finkelman (New York: Bedford Books, 2003), 190. The circle of analogies between blacks, the insane, and children is complete when we consider, as Caroline Levander does, that the figure of the child was often implicitly racialized in the nineteenth century. As Levander shows, discussion of childhood raised "urgent national question[s] of where freedom ends and slavery begins" that was both analogous to and foundational for discussion of slavery and citizenship. See Levander, *Cradling Liberty: The Child, the Self, and the Racial State in American Culture* (Durham, NC: Duke University Press, forthcoming), ms. p. 16.

62. See Gilman, *Difference and Pathology*, 136–38.

63. For an analysis of the disputes over the census findings, see Patricia Cline Cohen, *A Calculating People: The Spread of Numeracy in Early America* (Chicago: University of Chicago Press, 1983; New York: Routledge, 1999), 175–204 (citations are to the Routledge edition).

64. Calhoun, in a letter defending slavery to the British ambassador, wrote that "the census and other authentic documents show that, in all instances in which the States have changed the former relations between the two races, the condition of the African, instead of being improved, has become worse. They have been invariably sunk into vice and pauperism, accompanied by the bodily and mental inflictions incident thereto—deafness, blindness, insanity, and idiocy—to a degree without example; while, in all other States which have retained the ancient relation between them, they have improved greatly in every respect—in number, comfort, intelligence, and morals." Quoted in Gilman, *Difference and Pathology*, 137.

65. "Who would believe," asked a writer in the *American Journal of Insanity* in 1851, "without the fact, in black and white, before his eyes, that *every fourteenth colored person in the State of Maine is an idiot or lunatic?*" Quoted in William Ragan Stanton, *The Leopard's Spots: Scientific Attitudes Toward Race in America, 1815–1859* (Chicago: University of Chicago Press, 1960), 65; see also 214n24 (original emphasis).

66. Lynn Gamwell and Nancy Tomes, *Madness in America: Cultural and Medical Perceptions of Mental Illness before 1914* (Ithaca, NY: Cornell University Press, 1995), 58–59; David J. Rothman, *The Discovery of the Asylum: Social Order and Disorder in the New Republic* (Boston: Little, Brown, 1971), 112.

67. W.M. Bevins, "The Psychological Traits of the Southern Negro with Observations as to Some of His Psychoses," *American Journal of Psychiatry* 1, no. 1 (July 1921): 69–78 (the quoted material is on pp. 68 and 72).

68. Norman Dain, *Concepts of Insanity in the United States, 1789–1865* (New Brunswick, NJ: Rutgers University Press, 1964), 69; Lawrence B. Goodheart, *Mad Yankees: The Hartford Retreat for the Insane and Nineteenth-Century Psychiatry* (Amherst: University of Massachusetts Press, 2003), 99.

69. Gilman, *Seeing the Insane*, xiii.

70. "Editor's Table," *Opal* 2, no. 11 (November 1852): 349.

71. "Hast Thou No Friend?" *Opal* 4, no. 4 (April 1854): 103.

72. Karen Sanchez-Eppler similarly studies the linkages between the work of colony and empire on the one hand and moral reform at home on the other. Taken together, these movements "locate[d] the otherness in need of civilizing both within and without" the national boundaries. See Sanchez-Eppler, "Raising Empires Like Children: Race, Nation, and Religious Education," *American Literary History* 8, no. 3 (Autumn 1996): 399–425 (the quote is on p. 403). Sanchez-Eppler has expanded this study in *Dependent States: The Child's Part in Nineteenth-Century American Culture* (Chicago: University of Chicago Press, 2005).

73. On the Quaker roots of moral treatment, see Anne Digby, *Madness, Morality, and Medicine: A Study of the York Retreat, 1796–1914* (Cambridge: Cambridge University Press, 1985). On Thornton, see Lamin Sanneh, *Abolitionists Abroad: American Blacks and the Making of Modern West Africa* (Cambridge, MA: Harvard University Press, 1999), 185–87.

74. On connections between humanitarianism and productivity, see Thomas Haskell, "Capitalism and the Origins of Humanitarian Sensibility," *American Historical Review* 90, no. 2 (April 1985): 339–61; and no. 3 (June 1985): 547–66.

75. See Sanneh, *Abolitionists Abroad*.

76. "Africa," *Opal* 1, no. 7 (July 1851): 50.

77. Finley and the declaration are cited in Sanneh, *Abolitionists Abroad*, 235, 236.

78. Cited in Douglas C. Baynton, "'A Silent Exile on this Earth': The Metaphorical Construction of Deafness in the Nineteenth Century," *American Quarterly* 44, no. 2 (June 1992): 221, 223.

79. "Exchanges," *Opal* 1, no. 2 (February 1851): 21.

80. "Editor's Table," *Opal* 2, no. 6 (June 1852): 187–88.

81. Lennard J. Davis, *Enforcing Normalcy: Disability, Deafness, and the Body* (London: Verso, 1995), 91–92.

82. Baynton, "'A Silent Exile on this Earth,'" 217. Baynton argues that the separatism of Deaf culture became threatening to the American mainstream after about 1860 when, in the wake of mass immigration, the presence of "foreigners" who refused to assimilate was perceived as a grave danger to the social body.

83. See Jill Lepore, *A Is for American: Letters and Other Characters in the Newly United States* (New York: Knopf, 2002), 91–110 (the quote is on p. 108).

84. See Megan Vaughan, *Curing Their Ills: Colonial Power and African Illness* (Stanford, CA: Stanford University Press, 1991); and Richard Keller, "Madness and Colonization: Psychiatry in the British and French Empires," *Journal of Social History* 35, no. 2 (2001): 295–326. The latter is a trenchant review article of this emerging field.

85. Ann Laura Stoler, *Race and the Education of Desire: Foucault's History of Sexuality and the Colonial Order of Things* (Durham, NC: Duke University Press, 1995), 7.

86. Amy Kaplan, *The Anarchy of Empire in the Making of U.S. Culture* (Cambridge, MA: Harvard University Press, 2002), 36.

87. Frantz Fanon, *Black Skin, White Masks*, trans. Charles Lamm Markman (New York: Grove Weidenfeld, 1967), 8.

88. Castel, *The Regulation of Madness*, 37.

89. On the history of the eugenics movement, see Daniel J. Kevles, *In the Name of Eugenics: Genetics and the Uses of Human Heredity* (New York: Knopf, 1985); and Diane B. Paul, *Controlling Human Heredity: 1865 to the Present* (New York: Humanities Press, 1995).

90. See Sharon L. Snyder and David T. Mitchell, *Cultural Locations of Disability* (Chicago: University of Chicago Press, 2006), 12–13, 24–25.

91. On Blumer and American psychiatrists' involvement in the eugenics movement, see Ian Robert Dowbiggin, *Keeping America Sane: Psychiatry and Eugenics in the United States and Canada, 1880–1940*, (Ithaca, NY: Cornell University Press, 1997). Blumer's support for ovariotomies and vasectomies is discussed on pp. 84 and 91.

92. See Dowbiggin, *Keeping America Sane*, 70–132. (The quote from Blumer is on p. 83.)

93. Martin Pernick, *The Black Stork: Eugenics and the Death of "Defective" Babies in American Medicine and Motion Pictures Since 1915* (New York: Oxford University Press, 1996), 175.

94. Dowbiggin, *Keeping America Sane*, 86–87.

CHAPTER THREE

1. See Constance M. McGovern, *Masters of Madness: Social Origins of the American Psychiatric Profession* (Hanover, NH: University Press of New England, 1985), 44–61.

2. On Woodward's training, see Gerald N. Grob, *The State and the Mentally Ill: A History of Worcester State Hospital in Massachusetts* (Chapel Hill: University of North Carolina Press, 1966), 47–49.

3. See McGovern, *Masters of Madness*, 87.

4. For a fascinating study of this shift in sensibility, see Charles E. Rosenberg, *The Trial of the Assassin Guiteau: Psychiatry and Law in the Gilded Age* (Chicago: University of Chicago Press, 1968).

5. Quoted in Gerald N. Grob, *Mental Institutions in America: Social Policy to 1875* (New York: The Free Press, 1973), 135.

6. Amariah Brigham, "Insanity—Illustrated by Histories of Distinguished Men and the writings of Poets and Novelists," *American Journal of Insanity* 1, no. 1 (July 1844): 27; A.O. Kellogg,

"Considerations on the Reciprocal Influence of the Physical Organization and Mental Manifestations," *American Journal of Insanity* 14, no. 2 (October 1857): 158. Kellogg's essays were later collected and reprinted as *Shakespeare's Delineations of Insanity, Imbecility, and Suicide* (New York: Hurd and Houghton, 1866).

7. A.O. Kellogg, "William Shakspeare as a Physiologist and Psychologist," *American Journal of Insanity* 16, no. 2 (October 1859): 136.

8. A.O. Kellogg, "William Shakspeare as a Physiologist and Psychologist," *American Journal of Insanity* 16, no. 4 (April 1860): 411.

9. Isaac Ray, "Shakespeare's Delineations of Insanity," *Contributions to Mental Pathology* (1873; repr., Delmar, NY: Scholars' Facsimiles and Reprints, 1973), 482, 507. This article was an expansion of an earlier piece that appeared under the same title in *American Journal of Insanity* 3, no. 4 (April 1847): 289-332. A latter-day version of this enterprise can be found in Paul Matthews and Jeffrey McQuain, *The Bard on the Brain: Understanding the Mind Through the Art of Shakespeare* (New York: The Dana Press; Chicago: University of Chicago Press, 2003). The authors argue that cognitive neuroscience provides tools to explain "the brain mechanisms that Shakespeare so wonderfully described" and that "Shakespeare's interest in the human mind has parallels in the work of brain scientists today" (16).

10. Brigham, "Insanity," 41.

11. See Roger Smith, "The Language of Human Nature," in *Inventing Human Science: Eighteenth-Century Domains*, ed. Christopher Fox, Roy Porter, and Robert Wokler (Berkeley: University of California Press, 1995), 88-111.

12. Lawrence W. Levine, *Highbrow/Lowbrow: The Emergence of Cultural Hierarchy in America* (Cambridge, MA: Harvard University Press, 1988), 9, 68.

13. Levine, *Highbrow/Lowbrow*, 33.

14. On the cult of Washington in nineteenth-century American politics and culture, see Michael Kammen, *A Season of Youth: The American Revolution and the Historical Imagination* (New York: Alfred A .Knopf, 1978); George B. Forgie, *Patricide in the House Divided: A Psychological Interpretation of Lincoln and His Age* (New York: W. W. Norton, 1979); Alfred F. Young, *The Shoemaker and the Tea Party: Memory and the American Revolution* (Boston: Beacon Press, 1998); and Benjamin Reiss, *The Showman and the Slave: Race, Death, and Memory in Barnum's America* (Cambridge, MA: Harvard University Press, 2001), esp. 52-70.

15. Cited in Bennett Simon, "*Hamlet* and the Trauma Doctors: An Essay at Interpretation," *American Imago* 58, no. 3 (Fall 2001): 707.

16. Benjamin Rush, *Medical Inquiries and Observations, upon Diseases of the Mind* (Philadelphia: Kimber and Richardson, 1812), 160.

17. John Mason Good, as quoted in George Farren, *Essays on the Varieties of Mania, Exhibited by the Characters of Hamlet, Ophelia, Lear, and Edgar* (1833; facsimile repr., New York: AMS Press, 1973), vi, 28.

18. Farren, *Essays on the Varieties of Mania*, 28.

19. Brigham, "Insanity," 36; John Charles Bucknill, *The Mad Folk of Shakespeare: Psychological Essays* (1867), 2nd rev. ed. (Folcroft, PA: Folcroft Press, 1969), viii. This work was originally published in 1859 as *The Psychology of Shakespeare* (London: Longman, Brown, Green, Longmans & Roberts).

20. Bucknill, *Mad Folk*, ix-x; see also Bucknill, *The Medical Knowledge of Shakespeare* (London: Longman and Co., 1860), 8-12, 290.

21. John Conolly, *A Study of Hamlet* (London: Edward Moxon and Co., 1863), 8. See also 52, 77-78, 155-56.

22. Henry Maudsley, *Heredity, Variation, and Genius, with an Essay on Shakspeare: Testimonied in His Own Brigingsforth* (London: John Bale, Sons, and Danielsson, Ltd., 1908), 129.

23. Maudsley, *Body and Will* (1873), cited in W.F. Bynum and Michael Neve, "Hamlet on the

Couch," in *The Anatomy of Madness: Essays in the History of Psychiatry*, ed. Roy Porter, W.F. Bynum, and Michael Shepard (London: Tavistock Publications, 1985), 289-304 (quote is on p. 291).

24. Helen Small, *Love's Madness: Medicine, the Novel, and Female Insanity, 1800-1865* (Oxford: Clarendon Press, 1996), 67, 62.

25. On the social position and aspirations of nineteenth-century American asylum superintendents, see McGovern, *Masters of Madness*.

26. See Ray, "Shakespeare's Delineations," 533; and "Hints to the Medical Witness in Questions of Insanity," *American Journal of Insanity* 8, no. 1 (July 1851): 51.

27. Shakespeare, *King Lear*, quoted in Kellogg, "William Shakspeare" (1859), 147.

28. Shakespeare, *Macbeth*, quoted in Brigham, "Insanity," 35.

29. Brigham, "Insanity," 28.

30. Ibid., 29.

31. Ray, "Shakespeare's Delineations," 487.

32. See Kellogg, "William Shakspeare" (1860), 420.

33. See Brigham, "Insanity," 37. The idea that this scene shows Shakespeare's medical foresight persisted well in to the twentieth century. Though his concern was primarily to show how mental functioning was understood in Shakespeare's time, Winfred Overholser, superintendent of St. Elizabeth's Hospital, claimed in a 1959 essay that the medical scene in *King Lear* represents "what today we would call the prolonged sleep treatment." See Overholser, "Shakespeare's Psychiatry—And After," *Shakespeare Quarterly* 10, no. 3 (Summer 1959): 349.

34. A.O. Kellogg, "Shakspeare's Delineations of Mental Imbecility as Exhibited in His Fools and Clowns," (Part II), *American Journal of Insanity* 18, no. 3 (January 1862): 181.

35. Kellogg, "William Shakspeare" (1859), 129-30.

36. Irving I. Edgar, *Shakespeare, Medicine, and Psychiatry* (New York: Philosophical Library, 1970), 181.

37. Shakespeare, *Much Ado about Nothing*, quoted in Edgar, *Shakespeare, Medicine, and Psychiatry*, 196.

38. Ibid., 186. See also 179, 187-89, 196.

39. See Duncan Salkeld, *Madness and Drama in the Age of Shakespeare* (Manchester: Manchester University Press, 1993), 13-16, 20-26. Salkeld implicates even Edgar in this critique, for Edgar claims that "psychoanalytic principles" are the best tools for understanding Shakespeare's creativity and his worldview. See Edgar, *Shakespeare, Medicine, and Psychiatry*, 288.

40. Michael MacDonald, *Mystical Bedlam: Madness, Anxiety, and Healing in Seventeenth-Century England* (Cambridge: Cambridge University Press, 1981), 33 ("common"), 178-179 ("vegetal"), 197 ("therapeutic"). For a reading of Shakespeare's tragedies in light of MacDonald's historical study, see Carol Thomas Neely, "'Documents in Madness': Reading Madness and Gender in Shakespeare's Tragedies and Early Modern Culture," *Shakespeare Quarterly* 42, no. 3 (Autumn 1991): 315-38. On American faculty psychology, see Thomas Cooley, *The Ivory Leg in the Ebony Cabinet: Madness, Race, and Gender in Victorian America* (Amherst: University of Massachusetts Press, 2001).

41. John Bender, *Imagining the Penitentiary: Fiction and the Architecture of Mind in Eighteenth-Century England* (Chicago: University of Chicago Press, 1987), 9, 6.

42. See Jan Goldstein, *Console and Classify: The French Psychiatric Profession in the Nineteenth Century* (Cambridge: Cambridge University Press, 1987), 65-66.

43. Elaine Showalter, "Representing Ophelia: Women, Madness, and the Responsibilities of Feminist Criticism," in *Shakespeare and the Question of Theory*, ed. Patricia Parker and Geoffrey Hartman (New York: Methuen, 1985), 77-94 (quote is on pp. 85-86). See also Kellogg, "William Shakspeare" (1859), 120; Kellogg, "William Shakspeare" (1860), 425. Pliny Earle, "The Poetry of Insanity," *American Journal of Insanity* 1, no. 3 (January 1845): 193-224, also

has several comparisons of patients to either Shakespearean characters or to Shakespeare himself.

44. Shakespeare, *Hamlet*, quoted in Sir H. Halford, "Observations on Insanity," *Boston Medical and Surgical Journal* 2, no. 27 (18 August 1829): 421.

45. Halford, "Observations on Insanity," 421-22.

46. See Kellogg, "William Shakspeare," (1860), 431; Ray, "Shakespeare's Delineations," 521; Conolly, *A Study of Hamlet*, 155-56. The maneuver was well-known enough that it figures in at least one novel of the period, Davis B. Casseday's *The Hortons: Or American Life at Home* (New York: D. Appleton & Co., 1866), 279-80.

47. See "Shakspeare as a Lawyer," *The Monthly Law Reporter* 25, no. 1 (November 1862): 1-18; and "The Growing and Perpetual Influence of Shakespeare," *The Christian Examiner* 67 (September 1859): 178-80.

48. Kellogg, "Shakspeare's Delineations of Mental Imbecility," 98.

49. The only literary figure who was invoked with anything near the frequency of Shakespeare in early psychiatric writings was Scott, but his insights, while formidable, were less worthy than Shakespeare's, because Scott "is known to have made mental maladies a special study," and he borrowed in his delineations of insane characters from medical books that would have given him an "accurate picture" of insanity—and thus an unfair advantage over Shakespeare. See Brigham, "Insanity," 27; Isaac Ray, "Illustrations of Insanity by Distinguished English Writers," *American Journal of Insanity* 4, no. 2 (October 1847): 97-112.

50. Kellogg, "William Shakspeare" (1860), 415.

51. A.O. Kellogg, "Considerations on the Reciprocal Influence of the Physical Organization and Mental Manifestations: The Cerebral and Circulatory Systems—Their Reciprocal and Sympathetic Influences," *American Journal of Insanity* 13, no. 1 (July 1856), 231.

52. Brigham, "Insanity," 41.

53. Ralph Waldo Emerson, "Shakspeare; Or, the Poet," in *Emerson: Essays & Poems* (New York: Library of America, 1996), 710-26 (quoted material appears on pp. 718 ["not until"], 720 ["in us"], 712 ["ground"], 710 ["heart"], and 725 ["science of mind"]).

54. See Paul Starr, *The Social Transformation of American Medicine* (New York: Basic Books, 1982), 30-59; and Goldstein, *Console and Classify*, 8-40.

55. Starr, *The Social Transformation of American Medicine*, 59.

56. See Starr, *The Social Transformation of American Medicine*, 30-59; and Joan Burbick, *Healing the Republic: The Language of Health and the Culture of Nationalism in Nineteenth-Century America* (Cambridge: Cambridge University Press, 1994), 15-56.

57. See McGovern, *Masters of Madness* and Grob, *Edward Jarvis and the Medical World of Nineteenth-Century America* (Knoxville: University of Tennessee Press, 1978).

58. For a discussion and anthology of such writings, see Roy Porter, *A Social History of Madness: The World Through the Eyes of the Insane* (New York: Weidenfeld and Nicolson, 1987).

59. Starr, *The Social Transformation of American Medicine*, 13.

60. Ray, "Hints to the Medical Witness," 51-52.

61. Kellogg, "Considerations on the Reciprocal Influence," 158.

62. Kellogg, "Shakspeare's Delineations of Mental Imbecility," 98.

63. Levine, *Highbrow/Lowbrow*, 31.

64. Kellogg, "William Shakspeare" (1860), 414-15.

65. Ibid., 429.

66. Gary Taylor, *Reinventing Shakespeare: A Cultural History, from the Restoration to the Present* (New York: Weidenfield & Nicolson, 1989), 168.

67. The most famous warning of this sort was Amariah Brigham, *Remarks on the Influence of Mental Cultivation and Mental Excitement upon Health* (Boston: Marsh, Capen and Lyon, 1833). Annual reports of most asylums from the 1830s through the mid-1850s listed "religious excite-

ment" and related formulations among the leading causes for the mental illness of patients. The best study of the asylum movement within the context of religious movements in the nineteenth century is Lawrence B. Goodheart, *Mad Yankees: The Hartford Retreat for the Insane and Nineteenth-Century Psychiatry* (Amherst: University of Massachusetts Press, 2003).

68. Kellogg, "William Shakspeare" (1860), 420.

69. Raymond Williams, *Culture and Society: 1780-1850* (New York: Columbia University Press, 1983), esp. xvi, 83-84.

70. Michael D. Bristol, *Shakespeare's America, America's Shakespeare* (London: Routledge, 1990), 16.

71. See Edward Jarvis, "On the Supposed Increase of Insanity," *American Journal of Insanity* 8, no. 4 (April 1852): 331-61; Isaac Ray, *Mental Hygiene* (Boston: Ticknor and Fields, 1863); and Brigham, *Remarks on the Influence*. See also Rothman, *The Discovery of the Asylum*, 109-29.

72. Jarvis, "On the Supposed Increase," 360.

73. See Grob, *Mental Institutions in America*, 168; Nancy Tomes, *A Generous Confidence: Thomas Story Kirkbride and the Art of Asylum-Keeping, 1840-1883* (Cambridge: Cambridge University Press, 1984), 280; and Foucault, *Madness and Civilization*, 254-55.

74. See Ray, *Mental Hygiene*.

75. See Tomes, *A Generous Confidence*.

76. Elaine Showalter, *The Female Malady: Women, Madness, and English Culture, 1830-1980* (New York: Pantheon, 1985), 38.

77. See Taylor, *Reinventing Shakespeare*, 196-97.

78. See "Editor's Table," *Opal* 2, no. 3 (March 1852): 92-93.

79. James C. Scott, *Domination and the Arts of Resistance: Hidden Transcripts* (New Haven, CT: Yale University Press, 1990), xiii.

80. "H.O.C.," *Opal* 4, no. 2 (February 1854): 51-52.

81. Scott, *Domination and the Arts of Resistance*, 154-56.

82. Mrs. George Lunt, *Behind the Bars* (Boston: Lee and Shepard, 1871), 71.

83. On this point, see especially Mary Elene Wood, *The Writing on the Wall: Women's Autobiography and the Asylum* (Urbana: University of Illinois Press, 1994).

84. Lunt, *Behind the Bars*, 323-324.

85. Ibid., v (in the preface).

86. Ibid., 17 ("Behind"), 59 ("inferior").

87. Ibid., 187-88.

88. Ibid., 83 ("was the finest," "great poet," "by purely,"), 116 ("ideal studies," "corroborated").

89. Ibid., 17.

90. Ibid., 86 (original emphasis).

91. See Ludmilla Jordanova, *Sexual Visions: Images of Gender in Science and Medicine between the Eighteenth and Twentieth Centuries* (Madison: University of Wisconsin Press, 1989).

92. See Showalter, *The Female Malady*, 50-73.

93. Andrew Scull, *Social Order/Mental Disorder* (Berkeley: University of California Press, 1989), 270; Nancy Tomes, "Devils in the Heart: Historical Perspectives on Women and Depression in Nineteenth-Century America," *Transactions and Studies of the College of Physicians of Philadelphia*, Series V, 13 (1991): 154-58. Tomes surveys the responses to Showalter's work in "Feminist Histories of Psychiatry," in *Discovering the History of Psychiatry*, ed. Mark Micale and Roy Porter (Oxford: Oxford University Press, 1995), 348-83 (see esp. 364-66).

94. Eugene D. Genovese, *Roll, Jordan, Roll: The World the Slaves Made* (1972; repr., New York: Vintage Books, 1974), 165.

CHAPTER FOUR

1. On McLean's elite standing among American asylums, see Edward Jarvis, *Insanity and Insane Asylums* (Louisville, KY: Prentice and Weissinger, 1841), 16. On McLean as a model for state institutions, see Robert Cassie Waterston, *The Condition of the Insane in Massachusetts* (Boston: James Munroe, 1841).

2. Michel Foucault, *Abnormal: Lectures at the Collège de France, 1974-1975*, trans. Graham Burchell (New York: Picador, 2003), 42.

3. Ibid., 118.

4. As Michael Ignatieff and Gareth Stedman Jones have pointed out—from differing ideological perspectives—Foucault, Rothman, and the other "social control" theorists of total institutions tend to fudge or abstract the question of who exactly is doing the controlling. See Stedman Jones, "Class Expression versus Social Control? A Critique of Recent Trends in the Social History of 'Leisure,'" in *Social Control and the State*, ed. Stanley Cohen and Andrew Scull (New York: St. Martin's Press, 1983), 39-49; and Michael Ignatieff, "State, Civil Society and Total Institutions: A Critique of Recent Social Histories of Punishment," in ibid., 75-105.

5. My characterization of romantic nostalgia comes largely from Michael Löwy and Robert Sayre, *Romanticism Against the Tide of Modernity*, trans. Catherine Porter (Durham, NC: Duke University Press, 2001). On the connections between American literary romanticism (including transcendentalism) and early American psychiatry, see Joan Burbick, "'Intervals of Tranquility': The Language of Health in Antebellum America," *Prospects: An Annual of American Cultural Studies* 12 (1987): 175-200; and Robert A. Gross, "'The Most Estimable Place in All the World': A Debate on Progress in Nineteenth-Century Concord," *Studies in the American Renaissance* 2 (1978): 1-15.

6. Daniel Walker Howe, *The Unitarian Conscience: Harvard Moral Philosophy, 1805-1861* (Cambridge, MA: Harvard University Press, 1970; 2nd ed. Middletown, CT: Wesleyan University Press, 1988). On transcendentalist group formation within the culture of Unitarianism, see Lawrence Buell, *Literary Transcendentalism: Style and Vision in the American Renaissance* (Ithaca, NY: Cornell University Press, 1973), 23-54.

7. William Ellery Channing, "Likeness to God" (1828), in *Transcendentalism: A Reader*, ed. Joel Myerson (New York: Oxford University Press, 2000), 7.

8. Howe, *The Unitarian Conscience*, 80.

9. Steven Mintz, *Moralists and Modernizers: America's Pre-Civil War Reformers* (Baltimore: Johns Hopkins University Press, 1996), 22; Howe, *The Unitarian Conscience*, 10-12.

10. Robert E. Burkholder, "Emerson, Kneeland, and the Divinity School Address," *American Literature* 58, no. 1 (March 1986): 1-14.

11. Helen Lefkowitz Horowitz, *Rereading Sex: Battles Over Sexual Knowledge and Suppression in Nineteenth-Century America* (New York: Random House, 2002), 77.

12. See Edwin Gittleman, *Jones Very: The Effective Years, 1833-1840* (New York: Columbia University Press, 1967), 75-76.

13. Barbara L. Packer, "The Transcendentalists," in *The Cambridge Literary History of American Literature*, ed. Sacvan Bercovitch (Cambridge: Cambridge University Press, 1995), 331-49 (the quote from Locke is on p. 338).

14. See Ronald Story, *The Forging of an Aristocracy: Harvard and the Boston Upper Class, 1800-1870* (Middletown, CT: Wesleyan University Press, 1980), chapters 2 and 3; Robert D. Habich, "Emerson's Reluctant Foe: Andrews Norton and the Transcendental Controversy," *New England Quarterly* 65, no. 2 (June 1992): 208-37.

15. I owe this insight to Lawrence Buell, who reads Emersonian selfhood as profoundly impersonal: "The more inward you go, the less individuated you get." Buell, *Emerson* (Cambridge, MA: Harvard University Press, 2003), 65.

16. Quoted in Stephen Whicher, *Freedom and Fate: An Inner Life of Ralph Waldo Emerson* (New York: A. S. Barnes), 20.

17. Ralph Waldo Emerson, "Divinity School Address," in *Essays & Poems* (New York: Library of America, 1996), 80–81, 83.

18. Packer, "The Transcendentalists," 367.

19. Emerson, "Divinity School Address," 88 ("go alone"), 89 ("without mediator"), 83 ("the need"), 89 ("yourself a newborn bard").

20. Quoted in Burkholder, "Emerson, Kneeland, and the Divinity School Address," 9, 10.

21. Habich, "Emerson's Reluctant Foe."

22. Andrews Norton, "The New School in Literature and Religion" (August 27, 1838), in Myerson, *Transcendentalism*, 247–48.

23. Ibid., 248–49 (see also p. 246).

24. Unless otherwise noted, all details of Jones Very's biography are taken from Gittleman, *Jones Very: The Effective Years, 1833–1840*.

25. "Rev. Jones Very: College Life of Jones Very," *Salem Gazette* (n.d., May 1880); in Wellesley College Library English Poetry Collection scrapbook *Letters of Jones Very to Ralph Waldo Emerson, 1838–1846*, Wellesley, MA.

26. Rev. J.T.G. Nichols, "1836. Jones Very, at Salem, May 8" in the *Harvard Register* (1880); in the Wellesley College Poetry Collection scrapbook *Letters of Jones Very*.

27. Gittleman, *Jones Very*, 174.

28. Odell Shepard, ed., *The Journals of Bronson Alcott*, vol. 1 (1938; repr. Port Washington, NY: Kennikat Press, 1966), 107.

29. Quoted in Helen R. Deese, Introduction to *Jones Very: The Complete Poems*, ed. Helen R. Deese (Athens: University of Georgia Press, 1993), xi–lv (quote is from p. xix).

30. Jones Very, "Shakspeare," in *Essays and Poems* (Boston: Charles C. Little and James Brown, 1839), 40.

31. Sharon Cameron, "The Way of Life by Abandonment: Emerson's Impersonal," *Critical Inquiry* 25, no. 1 (Autumn 1998): 1–31.

32. Emerson, "The Divinity School Address," 89. The important distinction is that Very believed that he alone had this ability, whereas Emerson believed that Shakespeare spoke "to the Shakspeare in us"—that is, all of us. Emerson, "Shakspeare; Or, The Poet," in *Essays and Lectures*, 720.

33. Gittleman, *Jones Very*, 165–66; Carlos Baker, *Emerson Among the Eccentrics: A Group Portrait* (New York: Viking, 1996), 121–22. It should be noted, however, that Emerson did use several additional Divinity School students as a sounding board for the composition of his address. See Ralph Waldo Emerson, *Journals and Miscellaneous Notebooks*, vol. 5, ed. Merton Sealts, Jr. (Cambridge, MA: The Belknap Press of Harvard University Press, 1965), 471.

34. Letter from Jones Very to Henry Whitney Bellows, December 29, 1838, Boston Athenaeum. This letter has been reprinted in Harry L. Jones, "The Very Madness: A New Manuscript," *College Language Association Journal* 10 (1967): 196–200; and in Deese, ed., *Jones Very* (see the introduction).

35. Henry Ware, Jr., "The Personality of the Deity," in Myerson, ed., *Transcendentalism*, 258–59.

36. Quoted in Gittleman, *Jones Very*, 188–89.

37. The essay was published as "Shakspeare" in Very, *Essays and Poems*, 39–82.

38. Quoted in Gittleman, *Jones Very*, 219.

39. Elizabeth Palmer Peabody to William P. Andrews, November 12, 1880; repr. in *The Letters of Elizabeth Palmer Peabody, American Renaissance Woman*, ed. Bruce A. Ronda (Middletown, CT: Wesleyan University Press, 1984), 406–7.

40. On Upham and Brazer's religious views, see Alfred F. Rosa, *Salem, Transcendentalism, and*

Hawthorne (Rutherford, NJ: Fairleigh Dickinson University Press, 1980), 99–108, 148–49; see also William R. Hutchison, *The Transcendentalist Ministers: Church Reform in The New England Renaissance* (New Haven, CT: Yale University Press, 1959).

41. Helen R. Deese, "The Peabody Family and the Jones Very 'Insanity': Two Letters of Mary Peabody" *Harvard Library Bulletin* 35, no. 2 (Spring 1987): 219–20.

42. George B. Loring to James Russell Lowell; Richard Henry Dana to William Cullen Bryant; quoted in Gittleman, *Jones Very*, 228.

43. Howe, *The Unitarian Conscience*, 77; Buell, *Literary Transcendentalism*, 23–54; Habich, "Emerson's Reluctant Foe"; Packer, "The Transcendentalists," 392–423.

44. Gittleman, *Jones Very*, 226.

45. Norman Dain, *Concepts of Insanity in the United States, 1789–1865* (New Brunswick, NJ: Rutgers University Press, 1964), 187. Dix's biographer, David Gollaher, calls Channing her "surrogate father" and suggests that her interest in ameliorating the condition of the insane was prompted by his "confidence in the redemptive power of moral education." Gollaher, *Voice for the Mad: The Life of Dorothea Dix* (New York: Free Press, 1995), 78.

46. Waterston, *The Condition of the Insane*, 11. Waterston's friendship with Very is chronicled in a letter memorializing the poet on his death in 1880. Robert Cassie Waterston to William P. Andrews, August 18, 1880, in Wellesley College Library English Poetry Collection, *Notebook of William P. Andrews on Jones Very*, Wellesley, MA.

47. Dain, *Concepts of Insanity*, 188.

48. Ibid., 193.

49. Charles Wentworth Upham, *Lectures on Witchcraft: Comprising a History of the Delusion in Salem, in 1692* (Boston: Carter, Hendee, and Babcock, 1831), 99.

50. Ibid., vii.

51. Ibid., vi.

52. On Kneeland's support of Emerson, see Packer, "The Transcendentalists," 407.

53. Thomas S. Szasz, *The Manufacture of Madness: A Comparative Study of the Inquisition and the Mental Health Movement* (1970; repr. Syracuse, NY: Syracuse University Press, 1997), xxiv.

54. The quotes are taken from Gittleman, *Jones Very*, 161, 284.

55. Robert D. Arner, "Hawthorne and Jones Very: Two Dimensions of Satire in 'Egotism; Or, the Bosom Serpent,'" *New England Quarterly* 42, no. 2 (June 1969): 267–75.

56. Gerald N. Grob, *Mental Institutions in America: Social Policy to 1875* (New York: The Free Press, 1973), 7.

57. Morrill Wyman, *The Early History of the McLean Asylum for the Insane* (Cambridge, MA: Riverside Press: 1877), 13.

58. Jarvis, *Insanity and Insane Asylums*, 16.

59. Ibid., 18.

60. Ibid., 17.

61. Wyman, *The Early History of the McLean Asylum*, 12.

62. Ibid., 1–2.

63. Gerald N. Grob, *The State and the Mentally Ill: A History of Worcester State Hospital in Massachusetts* (Chapel Hill: University of North Carolina Press, 1966), 92.

64. Ibid., 49–50.

65. Gittleman, *Jones Very*, 223–24.

66. Very to Bellows (see note 32 of this chapter).

67. Wyman, *The Early History of the McLean Asylum*, 12.

68. Luther Bell, *An Hour's Conference with Fathers and Sons, in Relation to a Common and Fatal Indulgence* (Boston: Whipple and Damrell, 1840), 86. While I do not have space here to consider the question of Very's sexuality and his supposed madness, Holly Allen has intriguingly suggested to me that his renunciation of romantic attachments to women and his frantic intellectual

courting of Emerson—coupled with his stay at an aggressively desexualizing institution—might open up an interesting "queer" reading of Very's story. Against this notion, Helen Deese speculates that Very suffered from temporal lobe epilepsy, which "is characterized by a syndrome including the following symptoms: hyperreligiosity; hypergraphia, the uncontrollable compulsion to write; 'stickiness,' the reluctance to end conversations" (she cites Hawthorne's comment that Very "is somewhat unconscionable as to the length of his calls"), "transient aggressiveness, rarely leading to violence; and altered or decreased interest in sex" (Deese, ed., *Jones Very*, xxxiv).

69. Elizabeth Palmer Peabody to Ralph Waldo Emerson, October 20, 1838; repr. in Ronda, ed., *Letters of Elizabeth Palmer Peabody*, 215-17.

70. Mary Peabody to Elizabeth Palmer Peabody, November 24, 1838; repr. in Deese, "The Peabody Family and the Jones Very 'Insanity,'" 218-29.

71. Elizabeth Palmer Peabody to Ralph Waldo Emerson, October 20, 1838.

72. Ralph Waldo Emerson, *Journals and Miscellaneous Notebooks*, vol. 7, ed. A.W. Plumstead and Harrison Hayford (Cambridge, MA: The Belknap Press of Harvard University Press, 1969), 116-17.

73. Ibid., 122.

74. Ibid, 123.

75. Emerson, "Friendship," in *Essays & Poems*, 347.

76. Jones Very, "Help," *Jones Very: The Complete Poems*, 117-18.

77. The retort is quoted in Elizabeth Palmer Peabody to Ralph Waldo Emerson, November 12, 1880 and is taken at face value in Gittleman, *Jones Very*, 337. The source is apparently a letter from Emerson to Elizabeth Hoar, dated September 12, 1840, in which he is discussing the preparation of a selection of poems by William Ellery Channing the Younger for publication in the *Dial*. Discussing Channing's "bad grammar& his nonsense," he wrote: "As it fell in the case of Jones Very, cannot the spirit parse & spell?" (repr. in *The Letters of Ralph Waldo Emerson*, vol. 2, ed. Ralph L. Rusk [New York: Columbia University Press, 1939], 331).

78. Quoted in Gittleman, *Jones Very*, 258.

79. [Ralph Waldo Emerson], "*Essays and Poems*. By Jones Very," *The Dial: A Magazine for Literature, Philosophy, and Religion*, 2, no. 1 (July 1841): 130-31.

80. Gittleman, *Jones Very*, 165; Baker, *Emerson among the Eccentrics*, 141; Deese ed., *Jones Very*, xix; Sarah Turner Clayton, *The Angelic Sins of Jones Very* (New York: Peter Lang, 1999), xi. On the surface, Yvor Winters's comment that "Very's poems bear witness unanswerably that he had the experience which Emerson merely recommends" seems in line with this idea; but Winters tries to show that Very's mysticism was closer to the Puritan and Quaker traditions than to transcendentalism or Unitarianism. See Winters, "Jones Very and R.W. Emerson: Aspects of New England Mysticism," in *Maule's Curse: Seven Studies in the History of American Obscurantism* (Norwalk, CT: New Directions, 1938), 125-48 (the quote is on p. 127).

81. Quoted in John Stauffer, *The Black Hearts of Men: Radical Abolitionists and the Transformation of Race* (Cambridge, MA: Harvard University Press, 2001), 37.

82. Emerson to William Emerson, June 2, 1828; repr. in *The Letters of Ralph Waldo Emerson*, vol. 1, 235.

83. Emerson to William Emerson, June 30, 1828; repr. in ibid., 236.

84. Emerson to William Emerson July 3, 1828; repr. in *The Letters of Ralph Waldo Emerson*, vol. 7, 172-73.

85. Baker, *Emerson among the Eccentrics*, 4; Ronald A. Bosco and Joel Myerson, *The Emerson Brothers: A Fraternal Biography in Letters* (New York: Oxford University Press, 2006), 6.

86. This quote is from an entry from Edward Jarvis's diary dated June 30, 1828, and reprinted in Bosco and Myerson, *The Emerson Brothers*, 122.

87. Ralph Waldo Emerson to Josiah Quincy, Jr., December 10, 1836, in *The Letters of Ralph Waldo Emerson*, vol. 2, 49-50.

88. Two historians who note the lack of intellectual dissent against psychiatric culture are David J. Rothman and Nancy Tomes. See Rothman, "Introduction to the 1990 Edition," *The Discovery of the Asylum: Social Order and Disorder in the New Republic* (Boston: Little, Brown, 1971; 1990), xxxix; and Tomes, *A Generous Confidence: Thomas Story Kirkbride and the Art of Asylum-Keeping, 1840–1883* (Cambridge: Cambridge University Press, 1984), 86–88.

89. On the autonomy of the psychiatric profession, see Paul Starr, *The Social Transformation of American Medicine* (New York: Basic Books, 1982), 72–75; Constance M. McGovern, *Masters of Madness: Social Origins of the American Psychiatric Profession* (Hanover, NH: University Press of New England, 1985), 44–61.

90. Very was only the first of many of well-known poets and writers—stretching out over nearly two centuries—to receive treatment there (see epilogue). For a breezy but informative history of McLean, see Alex Beam, *Gracefully Insane: The Rise and Fall of America's Premier Mental Hospital* (New York: Public Affairs, 2001).

91. Robert Fuller, *An Account of the Imprisonment and Sufferings of Robert Fuller, of Cambridge* (Boston: privately printed, 1833), 17.

92. Erving Goffman, *Asylums: Essays on the Social Situation of Mental Patients and Other Inmates* (New York: Anchor Books, 1961). In Goffman's terms, each patient comes to the institution with a "presenting culture," which must be changed through "disculturation" or "untraining" (13).

93. This despite his youthful claim in his journal that he had "so much mixture of *silliness* in my intellectual frame that I think Providence has tempered me against this." Emerson, *Journals and Miscellaneous Notebooks*, vol. 3, 137.

94. Quoted in Burkholder, "Emerson, Kneeland, and the Divinity School Address," 10.

95. Sleepless nights caused the postponement of at least one lecture. See *The Early Lectures of Ralph Waldo Emerson*, vol. 3 (1838–1842), ed. Robert E. Spiller and Wallace E. Williams (Cambridge, MA: The Belknap Press of Harvard University Press, 1972), 1.

96. Löwy and Sayre, *Romanticism Against the Tide of Modernity*, 17.

97. Emerson, *Nature*, in *Essays & Poems*, 43.

98. See Richard F. Teichgraeber III, *Sublime Thoughts/Penny Wisdom: Situating Emerson and Thoreau in the American Market* (Baltimore: Johns Hopkins University Press, 1995).

99. Emerson, "Self-Reliance," in *Essays & Poems*, 268.

100. Etienne Esquirol, *Mental Maladies: A Treatise on Insanity*, trans. Ebenezer Kingsbury Hunt (Philadelphia: Lea and Blanchard, 1845), 347.

101. Jarvis, "On the Supposed Increase of Insanity," *American Journal of Insanity* 8, no. 4 (April 1852): 359.

102. Emerson, "Self-Reliance," in *Essays & Poems*, 279.

103. On intellectual connections between transcendentalism and early psychiatry, see Burbick, "'Intervals of Tranquility'" and Gross, "'The Most Estimable Place in All the World.'"

104. Quoted in Thomas Cooley, *The Ivory Leg in the Ebony Cabinet: Madness, Race, and Gender in Victorian America* (Amherst: University of Massachusetts Press, 2001), 30.

105. Emerson to Margaret Fuller, November 9, 1838, in *The Letters of Ralph Waldo Emerson*, vol. 2, 173.

106. Emerson, "The American Scholar," in *Essays & Poems*, 54 (original emphasis).

107. Quoted in Burbick, "'Intervals of Tranquility,'" 176.

108. On the influence of Locke on the first generation of American asylum superintendents, see Dain, *Concepts of Insanity*, 59–62.

109. On the transcendentalists' "assault on Locke," see Packer, "Transcendentalism," esp. 350–61.

110. A letter from Peabody to Emerson, September 24, 1838, repr. in Ronda, ed., *Letters of Elizabeth Palmer Peabody*, 209–10 (original emphasis).

111. On the centrality of "Reason" to the transcendentalists' self-definition, see Buell, *Literary Transcendentalism*, 4–5, and Packer, "Transcendentalism," 354–56.

112. Emerson, *Nature*, in *Essays & Poems*, 26.

113. Packer, "Transcendentalism," 356.

114. See Clayton, *The Angelic Sins of Jones Very*, 41.

115. Shepard, ed., *The Journals of Bronson Alcott*, vol. I, 107–8.

116. Emerson, "The Over-Soul," in *Essays & Poems*, 392.

117. Shepard, ed., *The Journals of Bronson Alcott*, vol. I, 113–14.

118. James Freeman Clarke, "Religious Sonnets: By Jones Very," *The Western Messenger: Devoted to Religion and Literature* 6, no. 5 (March 1839): 308–11.

119. Gerald N. Grob, *Edward Jarvis and the Medical World of Nineteenth-Century America* (Knoxville: University of Tennessee Press, 1978), 43.

120. See Cooley, *The Ivory Leg in the Ebony Cabinet*, 16–26.

121. Dain, *Concepts of Insanity*, 57–62.

122. Emerson, *Nature*, in *Essays & Poems*, 48.

123. Quoted in Barbara L. Packer, *Emerson's Fall: A New Interpretation of the Major Essays* (New York: Continuum, 1982), 13.

124. Caleb Smith, "Emerson and Incarceration," *American Literature* 78, no. 2 (June 2006): 208 ("prison architecture"), 225 ("clapped into jail").

125. Emerson, "Self-Reliance," 276 ("men's prayers"), 270 (the centuries").

126. Ibid., 262–63.

127. Ibid., 263.

128. Sharon L. Snyder and David T. Mitchell, *Cultural Locations of Disability* (Chicago: University of Chicago Press, 2006), 37–43, 60.

129. "Religion," in *The Early Lectures of Ralph Waldo Emerson*, vol. 3, 273.

130. "The Protest," in ibid., 100.

131. Buell, *Emerson*, 162.

132. On Emerson's increasing conservatism, see Sacvan Bercovitch, "Emerson, Individualism, and Individual Dissent," in *The Rites of Assent; Transformations in the Symbolic Construction of America* (New York: Routledge, 1993), 307–52; and Mary Kupiec Cayton, "The Making of an American Prophet: Emerson, His Audiences, and the Rise of the Culture Industry in Nineteenth-Century America," in *Ralph Waldo Emerson: A Collection of Critical Essays*, ed. Lawrence Buell (Englewood Cliffs, NJ: Prentice Hall, 1993), 77–100.

133. Thomas Augst, *The Clerk's Tale: Young Men and Moral Life in Nineteenth-Century America* (Chicago: University of Chicago Press, 2003), 119.

134. See Buell, *Emerson*, 252.

135. Emerson, "The Fugitive Slave Law," in *Essays & Poems*, 993; and "The Fugitive Slave Law," *The Complete Works of Ralph Waldo Emerson*, vol. XI (Miscellanies) (Boston: Houghton Mifflin, 1903), 179.

136. Fuller, *An Account of the Imprisonment*, 16.

137. Ibid., 22.

138. Ibid., 29.

139. Elizabeth T. Stone, *A Sketch of the Life of Elizabeth T. Stone, and of Her Persecutions* (n.p., privately printed, 1842), 4.

140. Stone, *A Sketch of the Life of Elizabeth T. Stone*, 7.

141. Ibid., 17.

142. Ibid., 19.

143. Ibid., 22.

144. Ibid., 25

145. Ibid., 39

146. Deese, ed., *Jones Very*, 295.

147. Ibid., 283.

148. Very to Bellows (see note 34 of this chapter).

149. Cited poems are from Deese, ed., *Jones Very*: "The New Birth," 64; "The Garden," 69; and "He Was Acquainted with Grief," 85.

150. "The Foe," in Deese, ed., *Jones Very*, 151.

151. "Behold He Is At Hand That Doth Betray Me," in Deese, ed., *Jones Very*, 88–89.

152. Ibid., 89.

CHAPTER FIVE

1. Edmund Burke, *Reflections on the Revolution in France* (London: Penguin Classics, 1986), 90.

2. Ibid., 195.

3. Jan Goldstein, *Console and Classify: The French Psychiatric Profession in the Nineteenth Century* (Cambridge: Cambridge University Press, 1987), 109.

4. Quoted in Robert Castel, *The Regulation of Madness: The Origins of Incarceration in France*, trans. W.D. Halls (Berkeley: University of California Press, 1988), 61.

5. Amariah Brigham, "Insanity and Insane Hospitals," *North American Review* 44 (January 1837): 104.

6. Peter Weiss, *The Persecution and Assassination of Jean-Paul Marat as Performed by the Inmates of the Asylum of Charenton Under the Direction of the Marquis de Sade (Marat/Sade)*, English version by Geoffrey Skelton, verse adaptation by Adrian Mitchell (New York: Atheneum, 1965).

7. One of the few critics to attend seriously to the linkages between the psychiatric foreground and the racial background of the story is Jonathan Elmer, *Reading at the Social Limit: Affect, Mass Culture, and Edgar Allan Poe* (Stanford, CA: Stanford University Press, 1995), 142–48. Elmer argues that Poe's story registers antebellum fascination with "mixed states between freedom and incarceration" registered both in the popularity of fugitive slave narratives and the widespread interest in the legislative activities of Dorothea Dix (141). Another essay that analyzes Poe's treatment of incarceration and individual liberties as central threads in his work is Joan Dayan, "Poe, Persons, and Property," *American Literary History* 11, no. 3 (Autumn 1999): 405–25.

8. See Bernard A. Drabeck, "'Tarr and Fether': Poe and Abolition," *American Transcendental Quarterly* 14 (1972): 177–84; see also Louis Rubin, *The Edge of the Swamp: A Study of the Literature and Society of the Old South* (Baton Rouge: Louisiana State University Press, 1989), 162–67; and J. Gerald Kennedy, "A Mania for Composition: Poe's *Annus Mirabilis* and the Violence of Nation Building," *American Literary History* 17, no. 1 (Spring 2005): 1–35.

9. Martha C. Nussbaum, *Frontiers of Justice: Disability, Nationality, Species Membership* (Cambridge, MA: Harvard University Press, 2006), 160.

10. See Peter Brook's introduction (vi–vii) and Peter Weiss's "Author's Note on the Historical Background to the Play" (105–110) in *Marat/Sade*.

11. Weiss, *Marat/Sade*, 93.

12. Edgar Allan Poe, "The System of Doctor Tarr and Professor Fether," in *Poe: Poetry, Tales, and Selected Essays* (New York: Library of America, 1996), 700.

13. Ibid., 701.

14. A correspondent for a popular magazine, for instance, reported that "a survey of the scene" at an enlightened asylum in Scotland "imparted a feeling of awe; and now, for the first time, one could appreciate the sentiment which is felt in the east for idiots and madmen" "(A Ball at a Lunatic Asylum," *Littel's Living Age* 8, no. 93 [February 21, 1846]: 349).

15. Poe, "The System of Doctor Tarr and Professor Fether," 701.

16. Ibid., 709.

17. Ibid., 711.

18. Ibid., 713.

19. Ibid., 714.

20. Ibid., 714 ("counter revolution and "Gracious Heavens!"); Weiss, *Marat/Sade*, 101–2 ("the lunatics").

21. Poe, "The System of Doctor Tarr and Professor Fether," 715–16.

22. Ibid., 716.

23. See Drabeck, "'Tarr and Fether'"; see also Rubin, *The Edge of the Swamp*, 162–67; and Kennedy, "A Mania for Composition."

24. Kennedy, "A Mania for Composition," 16, 17.

25. Thomas Jefferson, *Notes on the State of Virginia* (New York: Harper and Row, 1964), 132–33.

26. See Elise Lemire, "'The Murders in the Rue Morgue': Amalgamation Discourses and the Race Riots of 1838 in Poe's Philadelphia," in *Romancing the Shadow: Poe and Race*, ed. J. Gerald Kennedy and Lilane Weissberg (Oxford: Oxford University Press, 2001), 177–204. Lemire's essay argues that these associations of Africans, orangutans, and violence were particularly urgent for Poe's readers in the context of the frequent race riots in Philadelphia in the late 1830s. Taken together, such studies primed white Philadelphians to view blacks as lustful and dangerous—much like the apes they were said to resemble—and that Poe's story helped to solidify their view that sexual mixing (or amalgamation) of blacks and whites was an unnatural abomination.

27. See Sander L. Gilman, "On the Nexus of Blackness and Madness," in *Difference and Pathology: Stereotypes of Sexuality, Race, and Madness* (Ithaca, NY: Cornell University Press, 1985), 131–49, esp. 142–48.

28. Sander L. Gilman, *Seeing the Insane* (Lincoln: University of Nebraska Press, 1996), 2.

29. Quoted in Allen Thiher, *Revels in Madness: Insanity in Medicine and Literature* (Ann Arbor: University of Michigan Press, 1999), 74.

30. Gilman, *Seeing the Insane*, 2–4.

31. Quoted in ibid., 62.

32. Quoted in ibid., 111.

33. See Ian Robert Dowbiggin, *Keeping America Sane: Psychiatry and Eugenics in the United States and Canada, 1880–1940* (Ithaca, NY: Cornell University Press, 1997); and Daniel J. Kevles, *In the Name of Eugenics: Genetics and the Uses of Human Heredity* (New York: Knopf, 1985).

34. Edward Jarvis, *Insanity and Insane Asylums* (Louisville, KY: Prentice and Weissinger, 1841), 6.

35. See Norman Dain, *Concepts of Insanity in the United States, 1789–1865* (New Brunswick, NJ: Rutgers University Press, 1964), 40–44; and Karen Halttunen, *Murder Most Foul: The Killer and the American Gothic Imagination* (Cambridge, MA: Harvard University Press, 1998), 219–38.

36. Pliny Earle, "The Poetry of Insanity," *American Journal of Insanity* 1, no. 3 (January 1845): 193–94. On Poe's relation to Earle see William Whipple, "Poe's Two-Edged Satiric Tale," *Nineteenth-Century Literature* 9, no. 2 (September 1954): 121–33.

37. Earle, "The Poetry of Insanity," 194–95.

38. Poe, "The System of Doctor Tarr and Professor Fether," 699 ("his very usual horror"), 716 ("fighting, stamping").

39. John Brown, *The History and Present Condition of St. Domingue* (Philadelphia: William Marshall and Company, 1837), 248. Thanks to Faye Felterman for this citation.

40. Weiss, *Marat/Sade*, 93.

41. Poe, "The System of Doctor Tarr and Professor Fether," 699.

42. Ibid., 703.

43. See Roy Porter, *Madness: A Brief History* (Oxford: Oxford University Press, 2002), 95; Porter, *Mind Forg'd Manacles: A History of Madness in England from the Restoration to the Regency* (London: Athlone Press, 1987), 119-20.

44. Poe, "The System of Doctor Tarr and Professor Fether," 699 ("the regulations"), 702 ("repose confidence").

45. Ibid., 702.

46. Ibid., 716.

47. Ibid., 703.

48. Ibid., 700

49. On the professionalism of nineteenth-century French psychiatrists, see Goldstein, *Control and Classify*, 8-40.

50. Hannah Arendt, *On Revolution* (New York: Penguin, 1963), 63.

51. Weiss, *Marat/Sade*, 76.

52. Brigham, "Insanity and Insane Hospitals," 91.

53. Klaus Doerner, *Madmen and the Bourgeoisie: A Social History of Insanity and Psychiatry*, trans. Joachim Neugroschel and Jean Steinberg (Oxford: Basil Blackwell, 1981), 127.

54. Ibid., 130. Dora B. Weiner, however, believes that Pinel's concern was to elevate the indigent insane "to the dignified status of medical patients in the newly formed republic." See Weiner, "'Le geste de Pinel': The History of a Psychiatric Myth," in *Discovering the History of Psychiatry*, ed. Mark S. Micale and Roy Porter (New York: Oxford University Press, 1994), 232-47 (see esp. 232).

55. Doerner, *Madmen and the Bourgeoisie*, 120.

56. Ibid., 98.

57. Ibid., 121.

58. Brigham, "Insanity and Insane Hospitals," 103.

59. Weiner, *"Le geste de Pinel,"* 237.

60. See Patrick Vandermeersch, "'Les mythes d'origine' in the History of Psychiatry," in *Discovering the History of Psychiatry*, 219-31.

61. Jarvis, *Insanity and Insane Asylums*, 6.

62. Quoted in Goldstein, *Console and Classify*, 74-75 (original emphasis).

63. Poe, "The System of Doctor Tarr and Professor Fether," 713.

64. See Doerner, *Madmen and the Bourgeoisie*, 124.

65. See ibid., 129; Goldstein, *Console and Classify*, 101; and Gerald N. Grob, *Mental Institutions in America: Social Policy to 1875* (New York: The Free Press, 1973), 41-44.

66. See Goldstein, *Console and Classify*, 83.

67. Poe, "The System of Doctor Tarr and Professor Fether," 702.

68. Ibid., 716.

69. David J. Rothman, *The Discovery of the Asylum: Social Order and Disorder in the New Republic* (Boston: Little, Brown, 1971), 110.

70. Benjamin Rush, *Medical Inquiries and Observations, Upon the Diseases of the Mind* (Philadelphia: Kimber and Richardson, 1812), 68-69.

71. Ibid., 71, 69.

72. Cited in Thomas S. Szasz, ed., *The Age of Madness: The History of Involuntary Mental Hospitalization, Presented in Selected Texts* (Garden City, NY: Anchor Books, 1973), 140.

73. See Dain, *Concepts of Insanity*, 14-23.

74. Quoted in Szasz, ed., *The Age of Madness*, 24.

75. See Nancy Tomes, *A Generous Confidence: Thomas Story Kirkbride and the Art of Asylum-Keeping, 1840-1883* (Cambridge: Cambridge University Press, 1984), 26-30.

76. See Szasz, ed., *The Age of Madness*, 26, 28.

77. Tomes, *A Generous Confidence*, 4-5.

78. Weiss, *Marat/Sade*, 4.

79. Castel, *The Regulation of Madness*, 64.

80. Nussbaum similarly asserts that the tradition of liberal social contract theory—from Locke and Kant through Rawls—founders on the question of nonrational social actors. "The classical theorists," she writes, "all assumed that their contracting agents" (those capable of freely and rationally entering into social bonds with each other for mutual benefit) "were men who were roughly equal in capacity, and capable of productive economic activity" (Nussbaum, *Frontiers of Justice*, 13).

81. "Celebration of the Birth-Day of Pinel at the State Lunatic Asylum, Utica, N.Y., April 11, 1846", *American Journal of Insanity* 3, no. 1 (July 1846): 78–87 (see pp.78–79 for the hymn and p. 80 for the poem).

82. F.O. Matthiessen, *American Renaissance: Art and Expression in the Age of Emerson and Whitman* (New York: Oxford University Press, 1941), xii n3.

83. See, for instance, Douglas C. Baynton, "Disability and the Justification of Inequality in American History," in *The New Disability History: American Perspectives*, ed. Paul K. Longmore and Lauri Umansky (New York: New York University Press, 2001), 33–57.

84. See Rosemarie Garland Thomson, *Extraordinary Bodies: Figuring Physical Disability in American Culture and Literature* (New York: Columbia University Press, 1997), 41–44.

85. The best overall study of Poe's treatment of race within the context of national politics is Terence Whalen, "Average Racism: Poe, Slavery, and the Wages of Literary Nationalism," in *Edgar Allan Poe and the Masses* (Princeton, NJ: Princeton University Press, 1999), 111–46.

86. See *The Poe Log: A Documentary Life of Edgar Allan Poe, 1809–1849*, ed. Dwight Thomas and David K. Jackson (1987; repr. New York: G.K. Hall, 1995), 633–34, 642.

87. See Kenneth Silverman, *Edgar A. Poe: Mournful and Never-Ending Remembrance* (New York: HarperCollins, 1991), 312–16.

88. Henry Maudsley, MD, "Edgar Allan Poe," *American Journal of Insanity* 17, no. 2 (October 1860): 152–98 (this essay was originally published in the April 1860 edition of the *Journal of Mental Science*).

89. See Philip Young, "The Earlier Psychologists and Poe," *American Literature* 22, no. 4 (January 1951): 442–54.

90. John Bryant also considers Poe's treatment of apes to be somewhat self-reflexive, but he finds this to be a matter of "sexual anxiety" that is ultimately "displaced" onto readers through rituals of humor. See Bryant, "Poe's Ape of Unreason: Humor, Ritual, and Culture," *Nineteenth-Century Literature* 51, no. 1 (June 1996): 16–52.

CHAPTER SIX

1. Robert Fuller, *An Account of the Imprisonment and Sufferings of Robert Fuller, of Cambridge* (Boston: privately printed, 1833), 29.

2. Moses Swan, *Ten Years and Ten Months in Lunatic Asylums in Different States* (Hoosick Falls, NY: privately printed, 1874), 85.

3. Quoted in Karen Halttunen, "Gothic Mystery and the Birth of the Asylum: The Cultural Construction of Deviance in Early-Nineteenth-Century America," in *Moral Problems in American Life: New Perspectives on Cultural History*, ed. Karen Halttunen and Lewis Perry (Ithaca, NY: Cornell University Press, 1998), 51.

4. Phebe B. Davis, *The Travels and Experience of Miss Phebe B. Davis* (Syracuse, NY: J.G.K. Truair & Co., 1860), 27.

5. Swan, *Ten Years and Ten Months*, 135.

6. One exception is the narrative of Robert Fuller (1832), whose account of his stay at McLean is cited above. Fuller's narrative, however, was written before the first state institutions were constructed.

7. Elizabeth T. Stone, *A Sketch of the Life of Elizabeth T. Stone, and of Her Persecutions* (privately printed, 1842), 35.

8. Swan, *Ten Years and Ten Months*, 91.

9. Mrs. George Lunt, *Behind the Bars* (Boston: Lee and Shepard, 1871), 36-37.

10. Rev. Hiram Chase, *Two Years in a Lunatic Asylum* (Saratoga Springs, NY: Van Benthuysen and Sons, 1868), 34-38.

11. Phebe Davis, *Two Years and Three Months in the New York Lunatic Asylum at Utica* (Syracuse, NY: privately printed, 1865), 24-25.

12. Ibid., 45.

13. Ibid., 50.

14. Chase, *Two Years in a Lunatic Asylum*, 92.

15. Swan, *Ten Years and Ten Months*, 55.

16. On causes for the decline of the asylum movement, see David J. Rothman, *The Discovery of the Asylum: Social Order and Disorder in the New Republic* (Boston: Little, Brown, 1971), 265-95. On cure rates and costs, see also Nancy Tomes, *A Generous Confidence: Thomas Story Kirkbride and the Art of Asylum-Keeping, 1840-1883* (Cambridge: Cambridge University Press, 1984), 290-93; on the effects of the Civil War, see Ellen Dwyer, *Homes for the Mad: Life Inside Two Nineteenth-Century Asylums* (New Brunswick, NJ: Rutgers University Press, 1987), 8; and Lynn Gamwell and Nancy Tomes, *Madness in America: Cultural and Medical Perceptions of Mental Illness Before 1914* (Ithaca, NY: Cornell University Press, 1995), 121; on the challenges posed by neurology, see Tomes, *A Generous Confidence*, 107, 292; and Norman Dain, *Concepts of Insanity in the United States, 1789-1865* (New Brunswick, NJ: Rutgers University Press, 1964), 133; on degeneracy and psychiatry, see Ian Robert Dowbiggin, *Keeping America Sane: Psychiatry and Eugenics in the United States and Canada, 1880-1940* (Ithaca, NY: Cornell University Press, 1997).

17. Quoted in Dowbiggin, *Keeping America Sane*, 72.

18. See Elizabeth Parsons Ware Packard, *The Prisoners' Hidden Life, or Insane Asylums Unveiled* (Chicago: privately printed, 1868); and Barbara Sapinsley, *The Private War of Mrs. Packard* (New York: Paragon House, 1991).

19. Quoted in Sapinsley, *The Private War of Mrs. Packard*, 45.

20. Packard, *Modern Persecution; Or, Insane Asylums Unveiled*, vol. 1, Introduction (Hartford, CT: Case, Lockwood, and Brainard, 1875; repr. New York: Arno Press, 1973), xxxii (citations are to the 1973 edition).

21. See Phyllis Chesler, *Women and Madness* (1972; repr. San Diego: Harcourt Brace Jovanovich, 1989), 10-16; Mary Elene Wood, *The Writing on the Wall: Women's Autobiography and the Asylum* (Urbana: University of Illinois Press, 1994), 25-47.

22. Packard, *The Prisoners' Hidden Life*, 84.

23. See Packard, "My Plea for Married Woman's Emancipation made before Connecticut Legislature in New Haven State House, June, 1866," in *Modern Persecution*, vol. 2, 393-406.

24. Packard, *The Prisoners' Hidden Life*, 335.

25. William Lloyd Garrison, "Speech at the Fourth National Women's Rights Convention," in *Against Slavery: An Abolitionist Reader*, ed. Mason Lowance (New York: Penguin Classics, 2000), 123.

26. Quoted in Sapinsley, *The Private War of Mrs. Packard*, 3.

27. Nancy Tomes, "Feminist Histories of Psychiatry," in *Discovering the History of Psychiatry*, ed. Mark S. Micale and Roy Porter (New York: Oxford University Press, 1994), 360.

28. Elaine Showalter, *The Female Malady: Women, Madness, and English Culture, 1830-1980* (New York: Pantheon, 1985), 5.

29. On Douglass's masculinist position as a writer and historical figure, see Deborah E.

McDowell, "In the First Place: Making Frederick Douglass and the Afro-American Narrative Tradition," in *African American Autobiography: A Collection of Critical Essays* (Englewood Cliffs, NJ: Prentice Hall, 1993), 36–58.

30. Chesler, *Women and Madness*, 15.

31. Ibid., xx.

32. Sandra M. Gilbert and Susan Gubar, *The Madwoman in the Attic: The Woman Writer and the Nineteenth-Century Literary Imagination* (New Haven, CT: Yale University Press, 1979), 85.

33. Showalter, *The Female Malady*, 5, 4.

34. Wood, *The Writing on the Wall*, 26.

35. Packard, *The Prisoners' Hidden Life*, 64.

36. Ibid., 326–27.

37. Sapinsley, *The Private War of Mrs. Packard*, 17. On Packard's love for McFarland, see also Thomas Cooley, *The Ivory Leg in the Ebony Cabinet: Madness, Race, and Gender in Victorian America* (Amherst: University of Massachusetts Press, 2001), 197–202.

38. Timothy A. Hacsi, *Second Home: Orphan Asylums and Poor Families in America* (Cambridge, MA: Harvard University Press, 1997), see p. 75.

39. Rothman, *The Discovery of the Asylum*, 218.

40. This is consistent with a pattern described famously by Mary Kelley in *Private Woman, Public Stage: Literary Domesticity in Nineteenth-Century America*(repr. ed., Chapel Hill: University of North Carolina Press, 2002).

41. Thomas J. Brown, *Dorothea Dix: New England Reformer* (Cambridge, MA: Harvard University Press, 1998), 168.

42. Gamwell and Tomes, *Madness in America*, 105.

43. Carroll Smith-Rosenberg, *Disorderly Conduct: Visions of Gender in Victorian America* (New York: Alfred A. Knopf, 1985), 208.

44. Sarah Apgar to Pliny Earle, May 24, 1847, in Pliny Earle Papers, American Antiquarian Society, Box 5, Folder 1, Worcester, MA.

45. W.B. to Pliny Earle, June 22, 1873, in ibid.

46. Smith-Rosenberg, *Disorderly Conduct*, see pp. 209–10.

47. The poetry of Lydia Sigourney was an exception. A close family friend of Amariah Brigham, she composed many flattering poems on asylum themes, some of which were read at official institutional pageants.

48. Fanny Fern, *Ruth Hall and Other Writings* (New Brunswick, NJ: Rutgers University Press, 1986), 109 ("fair rose the building"), 50 ("queenly"), 51 ("common female employments").

49. Ibid., 109.

50. Ibid., 111.

51. Ibid., 111.

52. E.D.E.N. Southworth, *The Hidden Hand* (Oxford: Oxford University Press, 1997), 394–95.

53. Ibid., 400.

54. Joanne Dobson, "The Hidden Hand: Subversion of Cultural Ideology in Three Mid-Nineteenth-Century American Women's Novels," *American Quarterly* 38, no. 2 (Summer 1986): 223–42 (the quote is on p. 234).

55. George Lippard, *The Quaker City or The Monks of Monk Hall: A Romance of Philadelphia Life, Mystery, and Crime* (Amherst: University of Massachusetts Press, 1995), 526.

56. Ibid., 538.

57. Greenhorn [George Thompson], *Dashington; Or, The Mysteries and Iniquities of a Private Mad-House* (New York: Frederic A. Brady, 1855?).

58. See David S. Reynolds, *Beneath the American Renaissance: The Subversive Imagination in the Age of Emerson and Melville* (New York: Alfred A. Knopf, 1988); Michael Denning, *Mechanic Accents: Dime Novels and Working-Class Culture in America* (London: Verso, 1987); and Shelley Streeby, *American Sensations: Class, Empire, and the Production of Popular Culture* (Berkeley:

University of California Press, 2002). Questioning the subversiveness implied by most of these analyses is Christopher Looby, "George Thompson's 'Romance of the Real': Transgression and Taboo in American Sensation Fiction," *American Literature* 65, no. 4 (December 1993): 651-72.

59. Thompson, *Dashington*, 54 (original emphasis).

60. See Christopher Castiglia, *Bound and Determined: Captivity, Culture-Crossing, and White Womanhood from Mary Rowlandson to Patty Hearst* (Chicago: University of Chicago Press, 1996).

61. Amy Schrager Lang, "Class and the Strategies of Sympathy," in *The Culture of Sentiment: Race, Gender, and Sentimentality in Nineteenth-Century America*, ed. Shirley Samuels (New York: Oxford University Press, 1992), 128-42 (quote is on p. 130).

62. Castiglia notes that many captivity narratives hinted at a protofeminist underplot that featured "confinement within the home, enforced economic dependence, rape, compulsory heterosexuality, prescribed plots." But before the women's movement of the 1840s, such texts were rarely overt in their appeals to women's rights (Castiglia, *Bound and Determined*, see esp. 4).

63. Packard, *The Prisoners' Hidden Life*, xii ("It is our legal position"), 158 ("this *slave* labor"), 316 ("Woman's love").

64. Chase, *Two Years in a Lunatic Asylum*.

65. The page from the *Twenty-Sixth Annual Report of the Managers of the State Lunatic Asylum for the Year 1868* is in turn pasted in the case book entry for Chase. See New York State, *Utica State Hospital Patient Case Files*, vol. 19, p. 416 (New York State Archives).

66. Ibid.

67. Luther Bell, *An Hour's Conference with Fathers and Sons, in Relation to a Common and Fatal Indulgence* (Boston: Whipple and Damrell, 1840), 24. On connections between reading and productivity in the reform imagination, see David M. Stewart, "Cultural Work, City Crime, Reading, Pleasure," *American Literary History* 9, no. 4 (Winter 1997): 676-701.

68. Bell, *An Hour's Conference with Fathers and Sons*, 11, 16.

69. New York State, *Annual Report of the Managers of the State Lunatic Asylum of the State of New-York*, vol. 8 (Albany, NY: 1851), 38-39.

70. Samuel B. Woodward, "Insanity, Produced by Masturbation," *Boston Medical and Surgical Journal* 12, no. 7 (March 25, 1839): 109.

71. Bell, *An Hour's Conference with Fathers and Sons*, 24, 48-49.

72. See Smith-Rosenberg, *Disorderly Conduct*, 46; Helen Lefkowitz Horowitz, *Rereading Sex: Battles over Sexual Knowledge and Suppression in Nineteenth-Century America*, (New York: Random House, 2002), 106.

73. Bell, *An Hour's Conference with Fathers and Sons*, 50.

74. Ibid., 51.

75. Quoted in Dain, *Concepts of Insanity*, 92.

76. Dwyer, *Homes for the Mad*, 90.

77. Quoted in Russ Castronovo, *Necro Citizenship: Death, Eroticism, and the Public Sphere in the Nineteenth-Century United States* (Durham, NC: Duke University Press, 2001), 69-70.

78. Quoted in Castronovo, *Necro Citizenship*, 76, 82.

79. Herman Melville, "Bartleby the Scrivener," in *Melville's Short Novels* (New York: Norton Critical Editions, 2002), 3-34 (quoted material in on pp. 16 and 17).

80. Cited in Horowitz, *Rereading Sex*, 102.

81. Ralph Waldo Emerson, "The American Scholar," in *Essays & Poems* (New York: Library of America, 1996), 51-71 (the quote is on p. 68).

EPILOGUE

1. See http://www.austenriggs.org/

2. Alex Beam, *Gracefully Insane: The Rise and Fall of America's Premier Mental Hospital* (New York: Public Affairs, 2001), 13.

3. http://www.mclean.harvard.edu/about/facts/

4. See T.M. Luhrmann, *Of Two Minds: An Anthropologist Looks at American Psychiatry* (New York: Knopf, 2000), esp. chapter 6.

5. Clifford J. Levy, "For Mentally Ill, Death and Misery," *New York Times*, April 28, 2002.

6. Alan Judd and Andy Miller, "Death in Georgia's Mental Hospitals," *Atlanta Journal-Constitution*, January 7, 2007.

7. Judd and Miller, "Feds to Probe State System," *Atlanta Journal-Constitution*, April 20, 2007.

8. Susanna Kaysen, *Girl, Interrupted* (New York: Vintage Books, 1994), 92-93.

9. See Sharon L. Snyder ad David T. Mitchell, *Cultural Locations of Disability* (Chicago: University of Chicago Press, 2006), 180-81.

Index